Philosophy in social work

The International Library of Welfare and Philosophy

General Editors

Professor Noel Timms

Professor of Social Work
University of Newcastle upon Tyne

David Watson

Department of Moral Philosophy
University of Glasgow

Philosophy in social work

Edited by

Noel Timms

Professor of Social Work
University of Newcastle upon Tyne

and

David Watson

Department of Moral Philosophy
University of Glasgow

Routledge & Kegan Paul
London, Henley and Boston

First published in 1978
by Routledge & Kegan Paul Ltd
39 Store Street,
London WC1E 7DD,
Broadway House,
Newtown Road,
Henley-on-Thames,
Oxon RG9 1EN and
9 Park Street,
Boston, Mass. 02108, USA
Printed in Great Britain by
Redwood Burn Ltd,
Trowbridge and Esher

British Library Cataloguing in Publication Data

Philosophy in social work. — (The international
library of welfare and philosophy).

1. Social service — Philosophy
I. Timms, Noel   II. Watson, David, b. 1946
III. Series
361'.001   HV31   77-30531

ISBN 0 7100 8786 1
ISBN 0 7100 8787 X Pbk

Contents

Philosophy in social work

Notes on the contributors

LEONARD HUNT is Lecturer in Social Work, King's College, University of Aberdeen, having previously worked with Family Service Units, latterly as a Unit organiser.

DAVID WATSON is Lecturer in Moral Philosophy at the University of Glasgow. His publications include 'Talking about Welfare', 1976 and the present volume, both as joint editor with Professor Noel Timms. He is a member of Strathclyde Children's Panel.

T.D. CAMPBELL is Professor of Philosophy at the University of Stirling. Among his publications are 'Adam Smith's Science of Morals', 1971.

ANGUS MCKAY is Lecturer in Moral Philosophy at the University of Glasgow.

R.F. STALLEY is Lecturer in Moral Philosophy at the University of Glasgow. His publications include a paper on self-determination in 'Self-Determination in Social Work', ed. F.E. McDermott, 1975.

R.S. DOWNIE is Professor of Moral Philosophy at the University of Glasgow. Among his publications are 'Government Action and Morality', 1964 and with Elizabeth Telfer 'Respect for Persons', 1969. He was chairman of the Working Party on The Teaching of Values in Social Work, set up by the Central Council for Education and Training in Social Work, whose Report was published in 1975.

EILEEN M. LOUDFOOT was Lecturer in Moral Philosophy at the University of Glasgow. Her publications include The Concept of Social Role, 'Philosophy of Social Science', 2, 1972, and with R.S. Downie and Elizabeth Telfer, 'Education and Personal Relationships', 1974.

BARRY WILKINS teaches Philosophy at University College,
Cardiff, and is concerned with moral, social and political
theory and their bearing upon the resolution of practical
issues in such areas as social work, medicine and socialist politics.

ALEXANDER BROADIE is Lecturer in Moral Philosophy at the
University of Glasgow.   His publications include Aris-
totle on Rational Action, 'Phronesis', vol. 19, 1974 and
Kant's Concept of Respect, 'Kant-Studien', February 1975.

P.D. SHAW is Lecturer in Logic at the University of Glasgow.

DONALD HOUSTON is Senior Lecturer in Social Work at the
University of Glasgow.

Acknowledgments

A number of Departmental Secretaries have helped in the preparation of the text, but in particular our thanks must go to Anne Valentine and Wilma White.

Noel Timms
David Watson

Introduction

Most of the papers gathered here were contributions to a
series of joint meetings of the Department of Social Administration and Social Work and the Department of Moral
Philosophy at the University of Glasgow. The meetings
were designed to encourage philosophers to look at traditional problems raised in the comparatively unfamiliar
setting of social work and social service and to encourage
social workers to philosophise. Those who attended the
meetings soon discovered the importance of encouragement!
One's experience and training can impose harsh criteria of
relevance, and stunt imagination. Even so, we gradually
rediscovered and came to value philosophy in social work
and now publish the papers so that students of philosophy
and social work might encounter each other's perspective,
and be stimulated by their interaction.

Any reflective consideration of social work reveals
that social work cannot be described or justified in a
straightforward way. This is presently brought to our
attention by the assertion that the days are gone when
'social work could largely rely, for the beliefs and
values informing or directing it, upon the consensus of
the wider society or upon the assumptions and standards of
other already established professions, such as law and
medicine'. Len Hunt in Social Work and Ideology goes on
to offer an analysis of the present crisis. It has, he
argues, created a vacuum which may be filled by ideology
or philosophy, by beliefs and values arbitrarily adopted
or which are the fruit of rational reflection. Hunt
argues that 'the continuance of social work as a disciplined and informed intervention in the lives of people in
the community' requires social workers to give more status
to reflection, and requires philosophers to recover from
their recent 'failure of nerve' and deal once again with
substantive issues.

1

The papers collected here, we believe, manifest such reflection on substantive issues in social work. Questions of the meaning of social service and of the distinction between charity and other forms of help are already important for the social worker and those who wish to understand the considerable development of social work and social service in the last two or so decades. Because of this development the actions of social workers and the attempted justification of these actions take on a new significance as they support or undermine citizen rights or as they reflect or hinder self-determination. Who authorises the social worker and what authority does he employ? Does the social worker act towards the person he is trying to help as a claimant, client or customer? These and many other questions call for a fresh analysis.

In Social Services in a Nutshell, David Watson discusses Robert Pinker's statement that 'social services represent a compromise between compassion and indifference'. Pinker's statement is *instructive*, and is used by Watson as a guide to moral principles which may be used to justify social policies with status-enhancing and stigmatising propensities: *respect for human beings* and *indifference to human beings*, respectively. The discussion of respect for *human beings* should encourage social work theorists, social workers and philosophers to look more closely at accounts of the more familiar principle of respect for *persons*.

Social services with stigmatising propensities may conflict with one important strand of welfare state ideology: that the recipients of welfare services are not in any way excluded from the basic status of citizen with all the rights that pertain thereto. This is the issue taken up by Professor T.D. Campbell in his paper Discretionary Rights. As D.A. Fowler (1975) has recently stressed, social control is as important an ingredient in social work as concern for the individual. Social work theorists and professional bodies (cf. BASW, 1973a) have stressed social workers' pastoral and therapeutic role. This ignores social workers' very real power. Once we recognise that social workers play controlling roles we are in a position to recommend ways in which they might be regulated. It is one striking implication of Campbell's argument that unless social workers' power is regulated by law in accordance with the principles of natural justice, social workers may themselves be the major obstacle to the implementation of welfare *rights*. Can the pastoral and therapeutic role be combined with such regulation of the controlling role? As Campbell says, 'if some progress is to be made towards a reconciliation of these seemingly

opposed outlooks some common vocabulary must be found
which can function both within the pastoral and the legal
way of viewing the social worker's task'. To this end
Campbell introduces and discusses the notion of 'discretionary "rights"'.

In Charity and the Welfare State Angus McKay attempts
to clarify the distinction between these two, and its consequences for welfare rights. Beveridge seems to have
thought that we have welfare rights only because we have
paid for services received. But in that case net beneficiaries of state welfare programmes have no right to
what they receive. They receive charity. If we want to
avoid this conclusion we need a different foundation for
welfare rights. McKay suggests needs. This has the
consequence that many organisations presently called charities are misnamed, for in serving needs they too satisfy
welfare rights. Contrary to the Beveridge view, such
'charities' do not go beyond the call of duty.

Campbell recognises that social workers make many judgments and argues that they be governed by the rule of law
and the requirements of natural justice. In Non-Judgmental Attitudes, in contrast, R.F. Stalley attempts to
clarify the textbooks' recommendation of a 'non-judgmental' attitude in social work. Stalley reveals the wide
range of approaches to social work which might be called
non-judgmental: refraining from all judgment of the
client; refraining from moral judgment; refraining from
moral judgment of the client, if not his acts; and so on.
Stalley argues convincingly that a number of approaches
which might be called 'non-judgmental' cannot be part of a
pastoral, therapeutic, or controlling social work. His
general conclusion is that there is no one simple account
which can be given of a non-judgmental attitude and that
the demand for such an attitude, if it is to be taken seriously, must be seen as a protest against a number of different faults which could infect social casework. While
agreeing that the recommendation of a non-judgmental attitude may be less a recommendation of a certain kind of
approach and more a warning against certain kinds of
approach, it might be suggested that Stalley's paper also
puts us in a position to remove the ambiguity, leaving us
with a clear demand which can be taken seriously as a
demand for a certain kind of approach to social work, and
not merely as a warning against certain kinds of approach.

In Aim, Skill and Role in Social Work, Professor R.S.
Downie and Eileen M. Loudfoot outline 'value-questions'
which 'must exist for every practising social worker'.
Their paper is a general guide to such inescapable problems, usefully categorised in relation to the aims, skills

and role of social work. Downie and Loudfoot stress the
importance of *practical judgment* as an element in social
work practice. Further, they argue that 'the need for
practical judgment of what we ought to do, granted our
knowledge, is inescapable; and therefore there are radical limitations to the possibility of expertise'.
The authors' conception of a social role is that of a
set of rights and duties. This makes room for an interesting defence of social work within an institutional
framework. To give one example, if the social worker 'is
not simply to be a busy-body he must have the *right to
intervene*, and if he has the right to intervene he must
have duties and responsibilities; the concept of social
role encapsulates these ideas of rights, duties and responsibilities' (cf. Watson, 1975). But theirs is a
defence which recognises that it is part of a debate.
Geoffrey Pearson (1975) has recently argued that 'the objectives of social work are *problematic*'. Downie and
Loudfoot remind us that not only the aims, but also the
place of skills and social role of social work, and the
relations of each of these to the others are problematic.
It should also be noted that Downie and Loudfoot suggest that the primary aim of social work is individual
self-realisation. In Social Services in a Nutshell,
Watson argues that though this may be so for casework, it
cannot be the primary value of all social services.
In The Morality of Law and the Politics of Probation,
Barry Wilkins shows that the objectives of work with pro-
bationers are also problematic. These are conventionally
identified as the prevention of further offences and the
rehabilitation of the offender in society. Using a host
of interesting illustrations, Wilkins reminds us that some
laws at least may be morally unacceptable and so further
offences committed in breach of them not for that reason
discouraged. Further, rehabilitation as an aim may reflect commitment to the social and political status quo
and nct help the client. Contrary to the Morison
'Report' (1962), Wilkins argues, there are times when the
client's interests and those of society are *not* identical.
A proper understanding of the social worker's therapeutic and controlling roles presupposes an understanding
of his *authority*. His therapeutic aims require him to be
an authority on certain matters and perhaps also to have
authority over a client. The latter is certainly part of
the context of control. In Authority and the Social
Caseworker, Alexander Broadie attempts 'to isolate those
features of the social caseworker's job that constitute
his authority'.
Being 'an authority on' a topic obviously requires

having specialist knowledge but, Broadie argues, it also
requires recognition by others - which in turn presupposes
some ability to articulate the specialist knowledge. The
author draws out various ways in which the client's recognition of the caseworker as an authority on his subject
can affect the therapeutic and controlling relationships.
This suggests that 'acceptance', of one sort or another,
must work *both* ways. The client must accept the caseworker as an authority on the matters in hand. We might
add that recognition by society at large has an equally
important part to play. Though the author does not concern himself with the professionalisation of social work,
his points are clearly relevant to this debate. The professional typically claims an area of expertise, he claims
to be 'an authority on' some topic and pursues recognition.

Downie and Loudfoot, as we have said, define a social
role as a set of rights and duties. The social worker's
role may, of course, include rights and duties which put
him 'in authority over' his client. Probation work is
the obvious example. Broadie makes two points relevant
to therapeutic aims in such a context of control. First,
in particular cases the authority need not be exercised;
second, the authority need not be authoritarian. Broadie
also discusses *authorisation* in relation to being 'in
authority over' someone. A caseworker, he argues, might
be authorised by his client, or a client by his caseworker, without either being in authority over the other.
Authorisation then, is not a threat to client or worker
self-determination. By the same token nor does being
authorised provide 'an infallible escape route' from moral
culpability. Representatives of clients and of welfare
agencies cannot entirely pass the moral buck.

The 'medical model' is a favourite for theorists describing social services. In Medicine and the Marketplace, P.D. Shaw reviews and comments upon the debate
about the delivery of medical welfare, and in particular,
blood. Should medical welfare be 'socialised' or governed by market forces? Shaw identifies the philosophical
roots of the debate: the idea that man is thoroughly
self-interested. He argues that economists' doubts about
the possibility of altruism are groundless. The way is
open then for a socialised medicine which depends upon and
promotes altruism. Altruism is a concept that should be
given much greater emphasis in the exploration of social
work and social service.

Shaw concludes that 'there is a very strong case
against a market in medicine, but that what holds for medical care does not necessarily hold for the provision of

welfare in general'. Readers might find it interesting
to consider whether Shaw's arguments for keeping medicine
free from certain market forces apply to other welfare
services. Shaw argues against a market in medicine, for
example, that consumer choice is of little value because
the consumer is in no position to assess the competence of
practitioners. Does this apply to 'consumers' of social
work services (cf. Mayer and Timms, 1970)? Broadie argues, in the paper included here, that for a caseworker to
be an authority on his subject there must be a recognised
uneven distribution of knowledge; this may also be true
for community workers. But in these cases what constitutes 'welfare' is more problematic than it is in medicine. As Downie and Loudfoot point out, 'the possession
of skills does not remove the necessity of making evaluative judgments and decisions', and as Stalley says, 'it is
sometimes only in the light of a particular moral view
that the client could be seen as having a problem'.
Doesn't a market give the consumer more control over what
is a problem? On the other hand, a market may result in
the poor being unable to purchase services to deal with
what they see as a problem. Here social service and
social control are inextricably bound together.

In Affirmation and Sacrifice in Everyday Life and in
Social Work, Donald Houston offers an explanation of 'the
absence of conviction displayed by social workers that the
work they do has any real value'. Of course, some social
workers are convinced of the value of their work, but few
of these can articulate the value. Houston's explanation
begins with a classification of interpersonal relations
according to the degree of self-affirmation and self-sac-
rifice of the participants. Broadly, Houston argues that
the absence of conviction or uncertainty about objectives
arises where social workers aim at *reciprocal* self-affirmation and sacrifice in a society which primarily endorses
unilateral self-affirmation and sacrifice, where social
workers treat clients as equals in a society which stresses their being unequal. Houston recommends commitment
to reciprocity.

Houston's paper is quite different in style from the
other papers but, like the others, rewards imaginative
reading. It is a paper about status-enhancement, about
an aspect of social control and about the aims and role of
the social worker, all themes of the other papers collected here.

1   Social work and ideology

Leonard Hunt

---

1   THE SEARCH FOR A VALUE-BASE

> And though the philosopher may live remote from busi-
> ness, the genius of philosophy, if carefully cultivated
> by several, must gradually diffuse itself throughout
> the whole of society, and bestow a similar correctness
> on every art and calling. (David Hume, 'Enquiry con-
> cerning Human Understanding', Sec. 1)

Until quite recently social work could largely rely, for
the beliefs and values informing or directing it, upon the
consensus of the wider society or upon the assumptions and
standards of other already established professions, such
as law and medicine, to whose work the practice of social
work sometimes serves in an ancillary role. These beliefs and values were little questioned among social
workers themselves, and often left merely implicit. So
far as they were expressed at all, they were expressed in
terms of some imprecise kind of utilitarianism.

My purpose in this paper is first, to review the
reasons why this situation has now changed, why social
work can no longer escape from needful and self-conscious
reflection upon the beliefs and values which its practice
commonly presupposes; and second, to consider our response to this need.

The continuance of social work as a disciplined and informed intervention in the lives of people in the community, demands a reflection upon the credentials of the
beliefs and values which it presupposes, now that these
are so much questioned, not only in society itself, but
even amongst present and intending social workers themselves.

The origins of our present predicament

Current discussion of such issues as the direction which
social work is taking, the nature of its ethical and
value-base, and the character of its persistent crises of
identity, both within social work literature and within
the context of practice and teaching, make very plain how
great is the anxiety to find a meaningful value-base for
social work practice (cf. Stevenson, 1971). The reasons
why there is such anxiety and interest in regard to these
fundamental questions, and to a much greater extent now
than before, are not difficult to see. Four closely
associated factors can be readily identified:

(a) The rapid expansion of social work itself
The Seebohm and Kilbrandon reports resulted in the creation of whole new social work enterprises involving the
amalgamation of different social work specialisms, each
with their own knowledge, skills and practice, into new,
complex, single departments.

(b) The development of generic courses
As long as social work was taught as a practice-based expertise, questions regarding its ultimate justification
could mostly be left in abeyance; now this is no longer
possible.

(c) The development of community work
This has served to heighten persistent problems regarding
the function of traditional social work in a way to which
I will refer in detail below.

(d) The growth of professionalism
This growth of professionalism or quasi-professionalism is
largely consequential on the other factors, being especially closely connected with what some have called the
bureaucratisation of social work, which has resulted from
the amalgamation of social work specialisms. The expansion of social work has meant a whole new career structure, accompanied by all the paraphernalia of large organisations. These include restraints on professional autonomy; the splitting of responsibility and accountability;
role definition; limitations regarding initiative; limited access to resources; and insistence on the acquisition of a range of skills which are thought to be non-
professional or administrative. It is difficult to say
precisely what the system will look like when the process
is complete, but at the moment it is bewildering and be-
devilling (cf. Rowe, 1974). This bureaucratisation has

inevitably engendered conflict, e.g., which branch of the
old professional divisions shall have primacy regarding
knowledge and practice?   Sometimes the old divisions were
very specialised;   in some cases there has been a struggle
to retain their old identity.   Whatever the outcome, the
tensions are unlikely to be resolved to everyone's satisfaction, and their repercussions are likely to persist.
Relevant to this present transitional period it is apposite to quote Nina Toren.   She writes:

> the knowledge base of social work is still, to a large
> extent, drawn from experience, i.e., generalisations
> inferred from many specific cases and a great deal of
> intuition is required in the application of this know-
> ledge.   At the same time the methods, and particularly
> the service orientation of social work, have attained a
> high level of development and crystallisation.
> (Etzioni, 1969, p. 146)

The disparity between growing organisational sophisti-
cation and naivety concerning the security of its value-
base was not apparent so long as social workers continued
to operate as a number of separate specialisms.   That is,
each branch specialised enough to have its assumptions and
s andards closely rooted in practice.   However, now that
the teaching of social work has become organised along
generic lines, the fragmentary nature of the subjects
forming a social work curriculum has inevitably made
itself evident.   We have a collection of disparate and
maybe in some cases, incompatible subjects, which are
welded together unevenly, or else merely continue living
separately and uncomfortably.   Social and economic history;   social policy and administration;   human growth
and behaviour;   social philosophy;   and a whole variety of
sociological, psychological and psychiatric perspectives,
which inevitably include references to ethics, law and the
wider society.   It is my view that at many points these
perspectives clash philosophically and ideologically, that
is, with regard to the beliefs and values which they involve or in the way in which questions about these beliefs
and values are approached.

This type of clash did not, I think, occur so frequently in the past, because many social work courses were concerned with a training which concentrated on practice
models and did not involve having a frequently questioned
theoretical base.   Social work training was concerned
with the acquisition of expertise, knowledge, skills and
techniques securely based on practice.   Before generic
social work courses came into existence, social work
courses were intended to equip practitioners for a variety
of different specialised fields.   Within this context,

problems relating to values were mostly left to individuals to resolve, or simply treated as given, within the
process of training, which itself showed some analogy to
apprenticeship.   Theoretical or technical doubts were
allayed by the continuing existence of professional specialisms with their own traditions.   In this way a whole
series of professional standards regarding excellence was
established, e.g., probation, medical social work, child
care and psychiatric social work.   Some of these specialisms commanded a body of knowledge or theory to some
degree systematic: law, in the case of probation and
child care;   knowledge of medical matters, in the case of
medical social workers;   psychoanalytic/psycho-dynamic
theory, in the case of psychiatric social work.   It is my
belief that regardless of how 'expert' this knowledge or
theory actually was, certain specialisms derived confirmation of their values and standards from the fact of
being ancillary to older, more established professions
such as law and medicine.   I have few doubts that within
social work generally, there has been resistance and re-
vulsion against genericism in training and practice, accompanied by nostalgia for the older methods.

The return to the less complicated past is today made
more difficult by the challenge posed by community work
writers and practitioners who frequently bring in ideological argument and controversy concerning fundamental
questions of aim and value.   What they do very effectively is raise certain systematic objections to traditional social work practice.   In their view, social work
is by definition about adaptation;   it is a form of
social control rather than social change, because in
choosing to deal with individuals it seeks to reconcile
them to the intolerable situation in which many of them
live.   Traditional social work, they argue, is manipulative, and profoundly conservative, because in assisting
the individual to function it means that any wider consciousness amongst the broad class of social work clients
is 'blocked' and, with it, any possibility of large-scale
social change.   Most importantly, it is held that traditional social work colludes with the injustice of a divided and profoundly unequal society.

Much of this may seem remote from the urgent concerns
of those presently exercised in actual social work practice and immediately confronted with pressing personal and
social situations.   Social work intervention on occasion
involves life-and-death issues;   it very commonly means
working with both individuals and families living on the
margins of 'normal' life in extreme physical, emotional
or mental distress.

Therefore, at this point the critical argument is
liable to take the following form: what has such an
urgent undertaking to learn from the foregoing hazy, imaginative speculation? Hasn't the community underwrit-
ten the value and purpose of social work, its willingness
to invest in its establishment and the expansion of it?
Is not what social work practice requires simply a tough-
minded, pragmatic approach to problem-solving, this to be
reinforced and accompanied by soundly based empirical research? This is a viewpoint cogently expressed by
Matilda Goldberg (1972):

> Social workers are finding out that their ideological
> and emotional commitment alone will be useless unless
> it is underpinned by hard evidence from research or
> reliable documentary sources.

Although prepared to admit the plausibility of this
last seemingly down-to-earth viewpoint I don't believe
that it answers many of the questions or meets the objections to traditional social work practice raised earlier.

Social work is vulnerable enterprise. It is undertaken on behalf of society which often regards it ambi-
valently as a regrettable necessity; what I mean is that
its authority lacks wholehearted community sanction and
approval. Moreover, the clientele of social work are,
with some exceptions, reluctant recipients, frequently in
conflict with the authority of social work, whether in
itself or as it represents the wider society. The professional culture is evolving formal professional associations but these are as yet embryonic and only gradually
acquiring sustained support. The available body of systematic theory is fragmented and open to serious dispute
from many viewpoints, and seems quite inadequate to deal
with the objections made against it whether by the ideo-
logue, some community workers or the unsympathetic layman.
This is particularly true in the case of other professions
who clash with social workers' judgments. The ethical
basis still waits to be established upon a firmer footing.

Things were not always like this. Raymond Plant, in
his recent book 'Community and Ideology' (1974, p. 6),
reminds us that social work practice in the nineteenth and
early twentieth centuries sprang from securely underpinned
and confident premises. It was a largely upper- and
middle-class undertaking, philanthropic, concerned with
treating individuals and their environment. It also enjoyed a close and sustained relationship with a 'good many
philosophers of the time who were theoretically interested
in and indeed actively engaged in social work of all
kinds'. This was, he shows,

largely the result of the moral and political theoris-

ing of Thomas Greene.   Many of Greene's Oxford pupils
took very seriously his teaching on the role of the
state, the nature of welfare and the notion of citizenship, and made either practical or theoretical contributions to social work.
Also there can be little doubt that the influence of other
well-established or widely influential worked-out systems
of thought, of Christian or of utilitarian inspiration,
had a consolidating influence.

Unfortunately, however seductive it seems, there is no
way back to the past; society has changed, the old assu-
rances have disappeared, and philosophy, for reasons which
we shall see later, has changed its complexion.   Social
work, however, continues to profess and practise commit-
ments to a number of values which are not self-evident or
at least are not universally agreed, and which require
formidable intellectual justification and defence;   that
is, of course, unless such values are consigned to blind
faith with all the evils of breakdown of communication and
limits to co-operativeness which follow such a position.

From my point of view this would be a counsel of des-
pair;   indeed one of the most disturbing features of the
contemporary world is the clamour of conflicting views and
opinions, each being left to depend for its justification
on moral force with very little empirical evidence or
rational argument.

The values to which I refer are ones to which present-
day social work is perforce committed to profess in practice.   These include the uniqueness and worth of each
individual human personality;   the right to self-determination;   the existence and value of freedom;   the existence of obligations;   plus a host of beliefs about the
'good life' and the 'good society', including social justice.   These are accompanied by ethical standards which
may be thought of as particularisations of injunctions to
love and respect one another.

Until Plant's book 'Social and Moral Theory in Casework' (1970) appeared, there had been very little contemporary philosophical treatment of these themes in relation
to social work.   What literature we have is mostly American and treats the values as given in volumes whose purpose is other than philosophical (cf. Hollis, 1967;
Biestek, 1957).

This vacuum left by the philosophers has not remained
entirely empty.   But what has been put into it has been
ideology, and the fruits of an ideological approach, where
only philosophy and a philosophical approach can properly
serve.

2   THE PHENOMENON OF IDEOLOGICAL THINKING

The term 'ideology' is notoriously difficult to use in any
disciplined or consistent way.   It has a vexed and complicated history.   It began early in the nineteenth century as a term signifying any set of ideals and broad
ideas underlying the sciences, by contrast with special
forms of knowledge; but now that it has passed into common usage, it has come to have varied and sometimes conflicting meanings.

Horowitz, in his book 'Philosophy, Science and the
Sociology of Knowledge' (1961, p. 79) is concerned to distinguish and carefully delineate the phenomenon of ideology.   'It has been increasingly used to signify a med-
iating point in the spectrum of human knowledge.'   Thus:

> ideology is (a) an amalgamation of true and false con-
> sciousness;   (b) a justification for either revolution-
> ary or reactionary interests and attitudes in political
> life; or (c) a rationalisation of irrational forms of
> social and psychological motivations.   In short, ideo-
> logy expresses that point in social knowledge at which
> interests connect up to a picture of reality.

An ideology involves 'a series of ideas related to defi-
nite social ambitions'.

There is in Horowitz's (1961, p. 80) view another intrinsic element in ideology and this is preparedness to
act; this involves an expansion of the above point about
social ambition: 'an ideology, in so far as its purpose
is to convince, contains an element of coercion.'   Marx
would have agreed with Horowitz that ideology is to be
contrasted with other forms of knowledge or bodies of
belief; and in associating with particular class positions he and Engels saw ideology's inevitable distortion
as embodying false consciousness and as set in contrast
with the truth of science which they understood to include
the scientific knowledge of dialectical materialism and
its historic goal.

The principal difficulty with the notion of ideology is
that later theorists, principally Mannheim and others, extended both the application and the implications of the
word 'ideology' (cf. Mannheim, 1936).   Mannheim saw it as
'an inclusive system of comprehensive reality - a set of
beliefs infused with passion which seeks to transform the
whole of a way of life' (1936, p. 40).   For Mannheim (and
others) ideologies are universal in their appeal.   We now
have two distinct but comparable views of ideology and
ideological processes.   The Marxists, for whom ideology
serves only a temporary role in the process whereby history unfolds (an unfolding which is partly through ideolo-

gical conflict and those other ideologues of various political persuasions), believe that ideology offers a more inclusive framework, but argue this may be arbitrarily selected and that it may have a more universal appeal than the class-limited ideology envisaged in the Marxist view.

I think these two broad views about ideology and ideological processes have co-existed uneasily. We have to separate the Marxist view of ideology as an inevitable distortion of the truth, even if only partial, and therefore regrettable, from the view of those who, like Mannheim, accept without regret the situation in which the need to resort to ideology is part of the human predicament.   Ideology for the latter is neither regrettable nor morally reprehensible.

From my viewpoint the most important element in this very common view of ideology, well represented in Mannheim, is the inevitability of choice, its urgency, and of choice unsupported by reason.   In this view, there is no escape from simply choosing between conflicting ideological outlooks with their differing moral entailments.   And it is envisaged that there are no external criteria of evaluation by means of which one could judge between the competing claims of conflicting ideologies.   The choice is arbitrary, it is claimed.   In choosing, one is defiant or dismissive of reason, if not actually contemptuous of it.   This choice is regarded as a matter for the will alone, undirected and unsupported by reason.

In this respect, those who, like Mannheim, argue the necessity of ideology, and of ideology determined by choice, if one is to take up any standpoint at all, come close both to the existentialists who also emphasise the primary importance of choice and choosing, and to some contemporary Anglo-Saxon philosophers such as Hare (1952), who think in terms of 'choosing' one's moral principles. Standing back from the various points of view which I have reviewed, it seems clear that the essence of what is involved in the ideological approach to questions, or of what is involved in what it is reasonable to call the 'ideological approach', does not lie primarily in the internal character of the body of beliefs and values held but in the way in which the body of beliefs and values is held.   For the purpose of my argument, the key distinction to be grasped is that between, on the one hand,

(a)   a body of beliefs and values such as (speaking in a very loose but common usage) a sociologist of knowledge might call an 'ideology' whether or not it would count as an 'ideology' for Marx or Mannheim, and, on the other hand,

(b)   the question of how this body of beliefs and values is held, or presented, to others to be held.

On the one hand, a body of beliefs and values (whether labelled 'an ideology' or not) can be held ideologically, or presented to others as to be held ideologically. By this I mean that the person holding the body of beliefs and values under consideration understands the holding of them to be incapable of support or justification from reason, and regards this as acceptable and appropriate, because he views ultimate questions of belief and value to be ones upon which rational discussion, with the reflective analysis and weighing up of arguments and considerations such as might be adduced in discussion, can have no decisive bearing; commitment or faith in ultimate matters being, in his view, merely the expression of an ultimately arbitrary choice or act of will.   On the other hand, a body of beliefs and values (perhaps even the same ones other people hold merely ideologically) can be held philosophically; by this I mean the person holding the body of beliefs and values regards the exercise of reason and reflection as having a bearing upon the truth and validity and assumes that, if true or valid, this body of beliefs and values will stand up to rational examination, and that the effect of examining it will not be to subvert it but to enlarge one's understanding, and that, contrariwise, if the body of beliefs and values is not sound, the exercise of reason will be liable to reveal this.

Thus, in my thesis, the fundamental conflict is between those who hold that views concerning beliefs, values and their prescriptive entailments, are to be adopted arbitrarily, urged upon us by the necessity of choice and without the benefit of reason and reflection; and those who hold that the choice of beliefs and values, although prompted by the shared human predicament of being persons confronted with conflicting systems, can, and must, be taken with the guidance of reason and reflection.   Therefore, beliefs and values held ideologically and those held philosophically will differ with regard to their rational status, even if to the sociologist of knowledge they present the same appearance.   This is not, of course, to claim that ideological beliefs and values will be devoid of intellectual content and argument, but that it is essentially characteristic of them, precisely qua ideological, that their holders do not reckon their basic elements either to need or to be capable of any kind of intellectual justification.   Conversion, unmediated by rational persuasion, is what they require.

If, as I have argued, ideological positions are taken up in this way arbitrarily and without benefit of reason or reflection, how do they exert their fascination and

appeal?   It is my view that reason and reflection, however difficult they may be to use to fruitful effect, and
however frail they may be with regard to their timing, and
resistance to strong emotion, are abandoned by us at our
peril.   The processes whereby ideologies gain their persuasive attractiveness are well described by Gellner, who
is concerned to stress two especially important characteristics of ideologies;   first, 'great plausibility, a
powerful click at some one or more points which give it
compulsiveness of a kind, and secondly, some great absurdity, a violent intellectual resistance generating offen-
siveness at some one or more points' (1959, pp. 231-2).
The first of these characteristics, acts, he claims, as a
kind of bait: an 'appealing outlook which must somehow
account for some striking features of our experience which
otherwise would remain unaccounted for or which would
otherwise be less well explained.'   The second, 'the
swallowing of an absurdity within the framework of the
acceptance of an ideology, represents a powerful *rite de
passage*, as in joining a tribal group.   The act of commitment, the investment of emotional capital, assures that
one does not leave it too easily.'
      In my account of the perplexities of ideology and ideo-
logical processes of thought, we have uncovered several
features which help explain their origin and attractiveness.   To Marx and his followers we owe a great deal for
showing how certain features of ideology relate to its
social origins and for helping us to understand the
rationalising of such origins to justify and prescribe
either change or conservatism.   Mannheim's attempt to
recommend the espousal of some universalised ideology as a
way of responding to questions and problems relating to
mankind's predicament, shows the dynamic aspect of the
ideological approach and, incidentally, suggests or indicates the ideological nature of Marxism itself.   Gellner
has shown clearly how persuasive ideology can be, and his
account goes some way towards explaining its current
vogue.   The contemporaneity of the phenomenon of ideology, and of the resort to an ideological approach, is not
in doubt.   What I wish now to go on to question is its
newness.

3 IDEOLOGY AND PHILOSOPHY

It is my belief that both positivism and ideology can be
seen as a response to the current situation in philosophy.
This reflects a profound scepticism concerning the capacity of reason and reflection to deal with the substantive

issues with which we are concerned both as individuals and
as social workers.   Contemporary Anglo-Saxon philosophy
suffers a crisis of nerve.   True, the type of critique
that it offered first of logical atomism, then of logical
positivism, has undermined the arguments relied upon in
the past in order to establish sceptical or nihilist positions in ethics or in metaphysics, by revealing how crude
and how remote from the facts are the assumptions and distinctions upon which these arguments depended, e.g., the
assumption that arguments could be unproblematically described as being of simply two kinds - deductive and induc-
tive, or that the notions of the analytic or the a priori
were very clear.   But while the basis for a systematic
scepticism appear thus to have been laid waste by the
practitioners of so-called 'analytic' philosophy, the
result has not been any large-scale move towards treating
more substantive issues.   The notion of philosophy as a
therapy which freed one from the drive to require answers
to pseudo questions, introduced by logical positivism, was
turned by their successors into a weapon against the
assumptions of logical positivism itself.   But the effect
of this has not been a release, enabling philosophers to
address themselves to questions that 'common sense' does
not appear to resolve in a generally agreed manner.
Rather in their attitude, the philosophers have retained
the same sceptical dispositions of their predecessors,
albeit without the same theoretical justifications;   and
in their practice they have continued to be preoccupied
with the preliminary task of preventing the subverting of
what common sense seems to agree on, rather than in ad-
vancing beyond this.   In the climate of professional
philosophical agnosticism and scepticism there exists a
vacuum for those for whom action is imperative;   action,
that is, based on beliefs and values which may not be defended rationally or philosophically.   It is this vacuum
which ideology seeks to fill.   It is my contention that
this situation is only partly reaction to current stress;
the resort to ideological solutions exemplified in an arbitrarily held but emotional powerfully rooted advocacy
of the 'good life' based on faith alone, has an older
philosophical history.   Morals based on the will alone,
or morals based on faith, and faith as an act of will,
undirected and unsupported by reason;   voluntarism and
fideism are the theological analogues of the ideological
approach.   Scepticism concerning the possibility of finding a philosophical basis for morals in the writings of
philosophers such as William of Occam reveal the begin-
nings of modern anti-intellectualism as well established
even in the fourteenth century.

Many philosophers subsequently have had doubts about
the rational evidence for, and defence of, beliefs and
values, particularly those affecting moral choices and
conduct.   Moving nearer to our own times Schopenhauer
claimed that it might be possible to live a moral life
but to seek rational justification is impossible.   Thus,
ideology and ideological solutions have the lure and
fascination of solving complex intellectual problems and
difficulties at one swoop.   Wearied by the continual
assault of rational scepticism on one's position, always
inevitably a position open to question, it is so tempting
to substitute emotional persuasion and advocacy for
reason.

Even Iris Murdoch (1970), who points out how an Anglo-
Saxon philosopher such as Hampshire ends up by holding
strangely similar views to Sartre on the ultimate impos-
sibility of reasons providing any direction to the will,
and who registers a lack of sympathy with their position,
none the less hovers in her earlier work in an interes-
tingly ambiguous position at this point:

the difficulty is, and here we are after all not so
very far from the philosophers of the past, that the
subject of investigation is the nature of man, and we
are studying this nature at a point of great conceptual sensibility.   Man is a creature who makes pictures of himself and then comes to resemble the picture.   This is a process which moral philosophy must
attempt to describe and analyse.   I think it remains
for us to find a satisfactory method for the explanation of our own morality and that of others, but I
think it would be a pity if, just because we realised
that any picture is likely to be half a description
and half a persuasion, we were to deny ourselves freedom in the making of pictures and the coining of explanatory ideas which our predecessors have used in the
past.   After all, both as philosophers and social
workers and as moral beings, we are concerned with the
same problems with which they were concerned.   Questions like What is freedom?   Can it be shown that men
are free?   What is the relation of morality to what we
believe concerning God and the hereafter?   It is a
merit of modern philosophers to be more conscious than
their predecessors of what the philosopher's activity
is.   We can become more patient and historical in ana-
lysing moralities and more daring and imaginative in
exploring our own without losing the benefit of that
consciousness.   (Murdoch, 1962, pp. 122-3)

One can note how Murdoch's points about building pictures
and coming to resemble them represent a position open to

question within philosophy, they accord with central
ideas in psycho-analysis which has been so fruitful a
source for social work itself. Her description of any
picture of man's nature as 'half a description, half a
persuasion' comes close to diagnosing the predicament of
ideology itself. This has been the persisting attraction
and persuasiveness of ideology, the phrasing of the question, 'isn't this picture really the right one?'

If my views are correct, the term 'ideology' serves to
pick out one of the chief ways in which people do come to
hold their views, beliefs and attitudes, a way which is
both ancient and continually possible. The fascination
of ideology is that it so nearly resembles philosophy, in
that it purports to answer the same substantive questions
which the philosopher also confronts (albeit often only to
turn aside from), differing only in that it regards the
pictures it presents and the valuations they evoke as removed from the sphere of rational discussion, whether for
justification or for rejection. As Gellner's discussion
indicates, the attractiveness of these pictures and the
persuasiveness of ideology and its procedures, although
not rooted in reason, is still rooted in something within
us, historically and socially formed and shaping the many
ways in which we experience ourselves and the world.

Those who attack ideology as a phenomenon about to dis-
appear, who thought for example that by unmasking the un-
scientific, or non-rational nature of it, they would cause
its demise, were wrong. What one is socially, economically and politically, does affect one's perception of the
world and the kinds of problems and dilemmas we inevitably
face. This is where the relativists are correct, but it
is not the whole explanation; with difficulty one can
become aware of the sorts of events and experiences which
have conditioned and informed such judgments and percep-
tions, and take these into account. Being conditioned is
not the same as being determined; and for some beliefs
and values to be arrived at in a way which is ideological
rather than rational, is not for all of them to be so.
This fact, that a certain historical and social setting
can make it natural, though not inevitable, for us to be
drawn to certain pictures of the world, and certain eval-
uations arising from them, independently of reason, is
clearly exemplified in the thinking of many involved in
social work today. The particular challenge of the more
militant community workers id ideological, and necessarily so; the social situations in which many of them operate are, by their very nature, ideology-producing, being
both group oriented and informed by models of change which
are primarily 'revolutionary', at least in intention.

Further, as the ideology-accepting viewpoint tells us, we are forced to make choices simply because life experience presents us with dilemmas.

Marx expressed vexation with traditional philosophy, especially its role as mere interpretation, and was determined not merely to interpret but to change the world. However, calls to action combined with impatience at the world's inability to change decisively, are not substitutes for evidence and arguments about the direction and values of the change advocated. When faced with perplexity regarding one's overall direction, and the near-agonising problems of decision taking, it may be difficult to resist the solution of unhesitating and seemingly decisive answers. Ideology or irrationalism can ultimately give no guidance as to what we should choose; questions relating to why course A rather than course B cannot be resolved satisfactorily by reference to the necessity of ultimately arbitrary choice.

This is the sinister aspect of ideology, and the one which it is most important to grasp. Views about the world are reduced to the status of arbitrary choices and perspectives. Statements are reduced to the status of unsupported and unsupportable opinions. The most obvious effect of this is to polarise individuals and groups, leaving no middle or neutral ground to which they can appeal in order to communicate with one another or make themselves understood. Once one assumes that all ultimate beliefs and values (e.g., the ones I mentioned as presupposed in customary social work practice) are outside the scope of rational discussion, and incapable of receiving any confirmation through the reflective exercise of reason, the effect is to dry up the springs of learning and co-operation between those who disagree with one another in regard to the fundamental questions.

Moreover, once the issues are removed from the sphere of reason, they are liable in practice to be decided by power alone.

4   CONCLUSIONS

We began by considering the tasks of social work, and it is to this that I want to return. Without community sanction there could not be any social work as we know it; this is the axiom on which my view of it is based. Social work in whatever shape or form is an extremely difficult enterprise; it involves intervening in the lives of others, sometimes at their request, but more frequently on the community's behalf. As a profession it must try

to sustain itself by what it thinks and believes its
principles are, what practice tells it to be true, while
inevitably remaining sensitive to what may be shifting
values in the wider society that it serves. Some varieties of social work practice confront agonising dilemmas,
especially at the margins. By these margins I mean where
the principles of social work indicate one form of action
and the wider society demands another. Social work practice must seem an extraordinary undertaking; seeking to
help (now such an absurd motive in itself) individuals,
family or communities in distress situations - whatever
shape these may take - with only the unwitting approval of
the wider society. Social workers are particularly vulnerable to both criticism and anxiety regarding their own
motivation; in the recent past such anxieties were fos-
tered by guilt about lack of personal worth or failure to
achieve integrity. This situation is now complicated by
the criticism that most forms of social work intervention,
particularly traditional ones, are a form of social control; serving not only to stifle but to perpetuate some
of the worst forms of social injustice.

There have, of course, been a number of attempts to
locate and describe the motivation of social workers.
Halmos did so most cogently in his 'The Faith of the
Counsellors' (1965), where he depicted social workers as
the politically disaffected heirs of an old tradition of
caring, who seek to lovingly help their fellows. In a
humanist world this can only be undertaken with scientific
or quasi-scientific sanction and approval. Social workers are, therefore, in his view, the priesthood of a sec-
ular religion, dressed for intellectual respectability in
whichever scientific ideology happens to hold sway.
Whatever the truth or shortcomings of such a viewpoint, it
illustrates the precariousness which social workers experience in their dealing with clients in the wider society.
The dilemmas which result from this uncertainty are liable
to appear as an almost inevitable accompaniment to whatever one does. They are exhausting and there is a con-
stant temptation to reach for what seem to be all-embrac-
ing solutions of a certain ideological sort. This temptation, I think, must be resisted.

It is often remarked that philosophical matters are too
important to be left to philosophers. It is my belief
that social work values are too serious to be consigned to
ideologues and ideological ways of thinking which may subordinate social work to their own particular ends. I
hope it is not too fanciful to see the predominance of
ideologies and ideologues as an indication of crises in
our society. Historically, ideological battles have been

fought in the streets; if one thinks of the kinds of
power conflicts that are ultimately generated by them this
is not surprising.   In the absence of belief in the
ability of our minds to discover any truths about the
human condition which are in any real sense binding, and
in the rejection of tradition which follows inevitably
from such a position, ideological ways of thinking are
bound to predominate.   The end of this process can only
be the attempt to resolve conflicts of world view, not by
reason, but by unmediated conflicts of power.

So long as philosophy and philosophers remain with-
drawn from the consideration of substantive issues, it is
inevitable that ideology should flourish; after all, in
these circumstances it has no rival.   The current situation as the philosophers withdraw from considerations of
the issues we have mentioned, is absurd and self-defeat-
ing.   Philosophy and philosophers are involved in the
world, however remote the realm and language of their dis-
course may seem.   This is what I understand Hume to be
saying.   Whatever is, or is not being said, the language
used, and to some extent what is actually happening in the
wider society, will reflect the role philosophy is playing
at any particular historical moment.   Of course, philosophy has some excuse for its own withdrawal, namely the
undoubted need to overhaul and scrutinise its own assumptions and tools, and its preoccupation (in some quarters)
with avoiding a complete subversion of what appears to be
the basis of any common sense.

But if the current predominance of ideology and ideological solutions is to be challenged, then philosophy
must play its part.   In order for this to happen, philosophy and philosophers have to recover from the failure
of nerve to which I have referred, and rekindle interest
in the real world and real issues, which we all persist
in being concerned about.

This is a matter of urgency, because the present situation is not only uncomfortable philosophically, but those
values which our society professes as central to it (and
which social work happens to hold in one form) are being
continually eroded by both scepticism and ideological
assault.   My examination of the dilemmas facing the individual social worker and the profession in their search
for a secure value-base has revealed a number of possible
approaches.   These are: the historical; the pragmatic-
instrumental; the ideological; and the 'existentialist'.
Obviously these categories do not appear in print and
rarely in verbal exchanges as clearly as I am concerned to
depict them, but one can discern their style and characteristic modes of expression quite readily.

In section 1 I referred to nostalgia for a past when
the basis for practice could be assumed and workers could
concentrate on developing their technical knowledge and
skills.   This approach is shown by Baker in The Challenge
for British Casework (1973):

> Casework as a specific method of helping involves a
> helping process which is illuminated by knowledge and
> underpinned by principles, assumptions, ethics and
> social values.   Each of these components demands con-
> tinuing empirical research and further critical theo-
> retical development but even more important *now* is to
> practise and teach what is already known about helping
> troubled people.

I am sure these are sentiments for which there is a great
deal of sympathy amongst social workers, they constitute
a mixture of conviction, faith and assertion but there is
no acknowledgment as to how the 'underpinning values' were
arrived at, nor whether the 'principles, assumptions,
ethics' referred to are in harmony or conflict, nor on how
or what they are based.

Barbara Wootton exemplifies the pragmatic approach;
her published lecture A Philosophy for the Social Services
(1975), turns out to be a plea for 'good communication and
simplicity'.   Nowhere is there a mention of philosophy;
the lecture consists of the advocacy of a 'welfare rights'
approach to 'clients' coupled with exhortations to social
workers to abandon pretence at professional knowledge and
vocabulary, which is evidently regarded as pretentious
nonsense.   Lady Wootton's hard-headed approach involves
both socialist and utilitarian values which are assumed
because there are no dilemmas or arguments anywhere to be
seen.   Those who believe that research can somehow 'show'
the truth of social work in practice in a way which es-
capes the problems of the values and assumptions upon
which it is based exemplify the instrumental approach.

The ideological approach is articulated clearly by
Popplestone in The Ideology of Professional Community
Workers (1971); having identified certain skills and
strategies for the developing profession he says:

> All this suggests an unashamedly conflict view of
> social relations with an articulated ideology that will
> itself have some appeal to clients and offer them the
> possibility of identifying with it, and perhaps some
> sympathy with the general working-class struggle.

In a more extreme form, similar views can be found in
'Case Con' (April 1972), wherein supporters set out their
ideological value orientation and their aims.   Clause One
of their basic premises committed supporters to a belief
in the working-class struggle as a means of achieving

socialism.   Clauses Two and Three demanded social work
involvement with grassroots organisations such as claim-
ants' unions and tenants' associations, in the hope that
social workers would play their part in hastening the
advent of the revolution.   Ideology and ideological processes approaches have of course been the substance of
this paper.   I write as one who has found their lure difficult to resist on occasions;   however, it is my view
that they are not merely divisive but ultimately destruc-
tive.

There are other approaches to social work which do not
claim or acknowledge an overt justification;   the kind of
social workers Halmos referred to.   Such individuals, if
aware of the intellectual precariousness of their value-
base find confirmation and justification in their actual
practice.   Others find support in the 'existential'
writers such as Rogers (1961) and Frankl (1967), and claim
that the worker/client relationship is sacrosanct and that
in the reciprocity of the genuinely helpful relationship
which can be established is to be found the meaning and
value of what they undertake, but which they claim is difficult to express in words.   Again it is easy to be sympathetic to such a viewpoint;   in a real sense the sometimes urgent business of social work cannot be suspended
while a careful analysis of its assumptions is carried out
by philosophical analysts concerned about the veracity of
any claims for justification.   Elsewhere in social work
literature there are writers (Smith, 1973;   Wilkes, 1973)
who are aware of the problems engendered by value conflicts, but who appear to believe that it is sufficient
to have identified such conflicts, or alternatively seek
consensus from the wider society.   Such consensus, as I
have already indicated, may not be forthcoming and even if
it were, there are dangers inherent in it.   Consensus is
not a magic way of arriving at objectively correct, or
right solutions, but rather merely represents one particular way of resolving conflicts;   allowing for one particular mode of the exercise of power.   Those who pay the
price of consensus are those excluded from it.

Philosophy is largely absent from social work discussion and literature and there are many reasons for this
state of affairs.   The current predominant schools of
Anglo-Saxon philosophy often seem remote from the business
of everyday life;   their observations and conclusions
curiously commonplace and uninviting.   There can be
little doubt that social work practice is urgently concerned with substantive human problems which were known
and treated as such in traditional philosophy, but as I
have shown, the present climate makes such an undertaking

very difficult.   None the less I believe a rational,
critical approach to the problems we have been discussing
is both possible and necessary.   I think a careful delin-
eation and analysis of one's assumptions, the basis they
have, and their entailments, although a prerequisite for
philosophy, is not the end of the enterprise;   to para-
phrase a well-known dictum of Austin's, analysis must be
the beginning-all but it is certainly not the end-all of
philosophy.

Such an approach does not afford a blueprint for an
ideal society but it does provide a range of evaluative
criteria.   For example, it is possible for one to be concerned about social justice without being committed to
socialism;   it is possible to accept the Marxist emphasis
on the role that economics plays in political and social
processes without accepting the Marxist ideology and its
solutions;   one may accept Freud's profound understanding
of the way in which persons develop without accepting his
reflections concerning man's ultimate nature, history and
civilisation.

The framework I propose also provides means by which
one can examine the kinds of choices open to us in their
rational and ethical implications.   Choices by definition
have both opportunities and risks as their entailments;
these we cannot avoid as private individuals or as social
work advocates.   Such choices seem to be to constitute
the essence of social work practice and, if I can end on
a grandiose note, of life itself.

2   Social services in a nutshell

David Watson

1

According to R.M. Titmuss (1968, p. 21) what lies at the
centre of our focus of vision in the study of social administration is the objectives of services, transactions
and transfers, in relation to social needs. We are concerned, for example, with such questions as 'What is the
point in having a National Health Service?', 'Why ought
we to provide industrial retraining centres?', 'Why ought
we to offer "sheltered" accommodation to former mental
hospital patients returning to the community?', and so on.
As Titmuss puts it:

> It is the objectives of these services, transactions
> and transfers in relation to social needs, rather than
> the particular administrative method or institutional
> device employed to attain objectives, which largely
> determine our interests in research and study, and the
> categorisation of these activities as social services.
> (1968, p. 21)

Even if Titmuss is thought to exaggerate the place of
the study of the welfare objectives of social policies in
the study of social administration, if such objectives are
studied at all, students of social administration and
students of philosophy have at least some interests in
common. Plato's 'Republic', for example, a text widely
used in the teaching of philosophy, in Books 3 and 7 includes a detailed account of an education service and its
objectives discussed in relation to the social needs of
members of various social classes.

In this essay I present a conceptual analysis of a
statement which may be said to describe social services
'in a nutshell'. The statement in question is made by
Robert Pinker in his book 'Social Theory and Social
Policy' (1971). He says:

Social services represent a compromise between compassion and indifference, just as they reflect our dispositions both to remember and to forget our social
obligations. (p. 135)

My discussion will centre on the first part of this
statement, that is, on the view that social services represent a compromise between compassion and indifference.
Pinker has in mind local authority social services in the
United Kingdom, and I shall also restrict discussion to
these social services. The analysis, however, might be
applied more widely by trading on the relation between
Pinker's statement and Wilensky and Lebeaux's earlier
statement that social welfare services in the *USA* 'represent a compromise between the values of economic indivi-
dualism and free enterprise on the one hand, and security,
equality, and humanitarianism on the other' (Wilensky and
Lebeaux, 1958, pp. 138-9).

The chapter from which the nutshell is taken offers
what Pinker describes as a provisional classification of
social services 'in terms of their status-enhancing and
stigmatising propensities' (p. 135).   I propose to examine the nutshell as a guide to the *principles of evaluation* which justify social policies with these propensities.   Such principles play an important part in the
identification of 'social needs' and the recommendation
or criticism of the objectives of social policies in relation to those needs.   I shall not develop this latter
point, but make it in order to stress that there is a
place within the study of social administration, on Titmuss's account, for analyses of the *kind* I offer, whatever is thought of this particular example.

I do not claim, or deny, that the description to be
examined is equally apposite in the description of all
social services, nor that other descriptions might not
lead to other principles of evaluation justifying social
services.   These are issues for another debate.   Further, I choose Pinker's description not in order to commit him to my analysis, but because the analysis of his
description serves well the introduction and development
of philosophical theses relevant to a particular justification of social services.

I take the following path.   First comes an account of
the sense in which social services might *represent* a compromise between compassion and indifference.   Second, the
compromise in question is considered in the light of a
philosophical account of the difference and relation between emotions and attitudes.   As a result of the argument of this section and because our search is for principles of evaluation used in *justification*, I proceed to

examine the view that social services represent a compromise between the *attitude* of compassion and the attitude
of indifference.   I first discuss the relation between
these attitudes in the light of a philosophical account
of the relation between attitudes and principles of
action.   We are then in a position to suggest principles
of evaluation which justify social policies with status-
enhancing and stigmatising propensities: *respect for
human beings* and *indifference to human beings*, respectively.   Such a result may seem strikingly uncontroversial.   However, there are objections to consider, and,
amongst others, I consider the widely canvassed, and sometimes different, principle of respect for *persons* as more
appropriate in the justification of status-enhancing
social policies.

2

First, in what sense might social services be said to *represent* a compromise between compassion and indifference?
   In the history of philosophy many great philosophers
have drawn an analogy between the state and man.   In the
'Republic' Plato is concerned with the nature of justice
and injustice in the individual.   After preliminary and
unsuccessful attempts to describe justice and injustice
in the individual, Plato suggests a new approach.   He
says:
   Imagine a rather short-sighted person told to read an
   inscription in small letters from some way off.   He
   would think it a godsend if someone pointed out that
   the same inscription was written up elsewhere on a
   bigger scale, so that he could first read the larger
   characters and then make out whether the smaller ones
   were the same....   We think of justice as a quality
   that may exist in a whole community as well as in an
   individual, and the community is the bigger of the two.
   Possibly, then, we may find justice there in larger
   proportions, easier to make out.   So I suggest that
   we should begin by inquiring what justice means in a
   state.   Then we can go on to look for its counterpart
   on a smaller scale in the individual.   (Cornford,
   1941)
In this case the analogy is drawn in the hope that an
examination of a quality in the state will throw light
upon the nature of this quality in the individual.
   In the 'Leviathan' (1651) Thomas Hobbes uses the analogy to throw light upon the nature of the state, his
account of the state being deduced from the nature of man.
In his Introduction Hobbes says the state

is but an artificial man; though of greater stature
and strength than the natural ... in which the *sovereignty* is an artificial *soul*, ... the *magistrates*, and
other *officers* ... artificial *joints*; *reward* and
punishment ... are the *nerves*, ... the *wealth* and
riches of all the particular members, are the
strength....

It seems reasonable to say that in Plato's use of the
analogy, a quality in the state *represents* a quality in
the individual, and in Hobbes's use of the analogy the
state *represents* the individual.

It seems to me that Pinker is operating with the same
analogy and using it in the same way. In his use qualities manifested in the existence and operations of an
institution, or set of institutions, such as local authority social services, represent qualities in the individual. In particular, social services represent a compromise an individual might make between compassion and
indifference. Further, an understanding of the nature
of compassion and indifference as characteristics of an
individual helps us understand social services, which is
our purpose.

Though Pinker may not have any particular individual
or group of individuals in mind, we can ask *whose* compromise between compassion and indifference social services represent. Two answers come to mind. First, the
compromise represented might be a compromise made by
those whose sponsorship is required for the establishment, continued existence and operations of social services. Second, it might be a compromise made by those
employed in the provision of social services. A social
institution may naturally develop a measure of autonomy
which would justify our saying that it represents some
characteristic of its policy-makers, and of those who put
its policies into practice where they are allowed a
measure of discretion.

This second thesis is an interesting challenge to the
conception of social service staff, social workers, doctors, nurses and so on, as 'going the second mile'.
There is no reason to think that a compromise between compassion and indifference precludes going a second mile,
but indifference is something such folk may be thought
free from.

Since Pinker says that social services represent a
compromise between compassion and indifference *just as*
they reflect *our* dispositions both to remember and to
forget *our* social obligations, it seems that his thesis
is rather that the compromise represented is one made by
we who sponsor social services.

So far, it has been argued that Pinker's view is that, presumably in their operation, social services share some of the characteristics of their sponsors, and in particular the characteristic of compromising between compassion and indifference. (1)   I now turn to a closer examination of the compromise.

3

'Compassion' may signify an emotion or an attitude. Since indifference is, as I understand it, the absence of any emotions at the thought or mention of the object, 'indifference' signifies an attitude only.   Emotions and attitudes can be in conflict, as for example when one is strongly attracted towards someone but, perhaps because she is the boss's daughter, maintains an aloof attitude towards her.   Again one may maintain a favourable attitude towards an object which excites a strong repugnance, perhaps because she's the boss's daughter.   As J.O. Urmson (1968) says:

Often it will be our duty, and within our power, to do this; it is likely in such circumstances for it also to be our duty to try to overcome the emotion, but we may not succeed.   We can decide on our attitudes, but we can only take steps which are likely to result in a change of our emotions....   From the moral point of view it is particularly important that we can often choose to maintain an attitude which is out of accord with our feelings and emotions.   (pp. 42-3)

Further:

Our emotions are relatively beyond our control, completely so in the case of the less stable among us. We may try to suppress them, to discipline ourselves in ways which we expect to modify them, or to have them modified for us by psychotherapists; but we cannot simply choose which emotions to feel.   We can, however, choose our words and deeds, or most of us can most of the time.   Because of this we can to a great extent choose our attitudes and thus be immediately responsible for them, particularly those attitudes to which word and deed are of paramount importance. This, in its turn, explains why we can and do speak quite naturally of people adopting attitudes and maintaining them, of people being argued out of them, of logically consistent and inconsistent sets of attitudes, of well-based and ill-considered attitudes, and so on.   But we do not adopt or maintain our feelings and emotions; we are not argued out of them, even if

we may be in some way talked out of them;   though they
may be appropriate, they can hardly be well-based.
(p. 43)

The conceptual points made in these quoted passages are
particularly important.   Presumably we may say of the
policies of social service departments that they are
adopted and maintained, that they are argued successfully
for and against, that they are well-based and ill-considered, and so on, and this suggests that social service
department policies represent *attitudes*.   When we say
these things about the activities of such departments we
imply that their activities represent attitudes rather
than emotions, and if we see social services as representing some characteristic of its sponsors, we imply that its
policies represent the attitudes of its sponsors rather
than their emotions.

What *Pinker* says is that social services represent a
compromise between compassion and indifference.   If he is
using 'compassion' to signify an emotion, it is his view
that these policies represent a compromise between an
emotion and an attitude.   This is a useful point to make
because emotions can play a part not only in the success
of hospital flag days and local residents' participation
in community projects, but also in social welfare provision.   This is recognised when we say, for example, that
we are motivated to sponsor social services by 'frater-
nity' or 'a sense of community'.   These terms sometimes
signify an attitude, but they may also signify emotions
motivating a devotion of a kind resembling that felt to
brothers but extended to members of a community to which
one belongs (cf. Downie and Telfer, 1969, pp. 61-3).   Any
account of social services in the United Kingdom would be
incomplete if it did not refer to this component.

Even so, since I am concerned with Pinker's statement
as a guide to the principles of evaluation which justify
social policies with status-enhancing and stigmatising
propensities, I shall assume 'compassion' to signify an
attitude.   As we have seen, it is our attitudes rather
than our emotions which are well-based or ill-based, considered or ill-considered, argued for and against, so presumably we may say of attitudes but not of emotions that
they are justified or unjustified;   attitudes rather than
emotions are a guide to principles of evaluation used in
justifications.   As Urmson (1968) also says, emotions are
   importantly relevant to our attitudes;   but they are
   not predominantly or exceptionally relevant to them.
   Thoughts, beliefs, words and deeds are also relevant,
   and will be expected, as a matter of logic and not
   merely of psychological appropriateness, to vary in

character according as the attitude is one of interest, indifference, disdain, aloofness, friendliness, benevolence, hostility or approval.   But, though emotion, thought, word and deed are all logically relevant to the determination of an attitude, none is essential. (p. 42)

4

I propose now to consider the view that social services represent a compromise between the *attitude* of compassion and the attitude of indifference.   I shall discuss the relation between these attitudes and certain moral and social *principles*.   Such an approach is consistent with the conception of social administration mentioned at the beginning of the essay, on which the study of welfare *objectives* and of social *policy* lies at the centre of our focus of vision.

Broadly, principles of action are identical with policies.   If someone's policy as a social worker is to discuss marital difficulties only when both partners are present, then this is the principle of action he adopts, and vice versa.   Principles of action are related to *objectives* in two main ways.   They may be means to objectives.   For example, a nurse might have as an objective that the patient recover his health.   As a means to that end, the nurse might adopt a principle of scrupulous hygiene.   On the other hand, principles of action may themselves be, or encapsulate, objectives.   For example, someone might adopt a principle of honesty, with no objective in view other than being honest.

Such an approach also reflects something of the context Pinker himself provides for the statement with which we began.   He says 'social services represent a compromise between compassion and indifference just as they reflect our dispositions both to remember and to forget *our social obligations*' (my emphasis).   Social obligations are derived from social principles.   Further, welfare objectives and social policies are frequently justified or condemned by reference to their compatibility with adoption of given moral and social principles.   This can be more, or less explicit.   Here are four examples:

(a) 'It is cardinal to a proper health organisation that a person ought not to be financially deterred from seeking medical assistance at the earliest possible stage.'   (Aneurin Bevan, then Minister of Health, 2nd reading NHS Bill, 30 April 1946; 422 HC deb. 5S.)

(b)   'The acceptance of a prices and incomes policy as a
      part of a contract between the Government and the
      people is dependent upon the nature of our society.
      The Prime Minister cannot build a more just society
      "at a stroke".   One must build such a society brick
      by brick.   Everything one does must be infused with
      a determination to move towards one's socially
      planned and socially just goal.   Our complaint
      against the Government, and in particular the Prime
      Minister, is that brick by brick they have set out
      to create an unjust society.'   (Mrs Barbara Castle,
      Debate on the Queen's Speech, 6 November 1972, 845
      HC deb. 5S.)

(c)   'It has always been contrary to the principles of
      humanity to think and act exclusively;   now we can-
      not afford it.   The people of the less-developed
      countries must be helped to attain the basic needs
      which are every person's birthright or we shall all
      share the resultant misery.   That is not just idea-
      lism or sentiment;   it is a practical approach to
      international affairs.   It is indeed the approach
      that has guided the actions of my Government in both
      its domestic and its foreign policies.'   (Norman
      Kirk, late Prime Minister of New Zealand, 'Third
      World', vol. 3, no. 5, 1974.)

(d)   A Colonel ('Buffy'?) Wigg 'asked the Minister of
      Food if he will arrange for the increased supplies
      of beer to go to Dudley and Netherton in view of
      the special needs of heavy manual workers engaged
      in chain-making, mining and similar industries.'
      (24 June 1946, 425 HC deb. 5S.)

In their book 'Respect for Persons' (1969), R.S. Downie
and Elizabeth Telfer argue that there is a *logical* connection between an attitude and a principle of action:

in that if a person has a certain attitude towards
something he will necessarily adopt certain principles
of action towards it *other things being equal*, and the
general nature of the principles can be inferred from
knowledge of the attitude.   (p. 16)

They explain:

We need to add the qualification in order to allow for
conflicting attitudes.   Thus, if a man has an attitude
of fear towards cows, he will (other things being
equal) adopt a principle of avoiding cows;   but if he
has another attitude which is one of humiliation and
self-loathing towards the first attitude, he may well
make it a principle to walk through fields of cows as
often as he can, hoping to cure himself.   We can make
this point in another way by saying that principles of

action are logically connected with certain attitudes
in so far as these attitudes can be regarded as working
in isolation.   (pp. 16-17)

The qualification allows for the fact that some attitudes may override others and the principle of action
logically related to the overriden attitude not be
adopted.

On this view, having a certain attitude towards something is a sufficient condition of adopting certain principles of action towards it, other things being equal.
Without discussing this relation further, I should like
to go on to ask what principles of action are adopted by
someone with the attitudes of compassion and indifference?
Before this question is answered, one more general point
about attitudes may be noted.   As Downie and Telfer point
out, 'it is conceptually impossible for an attitude to
lack an object' (1969, p. 17).   Fear, for example, is
necessarily fear *of* something, aggression is necessarily
aggression *towards* something.   The objects of compassion
and indifference *in general* are difficult to identify.
We might be indifferent towards almost anything from
whisky to weasels but 'a being capable of suffering' might
label the object of compassion.   However, it is not so
difficult to identify the objects of these attitudes as
represented by social services.   Here the object of both
attitudes is, I shall argue, *a human being*.   The need to
argue this apparently uncontroversial claim will be understood when I consider alternatives.   More fully, the
object of compassion as represented by the social services
is a human being or human beings believed to be in need
of, or perhaps deserving, social service provision of some
good he, or they, ought to enjoy.   The object of indifference here is a human being or human beings *not* believed
to be in need of, or perhaps deserving, social service
provision of some good he, or they, ought to enjoy.   It
is a *human being* that is believed, or not believed, to be
in need of social service provision of supportive visits,
or a home help, or whatever.

I do not propose to include in this discussion an analysis of the concepts of need and desert.   Such an analysis may be found, for example, in S.I. Benn and R.S.
Peters's 'Social Principles and the Democratic State'
(1959).   However, I do want to stress that an evaluative
conception of a human being is entailed by the attitude of
compassion represented by the social services, while no
evaluative conception of a human being is entailed by the
attitude of indifference in this context.

To say that someone is in need is generally at least to
say that he does not possess what he ought to possess in

order to be *as a human being should be*. Thus, for example, we might say that a man needs freedom of speech in order to be self-determining. Or we might say that a severely disabled man needs a telephone in order to maintain and develop relationships with other human beings. In these cases we judge a human being to be in need when he lacks something he ought to possess in order to have characteristics we believe he ought to have, namely self-determination and the ability to maintain and develop relationships with others. Similarly, to say that someone deserves something is generally at least to say that he does not possess what he ought to possess in consequence of his being *as a human being should be*. Thus, for example, we might say of a man found with his hand in the till, that he deserves the benefit of the doubt if he has always previously been honest. Here we judge a human being to be deserving because he has previously displayed a characteristic we value in human beings.

The positive evaluation of some (though not necessarily all) human characteristics is, thus, through its objects in this context, entailed by the attitude of compassion. Since, I suggested, the object of indifference in this context is a human being or human beings not believed to be in need of, or perhaps deserving, social service provision of some good he, or they, ought to enjoy, it might also be suggested that *no* positive evaluation of human characteristics is, through its object in this context, entailed by the attitude of indifference. (To say this is not to say that a *negative* evaluation is entailed.)

I said earlier that Pinker's statement was to be examined as a guide to the principles of evaluation which justify social policies with status-enhancing and stigmatising propensities. Attitudes which, respectively, entail the positive evaluation of some human characteristics and no positive evaluation of human characteristics entail just such principles. The former clearly gives human beings, as such, status and entails, it seems to me, a principle which may be characterised as *respect for human beings*. Following Downie and Telfer (1969, p. 29), by 'respect' I signify an attitude of 'active sympathy' and a readiness at least to consider the applicability of other men's rules both to them and to ourselves. Their use of 'respect', and so mine too, will I hope be made clearer in my later discussion of respect for human beings in relation to their rival principle, respect for persons.

The relation between this notion of respect and compassion is indicated if we follow the account of compassion given, for example, by Bishop Joseph Butler in his

Sermon (V) Upon Compassion (1726).   He says: 'When we
rejoice in the prosperity of others, and compassionate in
their distress, we, as it were, substitute them for ourselves, their interest for our own; and have the same
kind of pleasure in their prosperity and sorrow in their
distress, as we have from reflection upon our own.'   In
serving their own interests men adopt certain principles
of action.   In substituting their interest for our own,
we consider the applicability of other men's principles
both to them and to ourselves.   Suppose your wife is due
home from the pub and you still haven't done the washing-
up, it may be in your interest to do it but not mine.
If I wash while you dry, that is, substitute your interest for my own, I have (other things being equal) considered the applicability of your principles to you and to
me: I have asked myself whether or not I ought to do it.
     The following objection might be made to this indica-
tion of the relation between compassion and respect by
someone who holds morality to be independent of interests,
who draws a distinction between categorical principles
('One ought to keep one's promises') and hypothetical
principles ('One ought to keep one's promises *if* one wants
to have friends').   On Butler's notion of compassion, as
substituting others' *interests* for one's own, an attitude
of compassion towards human beings entails respect for
them as creatures with interests.   It does not entail
respect for them as creatures with the ability to adopt
rules which are held to be binding on oneself and all
rational beings - the kind of creature which, according
to Downie and Telfer, their notion of respect is defined
to fit (1969, p. 29).   The objection is, then, that while
Butler's notion of compassion may be related to *a* notion
of respect, it does not entail Downie and Telfer's notion.
My use of 'respect' is, therefore, yet to be explained.
I shall not answer this objection now, but it will be answered later when I argue that, on the contrary, Downie
and Telfer's *account* of respect is *not* defined to fit only
creatures with the ability to adopt rules which are held
to be binding on oneself and all rational beings.   I
shall argue that as they use the term, respect might be
shown for human beings as creatures with interests and
such respect might, therefore, be entailed by an attitude
of compassion.
     To adhere to respect for human beings in the context of
social services is to recognise certain obligations to
human beings in need of, or perhaps deserving, social service provision of some good they ought to enjoy.   It
might be said that while respect for human beings entails
recognition of the status of human beings, it does not

entail *enhancement* of that status, and so cannot be the principle of evaluation which justifies social policies with status-enhancing propensities.   In reply I would say that a principle that entails simply recognition of the status of human beings may be used to justify *universal* social policies which *enhance* the status of human beings relative to other things (putting education, say, before economic growth and international prestige), and *selective* social policies which enhance the status of some human beings relative to others (putting Old Age Pension increases before expenditure on new schools, say).

The attitude of indifference neither gives nor denies human beings, as such, status, and entails, it seems to me, a principle which may be characterised simply as *indifference to human beings*.   To adhere to this principle in the context of social services is not to recognise obligations to human beings in need of, or perhaps deserving, social service provision of some good they ought to enjoy.   From the point of view of someone who does recognise such obligations, someone adhering to the principle of respect for human beings, this will clearly be seen as stigmatising: indifference to human beings is failing to show due respect for human beings.

The attitudes of compassion and indifference, and the principles which I have suggested are entailed by them, are such that a compromise might be reached, and reached in more than one way.   Suppose that in a particular society the principle of respect for human beings entails the positive evaluation of certain characteristics usually best developed and maintained through family life, such as emotional stability and the ability to make relationships with other human beings.   A compromise social service might promote family life but only half-heartedly.   A candidate for this description from among British social services would be the provision of Supplementary Benefit for deserted or unmarried women with children and an income thought inadequate for maintenance of a satisfactory family life.   Provision indicates positive evaluation of certain characteristics related to family life;   lack of provision would indicate our not valuing those characteristics;   inadequate provision indicates a compromise between compassion and indifference, and between the principles of respect and indifference.   This seems to me to be the most common form of compromise.   Those who regard present provision as inadequate, in any of the social services, may describe provision made as representing this compromise.

However, there are at least two other routes to a compromise.   A social service might adequately promote some

valued human characteristics but not others.   Again, suppose the characteristics developed and maintained through
family life to be valued, and now also self-respect.   The
former might be adequately promoted but not the latter.
A candidate for this description is hard to find, but suppose Unemployment Benefit to be adequate for the maintenance of family life.   Its provision indicates positive
evaluation of certain characteristics related to family
life, but we indicate not valuing self-respect if we deliver the provision in circumstances in which self-respect
is undermined - by not having facilities for confidential
interviewing, say.   The social service provided in this
way is a compromise between compassion and indifference,
and between the principles of respect and indifference.
In this kind of case we do not have half-hearted promotion
of a particular characteristic, but promotion of only a
part of a set of valued characteristics.

Incidentally, an objection might be made, against these
two kinds of case, that I assume that valued characteristics may be promoted independently, and this is false.
Self-respect, for example, cannot be ignored without cost
to characteristics maintained in family life.   This seems
to me plausible, and in that case social services will always represent a compromise between compassion and indifference, so long as not all members of the set of valued
characteristics are promoted adequately.

A third kind of compromise occurs when social services
have conflicting objectives.   For example, in Part III of
the 1948 National Assistance Act, an obligation is placed
upon local authorities to provide accommodation for homeless families.   This might be seen as indicating the
positive evaluation again of those characteristics usually
best developed and maintained in family life.   However,
no positive evaluation of such characteristics is shown
if the local authority in practice provides accommodation
only for women and children.   Further, one objective of
Part III of the 1948 Act is keeping families together,
while an objective of some local authority practice is
splitting up families.   It may be true, that this is just
a means to the objective of keeping the families together
later, in other accommodation, but in the short run, means
and end conflict and, I think it might reasonably be said,
a compromise between compassion and indifference emerges.

Support for respect for human beings as a principle of
action which is entailed by these attitudes represented by
social services has recently been expressed in A Code of
Ethics for Social Work (BASW, 1973a) and in The Inalienable Element in Social Work (BASW, 1973b).   In their
Statement of Principles, the authors of the Code declare

that 'Basic to the profession of social work is the recognition of the value and dignity of every individual human being, irrespective of origin, status, sex, age, belief or contribution to society' (1973a, section 3.2.1).   In The Inalienable Element in Social Work it is declared that 'All social work is based upon respect for the value of the individual' (para. 10).

Support for the view that a principle of acting with indifference to human beings is entailed by the attitudes represented by social services is summarised by Eileen Younghusband in the following passage from The Future of Social Work (1973, p. 33):

Nowadays, we are paying dearly for an innocent arrogance in which caseworkers often claimed to be able to make a significant intervention in almost every form of social problem.   These large, rather vague claims had a double boomerang effect.   First, if the claim was valid (which of course it wasn't) then, said some, we were acting as agents of the establishment, using essentially manipulative skills, which we dressed up as self-determination, to manoeuvre deviant people into conformity to accepted (i.e., middle class) standards of behaviour.   Secondly, most people have coping mechanisms that function most of the time, so social work, that is casework, is essentially a marginal activity with deviant or overwhelmed people and has nothing to contribute to the mainstream of ordinary social life. Moreover, deviance does not exist in its own right. It is a type of reaction to social conditions which is as predictable and as 'normal' as other reactions to these.

Thus, runs the argument, the only hope for social work, indeed the only decent thing to do, is to get into the mainstream of social action, to realise that it is simply irrelevant to act as the 'poor man's psychiatrist' when so much of the stress in people's lives is caused directly or indirectly by social circumstances, by poverty, bad housing, poor education, unemployment, being caught in the trap of powerlessness to change one's lot.   In these circumstances it is only structural change in society that will have any real effect.

We act with indifference to human beings when we ignore human characteristics, such as self-determination, and we act on the same principle in accepting a social structure in which, for many human beings who might otherwise possess them, these characteristics cannot reasonably be expected to develop to any significant degree.

5

A number of difficulties arise in connection with respect
for human beings as a principle of action entailed by
attitudes represented by social services, and I now want
to consider them.   First, it may be argued that although
some social provision, such as education or health services, is universal rather than selective, nevertheless
the widest classification under which users of social services generally fall is that of 'client', say.   'Respect
for clients' or even 'respect for human beings in need'
might plausibly be suggested as a principle of action entailed by attitudes represented by social services, but
not 'respect for human beings'.   Generally the object of
any attitude represented by social services must be a
human being *in certain circumstances* and not simply a
human being.   Social services do not generally cater for
so large a clientele.

In reply I admit the selectivity of most social service
provision but deny that this casts any doubt upon the
plausibility of 'respect for human beings' as the relevant
principle of action.   On the contrary, principles of
client selection reflect our positive evaluation of some
human characteristics.   A man would almost certainly not
be invited to attend the meetings of a group of parents of
school-refusers simply in virtue of being a human being.
But if he were invited in virtue of himself being a parent
of a school-refuser it would be in order to aid him, if
possible, to attain a measure of acceptance and understanding of his situation and to provide him with support
in any course of action he might implement to change it.
The client is selected as someone lacking, as regards this
situation at least, characteristics valued in a human
being.   In this case perhaps realism, understanding and
the ability to circumvent obstacles to one's goals, in
certain ways.

Second, it may be objected that the general principle
of action entailed by the attitude of compassion is not
'respect for human beings' but *'respect for persons'*.   In
valuing some human characteristics, it may be said, we
assert that human beings ought to be respected for what is
valuable in them, and what is valuable in them is what
makes a human being a *person*.   Such an objection may be
derived from Downie and Telfer (1969, ch. 1).

The principle of respect for persons has been offered
before, in particular to social workers.   Jonathan
Moffett (1968, p. 27) writes '"Respect for persons" is
more than anything the value that gives casework its particular character....   Its main purpose is to remind

caseworkers that they are dealing with human beings like
themselves.' The latter part of this quotation suggests
that Moffett would not draw a distinction between 'respect
for persons' and 'respect for human beings' despite basing
his account, as do Downie and Telfer, on the views of
W.G. Maclagan (1960), which are in turn derived from Kant.
Nor are the principles so clearly different in the more
detailed account of 'respect for persons' given by Raymond
Plant (1970, p. 11 ff.).   According to Plant, 'what is in
question is ... respect for a person *as* a human being'.
However, on Downie and Telfer's account, I shall argue,
the two principles are different, and so an objection to
my thesis arises.   For this reason I want to discuss
their account of 'respect for persons'.

In their use, 'person' is a fairly precise term, implying the possession of capacities to be self-determining
and rule-following (Downie and Telfer, 1969, p. 35).
Self-determination 'involves, in the first place, the
ability to choose for oneself, and, more extensively, to
formulate purposes, plans and policies of one's own.   A
second and closely connected element is the ability to
carry out decisions, plans or policies without undue re-
liance on the help of others' (p. 20).   Rule-following is
'the ability to govern one's conduct by rules, and indeed,
more grandly, to adopt rules which one holds to be binding
on oneself and all rational beings' (p. 21).

Respect for persons is a different principle from respect for human beings, I believe, for, as Downie and
Telfer recognise, not all human beings are persons: the
senile, certain categories of the mentally ill, and children, for example.   Respect for human beings allows, but
respect for persons strictly does not allow respect for
human beings who are not persons.   It must be made clear
that Downie and Telfer do not regard such human beings as
being outside the sympathy of practical concern for others
(Maclagan's 'active sympathy', 1960, p. 24).   But the
attitude of *respect*, and the ingredient of active sympathy, is seen as *extended* to human beings who are not persons (Downie and Telfer, 1969, p. 34).

Two points might be made in response to my claim that
respect for persons is a different principle from respect
for human beings.   First, if it is a different principle,
then it is not *significantly* different for, to repeat, the
attitude of respect may be extended to human beings who
are not persons.   Children do not possess capacities to
be self-determining and rule-following, but may develop
such capacities.   Again, the senile, though not possessing capacities to be self-determining and rule-following,
once possessed such capacities.   Certain categories of

the mentally ill present a greater difficulty for this
kind of analysis.   Congenital idiots never have possessed, do not possess, and never will possess capacities to
be self-determining and rule-following.   However, according to Downie and Telfer:

> The answer is that there are still sufficient resem-
> lances between them and persons to justify extending
> the language of *agape* [respect] to them, although it
> would not be possible to adopt such an attitude to
> them unless we first knew what it was to adopt it to-
> wards normal persons.   (1969, p. 35)

In sum, to the claim that respect for persons is a different principle from respect for human beings, it may be
replied that it is not importantly different because the
language of respect may be extended to all human beings
who are not persons, since they are 'potential persons'
(p. 34), 'lapsed persons' (p. 34), or share 'sufficient
resemblances' to persons.   Further, emphasis on respect
for *persons* brings out what a principle of respect for
human beings would obscure, namely the logical priority
of respect for persons in the full sense of 'persons'.
Respect for persons does not preclude respect for human
beings who are not persons, but it makes clear that the
attitude of respect is *extended* in the latter kind of
case.

I'm not sure why Downie and Telfer say that it would
not be possible to adopt an attitude of respect towards
human beings who are not persons unless we first knew what
it was to adopt it towards normal persons (p. 35), but I
think the explanation lies in the second point which might
be made in reply to my claim.   I have been using 'respect' in 'respect for human beings' as do Downie and Telfer in 'respect for persons'.   To repeat: 'respect'
signifies the attitude of *agape*: 'an attitude of active
sympathy and a readiness at least to consider the applicability of other men's rules both to them and to ourselves' (p. 29).   But in that case, it may be said, respect is primarily adopted towards persons rather than
human beings in general.   The attitude of respect in
question is 'defined to fit the concept of a person' (p.
29), '"a person" is the formal object of *agape*' (p. 29).
We cannot adopt an attitude of respect unless we know what
respect is.   On the account of respect in question, respect is for *persons*, and we must understand this before
the possibility of adopting the attitude to persons or
indeed to human beings who are not persons arises.   This
is what I think lies behind the statement that it would
not be possible to adopt an attitude of respect towards
human beings who are not persons unless we first knew what
it was to adopt it towards normal persons.

In sum, in reply to my claim that respect for persons
is a different principle from respect for human beings, it
may be said that the latter is indeed a different principle, but it is no alternative.   For, except by an extension under the principle of respect for persons, *respect*
for human beings who are not persons is logically impossible.

I should now like to comment on these two points, beginning with the second.

I want first to challenge the view that the attitude
of respect in question is 'defined to fit the concept of
a person'.   In the account accepted, the attitude of respect is defined in terms of two necessary and jointly sufficient components.   One is 'a readiness at least to consider the applicability of other men's rules both to them
and to ourselves' (p. 29).   This component does not, I
think, imply that the object of respect is 'a person', a
human being with the capacities to be self-determining
and rule-following.   This readiness may be an independently necessary condition of the attitude of respect, but
this necessity is not identical with, nor does it imply,
the necessity for the object of respect to be capable of
following rules whose applicability both to them and to
ourselves we must be ready to consider.   It may be true
that we cannot *respect* someone unless we are ready to consider the applicability of his rules both to him and to
ourselves *if he follows any*, but it does not follow that,
in order to be the object of respect, he must.

The other component is 'an attitude of active sympathy'
(p. 29).   In Maclagan's words, active sympathy is the
'sympathy of practical *concern for* others as distinguished
from simply *feeling with* them' (1960, p. 211).   In Downie
and Telfer's words, active sympathy for others is 'making
their ends our own' (1969, p. 25).   This component, I
believe, also does not imply that the formal object of
respect is 'a person'.

We may, of course, distinguish between what a man aims
at and what he might reasonably be expected to aim at.
Both may be said to be 'his end'.   If we understand
'making their ends our own' to mean 'aiming at what they
aim at', then, on this account of active sympathy the
second component *does* imply that the formal object of respect is 'a person'.   That Downie and Telfer *understand*
(as opposed to 'describe') active sympathy in this way
emerges in their account of the relation between passive
and active sympathy.   Here the other's ends are his aims,
and he is conceived of as exercising self-determination in
the pursuit of objects of inclination (pp. 26-7).

However, if we understand 'making their ends our own'

to mean 'aiming at what they might reasonably be expected
to aim at', the second component does not imply that the
formal object of respect is 'a person'.   Human beings who
are neither self-determining nor rule-following may have
ends in this sense;   they may be ends at which someone
might reasonably be expected to aim even if he is in fact
unable to choose these ends for himself, formulate purposes, plans and policies of his own, or govern his conduct by rules.   Using the language of Butler's account
of compassion: we may show respect even for such human
beings because it is in their interest that certain ends
be attained;   in that sense we may make their ends our
own.

On this alternative interpretation, active sympathy for
others is aiming at what they might reasonably be expected
to aim at.   'Active sympathy', thus understood, may be
directed towards human beings who are not 'persons' in the
full sense.   As an ingredient in the attitude of respect
it permits respect for such human beings, and it is false
that 'respect' 'has been defined to fit the concept of a
person' and that '"a person" is the formal object of
agape'.

Respect for human beings, is, then, a logically possible alternative to respect for persons. (2)   We must
now reconsider whether it is an importantly different
principle.

It will be recalled that, according to Downie and Telfer, it is possible to adopt an attitude of respect towards congenital idiots because 'there are still sufficient resemblances between them and persons to justify extending the language of agape to them'.   What resemblances there are is not made clear.   I should like to
supplement this remark by stating the obvious.   Both congenital idiots and persons are human beings.

The expression 'human being' can be used purely des-
criptively, serving simply to distinguish human beings
from other animals.   However, it can also be used evalua-
tively, serving to commend certain human characteristics,
to indicate those qualities of human beings which are
thought valuable.   According to Downie and Telfer, what
is valuable in a human being is what makes him a person.
They say that 'the concept of a person is ... an evaluative concept with something of the force of "that which
makes a human being valuable" implied in it' (p. 19), that
to say 'Persons ought to be respected' is to say 'Humans
ought to be respected for what is valuable in them' (p.
20), and finally they summarise 'We said that the formal
object of respect is "that which is thought valuable", and
that those aspects of human beings in virtue of which they

fall under this description - those aspects which are
thought valuable - are summed up by the expressions "a
person" and "personality"' (p. 29).

   This seems to me to be a correct account of the evaluative stance of someone adopting the principle of respect
for persons.   However, such a principle cannot justify
respect for congenital idiots.   The principle of respect
for persons implies that what is valuable in a human being
is what makes him a person.   A congenital idiot never has
possessed, does not possess, and never will possess what
would make him a person.   If the language of *agape* is
'defined to fit the concept of a person' (p. 29), then
there cannot be 'sufficient resemblances between them
[congenital idiots] and persons to justify extending the
language of *agape* to them' (p. 35).   Persons and congenital idiots are, *ex hypothesi*, unlike in the crucial par-
ticulars.

   Clearly a different view of what is valuable in a human
being might be taken; the expression 'human being' may
serve to commend rather more human characteristics than
the capacities to be self-determining and rule-following.
We might, for example, value the capacities to be emotionally secure, to give and to receive love and affection, to
be content and free from worry, to be healthy, and so on.
Of these only the capacity to *give* love and affection,
debatably, implies the capacities of a person.   If these
capacities were those commended by someone adopting a
principle of respect for human beings, then there *are* generally sufficient resemblances between congenital idiots
and human beings to permit respect for congenital idiots.
My remark that both are human beings may be developed by
saying that both have the capacity to be emotionally
secure, to receive love, and to be content and free from
worry.   Further, given my alternative interpretation of
'active sympathy for others' to mean 'aiming at what they
might otherwise reasonably be expected to aim at', respect
may be directed towards such human beings who are not persons without an extension of the language of *agape*.

   It was said earlier that an attitude of respect, even
when it is defined to fit the concept of a person, may be
extended to at least some human beings who are not persons, namely children and the senile.   We may value them
as 'potential' and 'lapsed' persons, respectively.   But
it is also true that we may value both for other characteristics than their (historical) relation to the capacities of a person.   Respect for children and the senile
may be associated with adoption of a principle of respect
for human beings on which, say, the capacities listed
earlier were valued.   Since children and the senile both

generally possess the capacities to be emotionally secure,
to receive love and affection, and to be content and free
from worry, they qualify for respect as human beings with
these capacities. We might respect children and the
senile even if they were not 'potential' and 'lapsed' persons, respectively.

This point also serves to rebut an objection which
might be made to the hypothesis, accepted by Downie and
Telfer and by myself, that 'a congenital idiot never has
possessed, does not possess, and never will possess what
would make him a person'. According to Errol E. Harris
(1968, p. 127):

> however difficult and extreme the case of insanity, and
> however apparently incurable, we can at least always
> hope for improvement. We cannot know for sure that
> the patient's internal make-up will not become so modi-
> fied as to rectify his outward behaviour, or that no
> new remedial techniques will be discovered to which he
> would respond. He remains therefore, a potential
> medium for the realisation of value and retains the
> right to be treated as an end in himself.

Persons and congenital idiots are, then, unlike in the
crucial respects, but it is possible that they may become
like, and so congenital idiots too are at least possible
potential persons.

It must be admitted that the methods used to identify
congenital idiots are not infallible. In recognition of
this fact we may value some of these human beings as possible potential persons. But it is also true, I think,
that we *know* that some individuals will never be persons.
And yet we might respect them. And even if those congenital idiots who are possible potential persons were
not, we might respect them too. It seems to me that
Harris fails in his attempt to show that 'every human
being, however immature or defective, who has any mental
capacity at all, is a person' (p. 129). On the other
hand, we may continue to assert that every human being is
worthy of respect if we take a different and wider view
of what is valuable in a human being.

At this point I should say that I do not regard my list
of what is valuable in human beings as definitive. I
have listed capacities which I believe are generally
valued in this society, and I would include the capacities
which make a human being a person. Nor do I want to suggest that any particular capacity is a necessary condition
of being a respect-worthy human being as the capacity to
be rule-following is a necessary condition of being a person. A particular child may not possess the capacity to
receive love and affection, a particular senile individual

may not possess the capacity to be emotionally secure, or
to be healthy.   Which, if any, valued capacities constitute necessary or sufficient conditions for being a respect-worthy human being, is another question I don't want
to go into here.   Even so, as Downie and Telfer (1969)
say in connection with the same problem raised for persons, 'a possible answer to the problem is to be found if
we try to compile a list of those features which constitute the "generic" human "self" or are the "distinctive
endowment of a human being"' (p. 19).

If we adopt this method, as do Downie and Telfer, our
list may not include the capacities to be emotionally
secure, to receive love and affection, to be content and
free from worry, to be healthy, and so on.   It is arguable **that** animals other than human beings possess these
capacities.   They are not *distinctive* of human beings.
This method might indeed lead to a list of valued capacities such that only *persons* qualify as respect-worthy
human beings.   But it is important to notice that the
method provides an answer to the question 'what is valuable *and distinctive* in human beings?', since some valuable capacities possessed by human beings are also possessed by animals other than human beings.   Since the
formal object of respect is 'that which is thought valuable', human beings ought to be respected for what is
valuable in them, but those aspects which are thought
valuable are not summed up by the expressions 'a person'
and 'personality', though these expressions may sum up
those aspects which are thought valuable and distinctive.

Having argued that respect for human beings is a logically possible alternative to respect for persons, I went
on to reconsider whether it is an importantly different
principle.   We may now say that if respect for human
beings implies valuing at least the human capacities
listed, including the capacities of a person, then respect for human beings is an importantly different principle from respect for persons.   Respect for human beings
permits respect to be directed towards children and the
senile for other characteristics than their relation to
the capacities of a person, which they do not possess.
Respect for human beings permits respect to be directed
towards known congenital idiots in virtue of their possession of at least some of the valued capacities.   Respect for persons does neither.

We should also consider a relevant empirical question.
Is the general principle of action entailed by the attitude of compassion represented by British social services
'respect for human beings' rather than 'respect for persons'?   It was maintained in the quotation from Young-

husband (1973) that social services in Britain typically
deal with human beings who are only to a limited extent
self-determining and rule-following.   However, it must be
admitted, I think, that *social work*, at least, typically
aims to encourage and develop these characteristics.   Admitting children into care, marriage guidance, supportive
casework with the depressed, discussion of rent arrears
and budgeting, discussion of the extent of the client's
own contribution to his problem and that of others, informing the client of the provision to which he is entitled and perhaps taking up his case, etc., may all be justified on the ground that they promote self-determination
and rule-following.   The principle of respect for persons, then, may plausibly be put forward as entailed by
compassion represented by social work.   But, of course,
social work activities also typically aim to encourage
and develop other human capacities such as the capacity
to receive love and affection and to be content and free
from worry (which is not to say that social workers necessarily encourage acceptance of any social conditions con-
tributing to the discontent; there is more than one route
to contentment).   The principle of respect for human
beings specified earlier is, therefore, also entailed by
compassion represented by social work.   Respect for human
beings entails, but entails more than respect for persons
and is thus the more fundamental principle entailed.

Further, social work is, of course, only one part of
the social services provided in Britain.   Education and
medical services may be said to promote self-determination
and rule-following, but it also seems fair to say that
these services also reflect a positive evaluation of other
human capacities.   Medical services include provision for
congenital idiots and others who are severely mentally
handicapped, and thus manifest respect for a category of
human being which the principle of respect for persons excludes from esteem.   Provision for congenital idiots must
be justified on grounds other than the promotion of self-
determination and rule-following, and I would suggest, may
be justified by reference to the principle of respect for
human beings specified.

I conclude, therefore, that though respect for persons
may be an important principle of action in social service
provision in Britain, respect for human beings is the most
general principle of action entailed by the attitude of
compassion represented by social work and by British
social services as a whole.

6

We began with the statement that social services represent
a compromise between compassion and indifference. Extra-
polation from this nutshell yielded the view that social
services represent a compromise between attitudes entail-
ing the principle of respect for human beings and the
principle of indifference to human beings.   In the chapter from which his statement is taken, Pinker sets himself
the task of describing social reality 'as it is' (1971,
p. 136).   It might, therefore, be said that to the extent
to which my account is intended to be faithful to Pinker's
statement, the particular capacities valued and encouraged
by particular existing social services should be identified.   That is, some attempt should be made to say more
fully what *we* value in human beings, to be more specific
about the principle of respect for human beings entailed
by compassion represented by particular existing social
services.
    I began by referring to a conception of social adminis-
tration on which there is a distinct area of interest
common to students of social administration and students
of philosophy.   The present point, I think, marks one
part of this area.   We might co-operate in the description of principles of action entailed by attitudes represented by these social services.   For the present, however, I have confined myself to drawing from the nutshell,
and, I hope, going some way towards identifying, the principles of action which, if Pinker is right, are compro-
mised in our social services considered as a whole.

NOTES

1   Pinker has also said 'The welfare institutions of a
    society symbolise an unstable compromise between com-
    passion and indifference, between altruism and self-
    interest' (1971, p. 211), and has characterised our
    social services as a compromise between 'the work
    ethic' and 'the welfare ethic' (1974).   There are in-
    teresting differences between these views and the
    statement from which I begin, but the later statements
    are, I believe, compatible with the present account.
2   Of course, Downie and Telfer *might* define 'respect' to
    fit their concept of a person.   In the case of the
    second component this would simply involve removing
    the ambiguity on which my objection turns.   If this
    were their ploy, then we might continue to talk of
    'respect' for human beings, but in the wider sense
    which I have argued they, albeit accidentally, allow.

3 Discretionary 'rights'

T. D. Campbell

It is assumed to be fundamental to the nature of the welfare state that the social services offered to the citizen
of such a state are theirs 'as of right'. What is meant
by this is not always clear but it certainly covers the
idea that the citizen who falls into certain objectively
definable categories, such as those of old age, sickness
or unemployment, has a legal entitlement to statutory
benefits. It also indicates that those who receive such
benefits are not to be regarded as inferior persons who,
because of their financial or other dependence on the
state, may be subjected to the arbitrary control of officials; that is, in a welfare state there should be no
status of 'dependent' removing the recipient of state-aid
from the position of an ordinary citizen, except in so far
as this is necessary for the protection of other citizens
(as in the case of some mentally subnormal people and some
delinquents). It is one important strand of welfare
state ideology that the recipients of welfare services are
not in any way excluded from the basic status of citizen
with all the rights that pertain thereto. (1)
One fundamental right of the citizen of a liberal democracy is the right not to be treated arbitrarily. By
this is meant that government action in relation to him
should be governed by properly enacted laws administered
according to the principles of Natural Justice. This
constitutional ideal of the 'Rule of Law' involves a variety of interconnected principles: that where a person's
interests are affected by government action this should be
only in consequence of legislation (that is the enactment
of rules which specify the benefits and/or burdens which
are to fall on specified classes of persons); that these
laws should be impartially administered (so that the benefits and burdens do fall on all members of that class and
only on members of that class of persons); and that any

disputes regarding the legality or fairness of executive
action as this affects the citizen is settled by a judicial procedure in which the disputants are given a hearing
by an impartial judge (that is one who is not in any way
a party to the dispute) in which the disputants have the
benefits of representation and access to relevant information, and have to answer only clearly formulated and specific charges or claims of which they have had reasonable
notice;   and that, in hearing the evidence, only considerations relevant to the disputed facts or laws in question
should be admitted.   More generally the rule of law has
been defined as 'a restriction on how the authorities may
reach a decision and what they may authorise ... in order
that their decisions shall not be justly liable to unfav-
ourable criticism' (Lucas, 1966, p. 107). (2)

The state's relationship to the citizen may always be
viewed and assessed in the light of these legal norms.
The rule of law requires that the citizen be treated in
accordance with public, general and constitutionally legitimate laws which enable him to know his rights and
duties, and, when these are in doubt or it is in dispute
whether or not he has infringed his duties or has been
denied his rights, he has access to a judicial procedure
which is designed to give his case an open, fair and impartial hearing which results in an enforceable decision.

Given this accepted background of the framework within
which democratic governments may, with constitutional
legitimacy, deal with their citizens, it would be expected
that to bring welfare services within the ambit of the
state would be to make their development and administration subject to the constraints of the rule of law.   This
is at least one of the assumptions which might be thought
to be supported by the usually undisputed proposition that
a welfare state confers welfare rights on its members.
We would therefore expect that the machinery of the welfare state would be created and administered in accordance
with the rights which the citizen is presumed to have in
relation to the other activities of the state.   That is
we would expect the legal norms embodied in the ideas of
natural justice and the rule of law to be observed within
the operations of the welfare state.

That these expectations would in some respects be dis-
appointed by a study of the procedures of welfare administration is to be explained historically by the continuity
between the modern welfare state and the tradition of poor
law administration and the associated public attitudes of
pre-welfare state days, and also by the inherent difficulties of applying the well-tried legal safeguards of the
civil and criminal courts to the complexities of innumer-

able welfare decisions without bringing the whole administrative machinery to a halt.   As presently constituted
the law courts have not the capacity to cope with the enormous number of disputes which at present arise within
the welfare services, let alone the number of disputes
which would arise were all potential and actual recipients
of welfare benefits and burdens able and minded to demand
their full legal entitlements.   Moreover, judicial procedure can be unsuited to the pressing and personal nature
of many disagreements about welfare provision.   It is not
surprising, therefore, that in so far as social workers
have regarded themselves as employing quasi-legal methods
this has tended to be restricted to the task of acquiring
reliable evidence for the purpose of social diagnosis and
treatment rather than as a necessary means for seeing that
their clients receive that to which they are entitled (cf.
Richmond, 1917).

Significant moves have, however, taken place which do
involve the application to the procedures of social administration of the standards of justice normally applied
in the courts (Wade, 1963, p. 4f.).   For instance, the
development of a complex system of administrative tribunals to hear and adjudicate on disputes between the individual citizen and the executive branch of government provides an interesting example of the way in which the extended activities of government, many of them to do with
the post-1945 creation of the welfare state, were gradually seen to require a system of judicial review in
which the principles which had long been accepted as
essential for the administration of justice in the courts
were applied to disputes between the individual and the
administrative arm of government.

Administrative tribunals, which can be traced back to
the National Insurance Act of 1911, were at one time regarded as principally an aid to good administration and
were usually seen as an adjunct to the departments whose
work they reviewed.   But their present status and function now approximates to that envisaged by the Franks
Committee in 1957, which urged that tribunals should, as
far as possible, be independent of the department with
whose work they were concerned, and that their procedures
should be marked by the familiar judicial characteristics
of 'openness, fairness and impartiality' (Franks, 1957).
This marked the recognition that the rights of citizens
were as likely, or more likely, to be infringed or affected by administrative action as they were by matters which
come before the criminal and civil courts of the land, and
that something approaching the procedures of these courts
should, therefore, be followed by the variety of ad hoc

administrative tribunals which had come haphazardly into
existence with the extention of the executive branch of
government.

Despite this progress towards justicising the procedures of executive action in the welfare state it is by
no means certain that there are as yet sufficient safeguards for the rights of all potential and actual recipients of welfare services.   Such safeguards may be all
the more necessary because of the social stigma which
still attaches to those who are unable, or it may be alleged unwilling, to 'look after themselves'.   This makes
it difficult for state-dependent persons to insist on
their rights without forfeiting the goodwill of those
officials on whom they depend, or think they depend, for
the satisfaction of their basic needs.

For instance, there is a tendency for decisions concerning the interests of 'difficult' or 'problem' families
or individuals to be left largely to the judgment of the
social work profession whose expertise is held to lie in
their ability to discover what is best for those in need
of the support of welfare services.   Thus in the case of
delinquents, debtors, neglected and emotionally disturbed
children and socially inadequate persons, it is the social
worker to whom it is often in practice left to recommend
and often to carry out appropriate treatment.   He is the
person who is meant to discover what is best for the individual or family concerned, and his judgment on these
matters is given a weight which may be difficult to reconcile with the idea that a person's interests should not be
adversely affected, or his prospects of receiving benefits
reduced, by the legally arbitrary acts of government officials.   The professional judgments of social workers,
based as they often are, or are supposed to be, on psychological and sociological theories about the causes and
cures of the difficulties in question, or simply on their
own experience, can rarely be interpreted as an application of legal rules or laws.

Yet, by the same logic which led to the creation of
administrative tribunals to ensure that welfare administration is carried out in accordance with the rule of law,
it follows that social workers, being amongst those who
are charged with putting welfare legislation into effect,
should fulfil their task according to the appropriate
legal norms in order that the rights of the citizens with
whom they deal may be respected.

What these legal norms are will depend in part on the
type of legal function which social workers are thought
to perform.   In so far as they are regarded as adminis-
trating unambiguous rules in clear-cut cases then the

norms of efficiency and accuracy will be most relevant to
ensuring that the citizen gets his rights.   In so far as
the social worker's role is more judicial in that it involves problems of the interpretation of rules and their
application to cases where the rule is not clear-cut or
where the facts are in dispute, then the stress will be on
the legal correctness of his interpretation of the rules
in question and the fairness of the procedure whereby it
is decided how the rules apply to the specific cases.
But, whether as administrator or judge, the social worker,
in so far as his decisions affect the interests of his
clients and other persons involved with the clients, must,
by the very nature of his position as an agent of the
state in relation to welfare provision, be seen as having
a legal role to play, and his activities ought, therefore,
to be guided and governed by the fundamental legal norms
of the rule of law.   Not only ought the social worker to
regard each case as potentially involving an adjudication
on the rights of the individuals concerned and attempt to
see that each client gets that to which he is entitled,
both in material terms and in personal services, either
from the social worker himself or from other agencies, but
also he ought to be prepared to accept and participate in
the judicial review of his own and other social workers'
decisions so that aggrieved individuals may have every
opportunity to contest, before an impartial adjudicator,
decisions which they regard as erroneous.   This does not
necessarily involve the possibility of an appeal to a
court of law, (3) although this is already recognised to
be appropriate where a person's liberty is at stake, but
certainly to a body which operates, like an administrative
tribunal, on the established principles of natural justice, so that the client is treated like an autonomous
individual with clearly specified rights, rather than as
a patient to be disposed of in accordance with the pater-
nalistic assessment of those whose special skill is to
know how to deal with socially inadequate persons.   Moreover, where a social worker's activities go beyond giving
advice which the client may accept or reject without any
loss to himself, other than the natural consequences of
ignoring good advice, and involves making decisions which
are in some way binding on the client or are made the
basis for decisions of others which are binding on him,
either because the client must comply with the judgment of
the social worker or risk losing the benefits he desires,
or because the social worker has the power either by his
own action or indirectly by his advice to another (maybe
judicial) authority to affect the client's interests
against his will, then his actions ought to be subject to

the same type of scrutiny as any other coercive action of the state.

This legal model of social work which, I have argued, should follow logically from the idea of a democratic welfare state, would not readily be accepted by most social workers as an apt analysis of their role. Social workers, especially caseworkers, more commonly see themselves as providers of the personal service of helpful care and advice to individual clients. That is, they would see themselves as having a pastoral or curative rather than a legal task to perform. In certain situations in child care and probation work they are accustomed to come before the courts to give an opinion on the basis of which the courts may determine such matters as whether a child should be taken away from its parents or a person put on probation, but they would see it as the task of the courts to safeguard the legal rights of the individuals concerned. It is the caseworkers' task to offer advice on what would be the most helpful course of action for their clients. That is, their professional expertise is felt to lie in the sphere of curative counselling, not in that of impartial adjudication on the rights of individuals as they are affected by the action or inaction of the state.

Social workers see themselves less as administrators of general rules than as concerned to assist specific individuals who are in need of their support and skill to help them through difficult social circumstances. In so far as welfare legislation does require the routine application of specific rules about entitlement to benefits this is thought to be work more suitable for administrative staff than for social workers. Bureaucratic work which can be made subject to the scrutiny of administrative tribunals is felt to be in a different category from the sort of personal service which is offered by social workers, and in particular by caseworkers, which is based on estanlishing the sort of personal relationship which cannot be reduced to the application of rules and thus to the language of rights and duties (which presupposes the existence of binding rules), since in the end it depends on the social worker's judgment which line of approach is suitable to each case. While the social worker may, therefore, be called upon to help to administer welfare benefits where there is some difficulty in applying the rules correctly to cases where the facts are difficult to ascertain, or the circumstances are unusual, it is felt that the social worker's distinctive contribution lies in a different sphere. In the language of Paul Halmos, social work involves counselling, or the philanthropic expertise of helping through caring-listening-prompting;

a form of personal service which requires the worker to be involved, with empathy and perhaps with love, in the situation of the client in order to provide the spiritual support which the troubled person needs to cope with his personal relationships and social responsibilities.

Halmos sharply distinguishes the work of counsellor from that of administrator: 'now that sustained government policies and elaborate administrative organisations are busily taking care of the stereotyped and classifiable ills, the counsellor can throw himself fully into the study of personal and intimate miseries' (Halmos, 1965, p. 28).   On the basis of the distinction between those professions whose principal function is to bring about changes in the body or personality of the client (the personal service professions) and the other professions (the impersonal service professions), Halmos explicitly contrasts the professions of clergy, doctors, nurses, teachers and social workers on the one hand with those of lawyers, accountants, engineers and architects on the other. The most important difference between them is that 'the amount of self-denial, matter-of-fact self-effacing personal care, and even human warmth and kindly solicitousness, required by professionals in health, welfare and education, is likely to be far more prominently in evidence than in the practice of law, accountancy and architecture' (Halmos, 1970, p. 26).   The classification is a significant one for it makes explicit the contrast which social workers often feel between the nature of their own work of which the goal is social and personal amelioration, and those whose task it is to administer the law in a fair and impartial manner.   This activity is essentially 'impersonal', it treats people according to their legal classification, not in accordance with the social or psychological diagnosis of their condition made by the experts in human health and happiness.

Yet to regard social work primarily in this light is to ignore the very real social power which is in the hands of the social work profession.   A brief survey of the functions of social workers indicates that their discretionary powers include: (a) Those permitted under the Children and Young Persons Act 1963 which gives local authorities the power to grant financial and material aid to families in need.   This is often done on the advice of social workers.   (b) The selection of foster parents after interviews by social workers.   (c) Decisions about whether to admit a child into care, to provide accommodation for homeless families or old people and how much assistance to give to unmarried mothers are amongst those made largely on the basis of social workers' opinions.   Rosalind

Brooke (Robson and Crick, 1970, p. 38), points out that:
'The Seebohm proposals, particularly if coupled with rec-
ommendations from the Royal Commission on Local Government
for much larger authorities, will mean a far greater concentration of power in the hands of officials and social
workers of the family service.'   For instance the fact
that there will only be one department of social work
dealing with a problem family may mean that the affairs of
that family are in the hands of one social worker who can,
therefore, as in the American system of social security,
acquire extensive power over the clients.

It is not simply that the advice of social workers is
taken seriously in courts of law where matters of individual liberty are concerned, for they also have in their
hand the key which can give many of their clients access
to a multitude of benefits which they desire.   Moreover,
the very personal services in which they specialise, which
may be typified by the activities of sympathetic understanding and wise advice and encouragement, may be regarded as a benefit to which the citizen of a welfare state
has, in certain circumstances of social difficulty, a
right.   Not all benefits are material benefits: advice,
information and kindly encouragement are valuable and
needed services whose just distribution is a matter of
importance.   It is now beginning to be recognised that
'effective social rights (interpreted as those things to
which the statutory social service entitle us) now cover
not only a guaranteed minimum income and medical care but
that somewhat vague and uncertain commodity "welfare"'
(Rodgers and Dixon, 1960, p. 15).   The neglect of the
social worker to fulfil his duty towards his clients in
respect to these non-material benefits may be just as in-
jurious to that client's welfare as the loss of financial
assistance which may result from the administrator's failure to provide him with his monetary entitlements.   If
the social worker has the duty to provide personal service
to this client then the client has a right to that personal service.

The intrusion of talk of rights into the description of
a relationship which is defined as personal raises difficulties.   Perhaps the explicit recognition of the obligations of the social worker as against the rights of the
client may make it more difficult to establish the sort of
curative relationship which the caseworker hopes to establish.   Perhaps the responses of the caseworker in situations where it is thought necessary to establish a personal relationship cannot readily be reduced to a manageable
set of formulae, in which case it will be difficult to
determine which acts of the caseworker fulfil his duty and

which of his acts do not, thus making the client's claim
to have a right to a certain type of assistance from the
caseworker too vague to be enforceable.   Perhaps the
whole nature of casework is incurably individualistic in
that it requires concentration on the particular case
without regard for the application of general rules. (4)
It may be that, for these sorts of reasons, the pastoral-
curative mode of social work is not fully compatible with
the legal mode;   it may be that they generate different
attitudes and practices which are to some extent irrecon-
cilable.   If this is the case then serious issues arise
for those who would allow the pastoral function of the
social worker to override the legal function, for this may
involve the denial of the basic rights of those citizens
whose interests are affected by the opinions and decisions
of welfare officers. (5)

These two modes of social practice are accompanied by
two sets of typical vocabulary.   The legal mode centres
round ideas of justice, equity, rights, entitlements, obligations, fairness, impartiality and so on.   The pastoral mode is associated with talk of needs, inadequacy,
care, empathy, supportiveness, and very often also the
technical language of psychiatry and sociology.   It takes
little reflection to see that it is difficult to envisage
a relationship which can be characterised by the participants using both sets of vocabulary.   On the pastoral
model, if the client is seeking his entitlement the social
worker is likely to see this interfering with the diagnosis and treatment which flows from establishing an empa-
thetic relationship.   Indeed a caseworker may be annoyed
and impatient when the client keeps referring to his
rights rather than his inadequacies.   This is not because
the caseworker thinks that the client has no rights, but
because he regards them as peripheral to the solution of
the client's problems.   The client's rights must not, of
course, be infringed, but the task of the caseworker is
not seen as one of determining his rights and making sure
that he gets them, but as one of overcoming the deficiencies of character and behaviour which have led him into a
position where he needs the support of the welfare services.

But if some progress is to be made towards a reconciliation of these seemingly opposed outlooks some common
vocabulary must be found which can function both within
the pastoral and the legal way of viewing the social
worker's task.   One possible concept which may bridge the
gap is that of 'discretionary rights'.   If pressed about
the sort of clash between the pursuit of social health and
the pursuit of social justice which I have outlined, the

caseworker may be inclined to agree that the client has
rights but that these rights are discretionary in that
they are mediated through the judgment of the caseworker
in his skilful assessment of the problems confronting the
client. The client has rights, the right to be treated
in the way most helpful to him compatible with the rights
of others, but what this way is depends on the assessment
of the caseworker: his rights are in this sense discretionary. The caseworker is to this extent like a medical
practitioner who has a duty to do what he can to promote
the health of his patient but this duty specifies only
that he does what he considers best for the patient, not
that he follows a clearly defined code of treatment.

This idea of a discretionary right does appear hopeful
as a formula for linking the rights of the client with the
professional judgment of the social worker. If it is a
coherent notion then it may enable the social worker to
retain his self-image of skilled personal caring assistance, something like that which is offered by the medical
profession, while still giving the idea of the rights of
the client a sufficient foothold in the social work relationship to be of some use to the client in the protection
of his interests. It may be, however, that the idea of a
discretionary right is a contradiction in terms in that if
a 'right' is discretionary it is not properly regarded as
a right at all. In this case the use of this phrase to
describe the social worker-client relationship may simply
confuse the issue bymmaking it appear that the client has
effective rights when this is not in fact the case. I
shall, therefore, consider what might be meant by the idea
of a discretionary right and see whether the sort of
rights which it is thought are protected by the rule of
law are compatible with treating citizens in accordance
with a scheme of 'discretionary rights'.

One thing which may be meant by a 'discretionary right'
is a right which a person has under a rule applied to particular cases by an official. That is, the official has
the task of deciding what rules apply to a client's situation and how these rules apply. This is the normal way
in which entitlement to particular levels of Supplementary
Benefit is determined by Supplementary Benefit Officers.
Such application may be regarded as administrative in that
it is the almost mechanical application of a rule book to
particular cases, but in so far as the facts of the situation are in doubt, or it is not clear which rule applies
to a marginal case, then the decisions are judicial in
that they are similar to those which have to be made by a
judge in a court of law who has to determine how relatively vague and often ambiguous laws apply to each case which
is brought before him.

It is doubtful if we should speak of discretion here if the process of applying rules to particular cases is looked on as a deductive process of showing that it follows from a statement of the rule and a statement of the facts of the case that the treatment prescribed by the rule is required.   But it is generally recognised that the actual practice of adjudicators and administrators of laws cannot be regarded simply in these syllogistic terms. Problems of selecting the relevant rule, of interpreting the rule, of ascertaining the facts, and seeing which facts are relevant to the rules selected, all call for a process of rational selection which cannot be encapsuled in any purely deductive model of argumentation.   The judicial and administrative process involves some elements of non-deductive reasoning which can never be wholly eliminated; it may, therefore, be held to involve the exercise of discretion even where a full and comprehensive and clear rule book is provided.   For although in theory an administrator may have no scope for exercising his own judgment on the cases before him, in practice there is always some scope, however limited, for the exercise of discretion, the discretion being that he has to exercise his own judgment as to what rule applies and what treatment is appropriate under the rules from his assessment of the facts of the case.   This I call discretion type one (discretion[1]).   It is not discretionary to the extent of it being up to the judge to say whether and how far he will apply the law in a particular case, but only to the extent of it being for him to decide how the law applies. No system of rules can be so automatic and mechanical as to avoid the necessity for some person to make such decisions about how the law applies.   It must always be the administrator's or judge's duty to exercise his judgment to this extent.

Rights which correlate with discretionary[1] duties are clearly rights in the full sense, since all rights follow from the existence of rules laying down obligations as to how some classes of human beings should treat other classes, and all rules require the exercise of discretion[1] for their application.   Where it is the official's duty to decide what are the rights of the citizen in a particular case and to act accordingly then the rights of the citizen may be called discretionary[1] in that the question of what treatment he is to receive will depend on the decision of the authorised adjudicator.

If all that is meant by saying that welfare rights are discretionary rights is that it is up to an official of the state to judge how the law applies to specific cases then, in so far as social workers are brought into this

process, this clearly demonstrates the administrative and/
or judicial function of the social worker, but it does not
in itself diminish the rights of the social worker's
clients.   Certain consequences do, however, flow from
making this legal role of the social worker explicit, in
that it can then readily be seen that it is appropriate
for the adjudicating process to be subject to the same
sort of requirements as the recognisedly legal activities
of the courts.   That is, the relevant rule books should
be readily available to the public; it should be required
that reasons be given for the decisions made, that, where
the factual evidence is in dispute, the relevant witnesses should be called and heard before an impartial judge
according to the rules of evidence; and that any client
who is not satisfied with his treatment should be able to
appeal to a higher authority about the decision which has
been made and be given every legal and financial assistance which is necessary to put his case satisfactorily.

To the extent that social workers are involved in
making this sort of decision about entitlements of their
clients they should no more regard it as a slight on
their professional judgment that their decision should be
challengeable in this way than it is thought a slight on
the professional standing of a judge that his decisions
are subject to revision by a higher court.   In practice
caseworkers may not be involved in making this sort of
discretionary decision except in cases which are sufficiently unclear or untypical to require the intervention
of a caseworker to investigate the situation in question,
and this means that the primary legal duty of determining
the rights of the client may be overshadowed by the caseworker's more normal role of applying his skills to sorting out the difficulties which lie behind a person's request for financial or other support from the state.   The
danger here is that the caseworker may confuse his task as
an adjunct to the fair administration of statutory benefits with his task as a pastor or counsellor and allow his
judgment about what would be beneficial for the client to
affect his opinion on what the client is entitled to.
This is to mix up discretion[1] with other types of discretion which we have yet to consider.   But where the social
worker is clear about the nature of his discretion in such
cases then no diminution of the rights of the clients is
in principle involved.

The dangers of caseworkers confusing their therapeutic
and their judicial functions parallel those which have
been pointed out in connection with the tendency for
courts to be turned into clinics for the treatment of
offenders:

If it is the treatment agency which exercises this
final authority [binding decisions], it is arguable
that it would have far too much power in its hands over
against the individual citizen.   Moreover, however
skilled it might be, it would still be subject to
human fallibility, and ever prone to forget that 'power
corrupts and absolute power corrupts absolutely'.   One
of the chief social roles of the court is to be impartial with no axe to grind and therefore able to protect
the small individual against the administrative leviathan ... in the interests of liberty there must be an
impartial tribunal ... for a binding decision to be
taken about an individual's way of life.   (Younghusband, 1964, p. 69)

It would be interesting to know, for instance, if the
Children's Panels, set up by the Social Work (Scotland)
Act as recommended by the Kilbrandon Committee (Cmnd 2306,
1964), which are empowered to order treatment and training
for children in need of compulsory care, including removing a child from its home (subject to right of appeal to
the Sheriff), are able to distinguish considerations of
justice from those of welfare.

A second meaning of 'discretionary' arises in the case
of rules or laws which permit a measure of latitude in
their application, as when the permitted benefits are
laid down but only to the extent that there is an official
maximum and an official minimum, or perhaps in the case of
a social worker's duty to offer personal assistance there
is a minimum attention which must be given to each case,
or the social worker is required to apply a rule with deliberately vague criteria. (6)   Here the discretionary
power of the social worker extends beyond the ordinary
judicial function of determining how the law applies in
each case, and involves an element of law-making in that
the social worker determines what is in practice the content of the law which he is going to apply, or, perhaps,
as his decision in one case does not bind future decisions
in similar cases, this is better regarded as the exercise
of an unregulated judgment to each case within the statutory limits.   That is, the law sets down a range of possible degrees and/or types of treatment and leaves it to
the professional skill of the social worker to determine
the exact nature of the treatment in particular cases.   I
will call this discretionary power type two (discretion^2).

If discretionary^2 power is itself governed by a rule
book laying down what is appropriate for the different
types of case which arise then it becomes equivalent to
discretionary^1 power.   This is the case with 'Code A'
issued by the Department of Social Security to regulate

the administration of welfare benefits within the legal limits laid down by Parliament. The only difference between this and discretionary[1] power is that the complete rule to be applied depends on the social worker putting together two complementary sets of rules, the first laying down the broad lines of appropriate benefits, or assistance, the second filling this out with guidance on how to deal with specific cases. In this case the same requirements of natural justice apply to discretionary[2] powers as to discretionary[1] powers. In practice it is likely that the reason for there being two complementary sets of rules is that the first is made public but the second is not. This clearly infringes the rule of law in that if the client does not know what the second set of rules lay down for his particulular case are then he will be unable to assess for himself whether he has been correctly treated and to make the appropriate appeals against the decision if he regards it as mistaken on points of fact or of law. Where part of the appropriate regulations are kept secret in this way, although it may be conceptually in order to regard the client as having a right to certain benefits or assistance since the social worker has an ascertainable duty to act towards him in a certain way, nevertheless this situation does not meet the full requirements of natural justice as there is an element in the treatment of the client which he cannot effectively challenge before an impartial adjudicator.

Apart from the conveniences of the administration of social welfare legislation, which may always be cited as a reason for denying social welfare clients the full rights which they would have under the rule of law, one argument for having 'secret' supplementary regulations is that the assessment on which detailed provision and assistance may depend requires the social worker to categorise the client in a manner which, were he aware of it, he might find offensive. That is it might be thought counter-productive for the social worker to inform the client that he regards his personality and behaviour to be of a certain type, but it may be that the regulations require that the social worker make such a judgment.

Granted that this is a fair picture of an actual situation it is clear that to make such regulations and the decisions made under them public would not be counter-productive from the point of view of Natural Justice (since the client might indeed be wrongly judged to be of a certain personality or disposition) but from the point of view of the pastoral-curative goals of the social worker; that is, we have a clash between the two models of social work with the priority being given to the non-legal one.

Assuming that this is the correct priority does this mean that there is inevitably a sacrifice of the rights of the client to his alleged welfare?   This would effectively be the case if the individual had no way of appealing against the decisions made under the 'secret' regulations, but while the idea of the possibility of appeal against the decisions of an administrator to an independent higher legal authority is an integral part of Natural Justice, it is not logically necessary that this appeal be initiated and argued by the individual himself; if we allow the possibility of the representation of the client's interests by a knowledgeable and able person who is independent of the administrative group whose actions are in doubt, then it is possible that, provided the representative has access to the 'secret' regulations, the rights of the client will be adequately protected, and will therefore be, in the fullest sense, rights.   A local ombudsman, for instance, might be given the task of checking administration which involves the use of discretionary^2 powers where these are governed by a secondary code.   The remaining disadvantage would be the public relations one of ensuring that justice is not only done but is seen to be done.

However, discretionary^2 powers may not reduce in this way to discretionary^1, for there may be no authoritative rule book to guide the discretionary decisions of the social worker.   This defect could be remedied by the development of case law from which the 'ratio dicidendi' of previous cases could be applied to future cases in the normal manner of the law of precedent.   The complexities and administrative burden of applying such a process to day-to-day welfare decisions make this little more than a logical possibility, although something like a system of case law might arise for settling a small number of disputed cases as they come before an appeals tribunal.   But such an appeals tribunal could hardly concern itself with the exercise of discretionary^2 powers without getting into a legal morass from which they could only be rescued by the creation of a book of rules.

But if there is no body of secondary rules and no case law to guide the discretionary^2 judgments of social workers then it is simply up to him to use his own 'judgment' without reference to any legally authoritative guide.   In such circumstances there is no way in which the social worker's judgments can, if they are within the prescribed limits, be legally wrong and so open to legal challenge, for he must be the ultimate judge in each situation since there exists no criterion against which to test his judgment, and no way of getting him to alter his decision except by a rhetorical appeal to him to 'change his mind'.

Further there is no way in which the citizen can fully
know in advance his entitlements and possible burdens,
and this not simply in the manner which occurs with every
law - for it is never possible to predict with absolute
certainty how the law will be applied in the courts - but
because there is a sense in which there is no law which
exists, either prior to or after the social worker's judgment has been made, which could be the basis for such a
prediction.   The imponderable is not how the judge will
interpret the law but, in a way, how the judge will make
the law (although it is not really a law he makes since it
is not binding on any other case).

The defence of the existence of such discretionary[2]
powers to social workers is likely to be an extension of
the arguments used to justify the granting of discretion
to judges in courts of law over sentencing, namely that it
allows consideration to be given to the likely outcome of
different modes or degrees of treatment in each case;
that is it enables the administration of law to be forward
looking to the individual and social benefits of different
courses of action, and not just backward looking to the
question of guilt in the light of the established facts
and the relevant law.   It is no coincidence that it is at
this stage that the courts seek advice from social workers
as well as from psychiatrists before passing sentence.
In the case of social work decisions the existence of discretionary[2] powers enables the social worker to treat each
case in the light of his assessment of the curative effectiveness of each line of action.   This is, in a sense,
what he is paid for; this is his distinctive task, or so
it might be argued.

It is interesting to note that the existence of discretionary power is justified in the Introduction to the Supplementary Benefits Handbook (1972, p. 1) by the argument
that:

the distinctive feature of the Supplementary Benefits
Scheme is its discretionary element, those powers
vested in the Commission which enable it to consider
the claims of individual circumstances.   By definition
no-one can claim as of right that a particular discretionary power should be exercised in his favour.   But
for the individual claimant the existence of these discretionary powers may be more valuable than a precisely
prescribed right because they give the scheme a flexibility of response to varying situations of human need.

Now it is clearly impossible to lay down rules governing
unforseeable circumstances, and it may, therefore, be
desirable to give the Commission discretionary powers to
deal with such circumstances, but this does nothing to

show that where it is possible to do so rules should not
be laid down.   This is not to say that discretionary
power cannot be used generously but it is to say that such
generosity is unjust if it is not a generosity which is
shown to all people in similar circumstances.   And where
discretionary power exists it is possible - some would say
likely - that it will often not be used generously.   Certainly it is a confusion to claim that such a scheme 'com-
bines basic rights with the flexibility which discretion
affords' (Supplementary Benefits Handbook, 1972, p. 1) as
if there were no conflict between rights and discretionary
powers.

A similar case is made out in favour of discretionary
power by Marshall (1965, p. 264) who argues that discretion is necessary in any service which is designed to satisfy particular individual need 'for the assessment of
need in any individual case, and of the measures that are
best suited to meet it, involve an act of personal judgment'.   But he too fails to see that even if discretionary power is used with good will as a 'positive, personal,
and beneficient' thing, nevertheless, so long as decisions
about what the welfare of potential recipients of relief
requires is a matter left to the good sense of individual
officials, the actions of these officials are to this
extent above the law and a client's interests are at the
mercy of the wisdom of that official's judgment as well
as the integrity of his character.

Thus the clash between discretionary[2] power and the
principles of the rule of law remain and the dangers of
this situation are apparent if we consider the possible
abuse of discretionary[2] power.   It is not simply that
the social worker may fail to give each case proper consideration because there is no redress for the individual
against his negligence, or that the social worker is a
fallible human being, for the social worker may use the
existence of discretionary[2] power as a weapon to change
the behaviour of the client in a manner which he considers to be desirable.   That is, discretionary[2] powers can
be used as a bribe, and the tendency for this to happen
is clearly shown by the practice within the old system of
charitable assistance where the aim of assistance was to
make people self-dependent, and the methods which were
used to this end, in addition to the fear of destitution,
the sense of shame associated with the receipt of benefit,
and the threat to civil rights, included the threat of
withholding benefits if certain behaviour patterns were
not changed to coincide with those which the charitable
organisation considered acceptable.   Where discretionary
powers are used as a threat or bribe for good behaviour we

have moved a long way from the idea of the rule of law for the law does not seek to buy good behaviour in this way, and the rights it confers are not normally conditional upon good behaviour other than that which is involved in not infringing the law.

The dangers to the legitimate interests of social work clients which are the result of existence of discretionary[2] powers are intensified when these are taken to their logical conclusion and the discretion which is given to the social worker is extended beyond that of deciding how to treat a case within relatively clear statutory limits, and involves giving the social worker a free hand with respect to his action in regard to specific cases which are brought to his attention.   Where this is the case I will talk of the social worker having discretionary powers type three (discretion[3]).   With discretionary[2] powers the social worker's only legally enforceable duty was to treat each case within the limits set; with discretionary[3] powers the social worker's only duty is to make some decision, even if it is for no action.

Since the rights which correlate with such a minimum duty are confined to the right for some consideration being given to his case, the individual client clearly has no right of a sort which would find an acceptable place within a system which embodies the principles of the rule of law.   Such a right is so vague as to constitute no effective right at all since it is not possible to say when it has been violated, provided the social worker has given a minimum of attention to the case; it is not, therefore, possible to appeal against such decisions or to know what a relevant argument would be were such an appeal possible.   At this point it appears that law ends and tyranny may begin.   However, in discussions of how discretionary decisions can be subjected to judicial review it is sometimes argued that, even where discretionary decisions are not governed by any code of rules, it is possible, nevertheless, for such decisions to be regarded as good or bad decisions, or perhaps reasonable or unreasonable.   Thus, for instance, Lucas (1966, p. 122) in discussing the responsibility of officials, argues that:

It is not enough for an official, as it would be for a private individual, to say simply 'I wanted to'....
He has not only to explain his actions, but to justify them.   He has to give the reasons why he did them, which were also reasons why he should have done them, and which would be reasons why anybody else similarly situated should act similarly.

And Titmuss (1971, p. 129) argues that discretionary power may make for more effective and humane administration in that where an official is simply applying a rigid code of case law he does not have to justify his decision, but if he is exercising discretion then he must make a reasoned case to his superior; his accountability thus makes his work more subject to rational criticism.   But, unfortunately, the superior is likely to judge the decision made on the basis of the policy he has to administer and the conveniences of his department rather than on the rights of the client which will be at the mercy of what seems 'rational' to the officials concerned.

In any case the notion of rationality employed here is rather nebulous.   A decision can be regarded as rational only in relation to some standard against which the outcome of the decision can be measured, but in the case of discretionary decisions no such standards are laid down. However, this would be denied by those who wish non-regulated discretionary[3] decisions to be open to criticism or review.   The argument employed at this stage is that not all standards are embodied in sets of rules; decisions can be assessed in the light of the policies or objectives in the context of which the decisions are made.   No discretionary power is so discretionary, it is argued, that it is not given to an official for some purpose.   The task of social workers, for instance, is to reduce distress and minimise the occurrence of socially disruptive and fiscally expensive behaviour.   The decisions of social workers can, therefore, be judged reasonable or unreasonable according to how far they contribute to the achievement of these goals, and indeed may be overruled as 'ultra vires' if they are not exercised for these purposes.

But if it is argued that the social worker's discretion ought to be guided by the purposes of the legislation which they are putting into effect, then this is a process fraught with dangers for the rights of the citizen. Apart from the fact that the purpose of legislation is not always clearly stated or is stated in such vague terms as to be open to a variety of contradictory interpretations by officials, the whole idea of treatment of citizens depending on what an authority considers likely to further some general policy objective is directly contrary to the idea that they should be treated in accordance with specific, public and clearly formulated rules in the light of which they can make rational decisions about their own future conduct.   To collapse the distinction between legislation and judicial procedure in this manner puts the individual at the mercy of the multitude of diverse applications of vaguely formulated policy objectives.   The aims of social work are usually stated without great pre-

cision.   Thus Slack (1966, p. 39) says that 'the very
purpose of their administration is to produce the conditions of what is regarded as the good life', and Halmos
speaking of the task of 'counsellors' says that 'their
common aim is health, sanity and an unspecified state of
virtue, even a state of grace, or merely a return to the
virtues of the community' (1965, p. 2).   Such vaguely
expressed goals could be used to license an almost limit-
less variety of treatment.

Even where it is possible to say that such decisions
are reasonable or unreasonable from the point of view of
government policy, this does not mean that we can say
whether or not they are acceptable from the point of view
of the rights of citizens, for under such a system the
individual has no rights except the right to be treated
in accordance with the policy of the political authorities
of the time or the policy which is imputed to those who
framed the legislation in question.   Such rights are no
rights at all because any specific interest of the individual in question has no legal standing against an appeal
to some general policy objective.

Just as the duty of the judiciary is to apply reasonable interpretations of the law and not to carry out the
state's wishes in the light of declared policy objectives,
so, in so far as his decisions affect the interests of his
clients, the social worker's powers ought to be curtailed
to a similarly distinct judicial function if the advances
towards the defence of individual rights which have been
achieved by the separation of legislative and judicial
powers are not to be lost in the sphere of welfare administration.   For it to be otherwise is to make the social
worker the tool of 'ultra vires' political power;   the
individual's right would amount to no more than the right
to be treated in accordance with government policy, a
position which is at variance with the ideal of the citizen as an autonomous individual who can plan his life and
act as he pleases within the framework of the law.

One reason why the idea of rights plays less of a part
in the administration of welfare than in the administration of the criminal law is because the compulsory powers
of the state do not feature so obviously in the former as
in the latter.   The state is thought of as making available welfare benefits of which the possible recipients may
or may not take advantage, in contrast to the exercise of
punitive powers in relation to violations of the criminal
law.   Where the use of compulsory powers does figure
quite obviously in the operation of the social services,
as where the children are being taken into care against
the wishes of themselves or their parents, or where the

probation service is concerned, there is a recognition
that it is necessary to have procedures to protect the
rights of those who are liable to lose their liberty or be
treated in some way which is against their wishes.   The
only place in the Seebohm Committee's Report, for instance, where there is any discussion of the rights of
clients, is where it is argued that there is a need to
strengthen the safeguards of the rights of parents and
children when children are taken away from their homes by
order of the court, for, as is pointed out, what was then
called 'a fit person order' could involve the detention of
a child up to the age of eighteen, which goes far beyond
the maximum period of what was an approved school order
which was three years (Seebohm, 1968, sections 190 and
269).

Since these matters do come before the courts the dangers to the rights of those involved is a great deal less
than is the case in the exercise of discretionary powers
which do not involve court proceedings.   But there are
dangers in the social worker's role in court proceedings,
for there is always the possibility that in welfare cases
the courts will adopt standards different from those which
they apply in criminal cases by being prepared to accept
the 'authoritative' evidence of social workers in a way in
which they would be disinclined to do with the testimony
of normal witnesses in a criminal trial, so that the
courts become rubber stamps for the decisions of social
work departments.   This is a danger which can to some
extent be countered by the provision of adequate representation for parents and children in such proceedings.

Similar safeguards do not seem, however, to be thought
necessary where the decisions to be made by the state concern not the loss of liberty but the loss of benefit or
personal assistance, and yet the interests of individuals
may be just as significantly affected by the failure of
the state to provide a welfare benefit as by the exercise
of its powers of compulsion over the individual.   Where a
local authority, for instance, decides not to admit a
person to accommodation for the aged or homeless, or a
social worker declines to give the sort of personal support which the client feels to be necessary, there is no
obvious way in which they can attempt to enforce their
right to such accommodation or attention.

It is sometimes argued that there can be no rights to
benefits of this kind because they are in short supply and
there is not, therefore, the means to help all those who
would, material circumstances permitting, be entitled to
such benefits.   Thus Marshall (1965, p. 268) argues that
welfare rights cannot be absolute and unconditional on the

grounds that 'if you concede to a poor person an absolute,
unconditional right to relief, the question then arises
how to deny him the right to become poor if he so wishes.
The obligation of the community to relieve destitution
must somehow be matched by a duty of the individual not to
become destitute, if he can help it' - and he goes on to
conclude that the award of benefits must be discretionary.
But even supposing that there is, in the case of welfare
'rights', a conditioning 'duty' of this sort, the question
of whether or not a person is fulfilling this duty need
not be left to the unfettered discretion of type 3, for
either there are or there are not objective tests of
whether or not a person can avoid being destitute; if
there are such tests then they should take the place of
discretionary[3] powers, and if there are not such tests
then the judgments of officials will be arbitrary and
should have no weight in deciding a person's eligibility.
In the absence of such objective tests the consequence of
using the discretionary[3] powers of officials to deter
'scroungers' is to diminish the rights of the remainder of
the needy, for,if there is no reliable way of distinguishing those who are poor by choice from those who are not,
then the latter must suffer the loss of their welfare
rights because they have no way of seeking redress if they
are classified as 'scroungers'.   Marshall seems to be
making the mistake of saying that if a right is not 'absolute and unconditional' in the sense that the right is
dependent on the fulfilment of an obligation, then it is
not a right at all because it correlates with a discretionary duty and not a proper duty.   But there is no
reason in logic or in practice why what he calls a conditional right may not correlate with a duty in the full and
proper meaning of the word.   However, it is true that
while a right does not, logically, cease to be a right if
it carries with it certain obligations (e.g., to spend
welfare benefits on food not beer), it is, nevertheless,
often regarded as part of the concept of the citizen as
an autonomous individual who should be able to live his
own life with a certain dignity and independence that his
rights should not be of this conditional sort.   Indeed,
if welfare rights were generally of this conditional sort
then these rights would not be similar to those enjoyed by
a citizen in most areas of his experience (cf. Keith-
Lucas, 1953, p. 1080).
     The general problem of the scarcity of resources can be
approached at two levels.   At the first level, taking the
fact of scarce resources as given, the issue becomes one
of distributive justice which requires that there be rules
to determine who has priority for the assistance avail-

able.   This is not something which must be left to the
discretion of social workers for it can be the subject of
political decision expressed in regulations whose enforcement can be carried out in an open and impartial manner
and which could be challenged and defended according to
the principles of the rule of law.   While this would cut
down the number of people who have a right to such benefits it would mean that those who have this right do have
what is properly regarded as a right, and not just a
prima facie claim on the consideration of the relevant
authority.

However, moving to the second level, it is possible to
question the unalterable nature of the alleged scarcity of
resources.   It would undoubtedly be expensive to make
welfare legislation open-ended, local authorities being
given the legally enforceable duty of providing services
of a certain type for all people in a given category, but
it is not inconceivable that this should be done.   In
fact it is a political difficulty and not a conceptual
difficulty which is involved when it is said that welfare
'rights' can't be enforced like ordinary rights because of
the scarcity of resources.

The image of social work as an instrument of political
policy is likely to be repudiated by the social work profession on the grounds that they have, within their legis-
lated rights and duties, the sort of independence of political influence which one would expect to find in the
case of professional work.   The social worker is, in
fact, more likely to see his discretionary[3] power as
being subject to the control of the norms of his profession, norms both of acceptable social goals such as the
rehabilitation of socially inadequate individuals and
families, and of professionally accredited techniques for
attaining these goals which are drawn from the social
sciences.

The whole purpose of the training of professional
social workers might be regarded as a preparation for the
time when the social worker has to exercise discretionary[3]
powers;   this is precisely what he is being trained to do;
this is what professional skill is all about.   It is a
common lay view that the job of the social worker is to
understand the needs of people in difficulty better than
they understand these needs themselves, and to show the
relevant skill in helping them to overcome the personal or
social inadequacy which the social worker has diagnosed.
And the feature of social work which makes it a profession
in the eyes of some of its practitioners is that it involves the skill of judging what is the right solution to
particular social and individual problems, not by the

mechanical application of rules laid down by non-profes-
sionals, but in accordance with the knowledge and expertise which is characteristic of the trained worker (cf.
Rodgers and Dixon, 1960, p. 11; Slack, 1966, p. 38).   It
is for this reason, it might be thought, that the social
worker is given a relatively free hand to decide what
ought to be done in particular cases.   His decisions may
indeed be criticised by his colleagues in the light of the
standards of the profession, but this is not legal criticism, just as the social worker's aims and skills are not
legal aims and skills.

Thus, for instance, it may be up to the social worker
to decide in the light of his diagnosis whether a certain
individual is capable of making his own decisions about
his future, or whether these decisions have to be made for
him by the social worker or some other authority.   This
is tantamount to the social worker deciding if that individual is to enjoy the normal rights of a citizen.   To
make this a matter of professional judgment indicates the
way in which the practice of making people's life-pros-
pects depend on the professional skill of a social worker
runs counter to the rights of the individual. (7)   It has
long been accepted that medical authority can be given the
status which enables us to deprive a person of their normal rights on the grounds of mental as well as physical
illness, although there is still a lively controversy
about the deprivation of rights on the basis of the diagnosis of mental illness,which is arguably not a scientific
process.   To give such a status to the opinions of social
workers about the social capacities of individuals may
also be acceptable in time if it can be shown that the
diagnoses given are sufficiently objective and verifiable
to count as part of a science of social behaviour, but
this will involve a major revision of the traditional idea
that a citizen does not require to prove that he is capable of making good use of his rights and freedoms before
he is allowed to enjoy those rights and freedoms.   To
make our capacity to make good use of our rights a matter
of professional judgment, and to make that professional
judgment the basis for determining whether or not we have
these rights is so clearly a prospect which endangers the
fundamental rights of the individual that the only way in
which it can be viewed with equanimity by anyone is if
that person regards the clients of social workers as a
small minority of inadequate persons amongst whom that
person could never find himself numbered.   But this is to
ignore one proposition which finds general acceptance
amongst students of social deprivation and distress,
namely, that these conditions are caused as much if not

more by social conditions outside the control of the individual's affected than by the inherent personal inadequacies of those individuals.   It is also incompatible with the manifest ideology of the social work professional ethic of which one central tenet is that the client should be self-directed (cf. Plant, 1970, pp. 6-34).

Whatever the cause of the social problems which it is the social worker's task to cope with it is a basic error to confuse the condition of being socially deprived or in need of welfare assistance with the legal status of the bearer of the rights of citizenship.   It is regarded as an advance from the older tradition of charitable social work that social workers do not make moral judgments on the basis of which they determine the deprived person's 'right' to benefits, but the extent of this advance may be doubted if the moral judgments of social workers are replaced by a professional 'scientific' judgment about the personal capacity of the individual to cope with his problems without decisions being made for him by those who are providing him with aid or seeing to the welfare of his children.   Social workers may feel that considerable progress has been made in that they are no longer 'judgmental', in that they do not go around making moralising comments and reports on the conduct and character of their clients.   But they are none the less still judgmental in that what they decide affects the future happiness of their clients and others who are or might be in contact with their clients, and the issue is whether or not they should be judgmental in a legal sense where their decisions follow from rules of sufficient precision and of a type to be acceptable to those who value the rule of law and are subject to procedures of judicial review, or whether they are to be judgmental in the skilled pastoral sense in which the knowledge and expertise available to and within the social work profession is the final authority on what is best for the clients of the profession and, therefore, on what is to be done or not to be done for or with them.   The fact that moral considerations do not affect their professional judgment does not mean that the rights of the client are not infringed.   It remains to be proved that the welfare and therapeutic benefits of allowing social workers discretionary[3] powers adequately compensate for the very real risk at which this puts the rights of that increasingly large class of persons who fall within the purview of the social worker.

NOTES

1   If as President Roosevelt had said, each man has a
    'right to life' and this meant that 'he had also the
    right to make a comfortable living' then each person
    in need had a right to share in the provision made by
    the government to meet the ravages of depression.
    Because he had this right, an applicant for public
    relief incurred no stigma, asked no favour, and was
    expected to express no gratitude. He, as well as
    his application, was treated with respect; his eli-
    gibility was determined in the light of legal re-
    quirements, available funds, and the claims of others
    equally in need of assistance.
    This change of attitude was crucial to what Woodroofe
    calls the new attitude to social casework (Woodroofe,
    1962, pp. 167 f.).
2   Examples of the 'rule of law', as it is applicable to
    administrative procedures are given by Wade (1963),
    they include: 'that no man should suffer without
    being given a hearing' (p. 9), 'that it is of the
    essence of justice that it should be dispensed in
    public' (p. 19); that 'the one who hears must decide'
    (p. 80), that 'reasons must be given for decisions'
    (p. 90).
3   The judicialising of social work practice need not
    mean handing disputes about welfare over to lawyers
    who are rightly feared by social workers as being un-
    interested in the speedy and fair settlement of
    'minor' disputes involving impoverished members of the
    community, but simply requires that judicial princi-
    ples be applied. The failure to make this distinc-
    tion vitiates some of the argument of Titmuss (1971).
    Even if there are overwhelming reasons for not having
    welfare disputes decided in public by judicial auth-
    orities not in the control of the executive it can be
    argued that some sort of procedures could be set up to
    obtain impartial opinions on the confidential but con-
    troversial decisions of social workers and social work
    departments. An example of this sort of procedure is
    given in a Report by Justice (1961, para. 56) which
    mentions the practice of the Home Secretary seeking
    advice from the Chief Magistrate of Bow Street before
    deciding to make a deportation order.
4   Social work has been ... an individualizing profes-
    sion. Government, although it may on occasion
    make use of equitable concepts which permit con-
    siderable discretion, is essentially a generalizing
    activity, proceeding on the assumption that men in

similar circumstances should be treated alike.
(Keith-Lucas, 1957, p. v)

5   One issue which I have only skirted is whether the
level of commitment to the interests of the client or
sympathetic identification with his situation required
for good social work therapy is compatible with the
necessary detachment for making impartial judicial
decisions.   On the view of Halmos this would not seem
to be the case (Halmos, 1965, p. 18):   There is 'an
absolute incompatibility between sympathy with the one
and sympathy with the many and this is because the
former is personal and the latter inevitably administrative, organizational, institutional, political and
therefore impersonal.'

6   There are many examples in social work of criteria
which are too subjective to be applied consistently in
practice, cf. Kathleen Woodroofe's account of how the
category of 'deserving' became 'not likely to benefit'
and then 'not assisted' (Woodroofe, 1962, p. 46).
But is it possible to get rid of the need to decide
who is 'willing to help himself' and who is 'work-
shy', and can objective tests of these characteristics
be devised or will it always be necessary to depend on
the intuitive judgment of welfare officials?   Or how
can one make an objective judgment about whether a
'socially acceptable situation exists' in order to
determine whether or not a child should be taken into
care?   Robson (1928) points out that judges have to
make decisions about 'imponderables' which 'depend on
subjective tasks and individual feelings' (2nd edn,
1947, p. 287) such as whether a ward of court should
be permitted to marry, and argues that this shows the
need for what he calls the 'judicial mind', which he
characterises as showing 'consistency, equality, certainty', being 'impartial, objective ... explicit in
its reasons ... he must suppress personal emotions and
instinctive prejudices and encourage his sense of
fairness' (p. 303).   It is, however, very questionable whether a judicial frame of mind can produce fair
decisions in the absence of the necessary regulative
framework against which to test the outcome.

7   Where the social worker sees himself as applying scientific ideas to the treatment of social problems it
is not surprising that he does not think of his job in
terms of the rights of his clients, since the image of
man as a self-directing rational being, on which
theories of human rights are based, is in conflict
with the deterministic image of human behaviour which
goes along with the scientific approach to his treat-

ment.   This point was forcibly argued some time ago
by Keith-Lucas (1953, p. 1082): 'The legal rights
established in the [Social Security] Act presumed recipients to be self-directing, rational beings.
Casework, despite its apparent acceptance of these
rights, was learning largely from a psychology that
held man to be basically irrational.'   Keith-Lucas
points out that (p. 1091):

once a positivist science becomes the rule of law,
or once a group in our society arrogates to itself
the right to judge or to treat another by the findings of such a science, no end to the process is in
sight.   What happens depends almost entirely on
the good will of the self-appointed 'social physi-
cian'....   Quis custodiet custodes?

4   Charity and the welfare state

Angus McKay

Social welfare benefits provided by the state, which in
Britain include cash payments and advisory services, are
akin to charitable trusts and societies in that both aim
at meeting certain needs of people. What, if anything,
is the difference between social welfare benefits and
charity? Is a welfare state a form of charity which happens to be run by the state, or is it an essentially different kind of thing from charity? People in Britain
sometimes register unease at being offered welfare benefits, or unwillingness to accept them, precisely because
they regard them as charity and do not wish to accept them
on this basis. The contrast, reflected in this uneasi-
ness, between 'charity' and 'what one is entitled to' or
'what someone has a duty to provide' is not, however, confined to British social consciousness. It is implicit in
a remark made by F.D. Roosevelt in 1931, when governor of
the state of New York, that when an ailing economy produces large-scale unemployment, 'To these unfortunate citizens aid must be extended by the government - not as a
matter of charity but as a matter of social duty' (quoted
in Woodroofe, 1962, p. 162). If we want to deny that
welfare benefits are 'charity' or are to be shunned as de-
tracting from a person's dignity, we must have some idea
in mind of the relation between the two.

One starting point for distinguishing social welfare
benefits from charity might be to say that to do something
for the sake of charity, or to be involved in a work of
charity, always presupposes a motive of a distinct kind.
Thus, it might be said, to give something for the sake of
charity or on behalf of a charitable organisation is to
give it for the sake of the recipient, and for no other
reason. For instance, if I send £20 to Oxfam, this
counts as charity if my motive is the disinterested one of
helping others in need. On the other hand, so the argu-

ment would go, those involved in operating a state welfare
scheme and those who contribute to it need not do so from
any such motives; a social worker might only be a member
of such a profession because he or she is interested in
the salary, or finds it an easy job, while members of the
public contribute to state social welfare because they
have to, or because it is in their own interests.   And
the state *might* have such services not only to take care
of those in need, but also in order to control or regulate
forces which would otherwise threaten the status quo, or
for a number of other possible reasons.

It is true that we do sometimes use 'charity' in such a
way as to suggest that an essential feature of a charitable act is that such an act is disinterested.   Such remarks as 'I'm not doing this from charity' suggest that we
are doing whatever is in question for some gain to ourselves rather than from a disinterested motive.   But although we undoubtedly do have such expressions, it does
not follow that the notion of 'a charitable society' or an
organisation such as Oxfam is such that it is to be distinguished from other forms of welfare in the way suggested.   One reason for denying the validity of that distinction is that it might be the case that some voluntary
workers or employees of a charitable institution choose to
do such work because they enjoy it, because it satisfies a
guilty conscience, because it's a convenient form of work,
or from many motives other than a disinterested one; I
might accept employment from Oxfam simply because it is
the only job I can get, but it does not follow from this
that I do not form part of a charitable organisation.   It
seems in such cases to be sufficient that the ends of the
organisation, for instance the relief of hunger, are
achieved, even if my motives in pursuing these ends are
not disinterested.   Similarly, the fact that a social
worker does the job because it is an easy one, or a chal-
lenging one, does not disqualify us from saying that what
he or she is doing in doing the job is 'relieving human
need', 'helping those with problems', or other such descriptions.   This suggests that interestedness or disin-
terestedness is not the sole criterion for distinguishing
social welfare and charity.   However, it might be replied
to this argument that a charity worker must *himself* be
disinterested for *his* act, as opposed to the agency's act,
to be an act of charity, and that the proposed criterion
still applies.   But even if this point is accepted, it
would still follow on the criterion that welfare workers
could not be disinterested in their actions.   And this is
clearly not the case.   So even if there is a distinct
motive which we sometimes call 'the motive of charity' it

will not suffice to distinguish state social welfare from charity.

A second way in which social welfare and charity are sometimes distinguished is to say that social welfare is essentially a state-run affair, while charity is a matter of private and voluntary aid.   Charity, therefore, would not exist unless individuals chose to operate such a scheme, whereas social welfare is something which the state runs.   But this does not amount to an essential difference - if there is no more to it than this, then it seems perfectly correct to say that the social welfare services are in essence a state-run charity scheme.

Of course, one possible reason for the state taking upon itself the responsibility for various kinds of services is that this is the simplest, and probably the only, way in which welfare benefits can be granted to people *as of right*.   And this does lead to a difference of a conceptual kind.   This is the view that social welfare is something granted as a legal right, whereas those who receive what is called charity receive something which, however nice to receive, is not something which is their's by right, either legal or moral.   It is precisely this view which makes it possible to draw the contrast mentioned in the opening paragraph between receiving as a right what is owed as a duty and receiving charity.   The remainder of this paper will be concerned with a discussion of the coherence of this view and its implications.

Let us suppose that there is a distinction between those things we have a right to, and which someone has a duty to provide, and those things which we may welcome receiving but which we cannot claim as a right.   Is this a suitable way of representing the difference between social welfare and charity?   The view that charity is essentially something which we cannot claim as a right has in the past been endowed with a rationale by some moral philosophers who have distinguished between *perfect* and *imperfect* duties.   In 'The Groundwork of the Metaphysic of Morals' Immanuel Kant employs this distinction: 'I understand here by a perfect duty one which allows no exception in the interests of inclination' (Paton, 1948, pp. 84-5n.).   Thus I have according to Kant a *perfect* duty to give the correct change to a customer who make a purchase in my shop;   I cannot, if I am to do my duty, give him less than I owe even if I feel so inclined.   On the other hand, there is another class of duties which Kant illustrates as follows: '[A man] is himself flourishing, but he sees others who have to struggle with great hardships ... and he thinks "what does it matter to me?"' (Paton, p. 86).   Kant wants to say that such a man has a duty to

help others, but that it is an *imperfect* duty.   That is
to say, for Kant, while I ought to give some of my income
to those in need, I have some choice in the matter, perhaps about which charity I give to, and to this extent I
can serve my own inclination.

As it is stated, it is possible to question the grounds
of this distinction.   Perhaps to some extent I can pick
and choose between charities; but the same is true of
Kant's example of a perfect duty.   If I owe £100 then I
may have no choice about repaying it, but I do have some
choice about whether to pay over ten £10 notes or one £100
note.   And one might in any case question how much choice
I ought to allow myself about which worthy causes to support.   Ought I really to give it all to the Dog and Cat
Home rather than to Oxfam?   However, let us allow that
some such distinction is ordinarily drawn in the way most
people consider such questions.   A more refined version
of this distinction, though one which is to some extent
implicit in what Kant says in the 'Groundwork' is to be
found in J.S. Mill's 'Utilitarianism' (1863).

According to Mill the distinction between perfect and
imperfect duties is really a distinction between those
duties which give rise to a correlative right and those
which do not.   (Mill is anxious to argue that this distinction marks the difference between those duties which
are duties of *justice* and those that belong to 'the other
obligations of morality'.)   Let us note for the moment
that he distinguishes between a duty which implies a corresponding right on the part of someone who can exact the
duty, and duties such as charity which Mill also regards
as an imperfect duty.   He says of charity that 'though
the act is obligatory, the particular occasions of performing it are left to our choice' (Mill, 1863, p. 305).
Further, 'No one has a moral right to our generosity or
beneficence, because we are not morally bound to practise
those virtues towards any given individual' (Mill, 1863,
p. 305).

Such, then, is the theoretical background to the view
of the relation between social welfare and charity which
we are considering.   In the case of social welfare benefits such as Unemployment Benefit, the recipient claims
these as a right guaranteed to him by the *state*.   It is,
thus, a legal right and, we can assume, is granted because
the government also thinks that such individuals have a
moral right to help.   On the other hand, in the case of
the receipt of charity, the individual is receiving something to which he has no moral claim, and he cannot,
therefore, complain to anyone if he is not given it.   As
mentioned above, such a scheme as this provides a frame-

work within which we can make sense of what is said by the
person who refuses to accept, for instance, Supplementary
Benefits, on the grounds that the right to them has not
been earned by being paid for, and they are, therefore, to
be regarded as charity.   It is presupposed by the remark,
made by Sir William Beveridge in laying the foundation of
the British welfare benefits system that 'by paying not,
indeed, the whole cost, but a substantial part of it, he
[the citizen] can feel he is getting security not as a
charity but as a right' (Beveridge, 1942, para. 296).

What is unsatisfactory about the above way of viewing
the present relation between social welfare benefits and
charity can be seen if we consider what it is that is
supposed to qualify a citizen in a country such as Britain
to rights such as the right to Unemployment Benefit, medical treatment from the National Health Service, etc.
Perhaps the most obvious answer to this question, and the
one which is explicitly stated by Beveridge, is that such
rights are earned by being paid for.   Now it is clearly
the case that the finances of the National Health Service
and other benefits of the welfare state are being paid
for, and are paid for, by members of the state.   However,
even a superficial examination of the manner in which the
social services are presently financed shows that it is
difficult to sustain the claim that an individual's right
to the welfare benefits supplied by the state is grounded
in the fact that he is in a significant sense paying for
these services.   In 1972, the income from insured persons' contributions to the National Health Service was
£233 million.   Expenditure on goods and services in that
year was £2240 m., and capital expenditure was £206 m.
So, as is well known, the health service is massively subsidised by central government funds, and contributions via
stamps amount to a small proportion of the total cost.
In 1972 the income from contributions to the National Insurance fund was £3048 m.;   the total expenditure was
£3483 m.   This included retirement pensions, Unemployment
Benefits, Sickness Benefits, Maternity and Death Benefits,
but excluded a further £725 m. spent on Supplementary
Benefits.   A government grant of £576 m. was made to the
fund, a grant which has been steadily increasing since
1946 when it was £60 m.   So approximately 16 per cent of
the cost of the scheme excluding Supplementary Benefits
had to be met by central government funds rather than
direct contributions from insured persons.   The other
main item of 'the social services' is education, which in
the case of state-run schools in Britain is almost solely
financed through local authorities in the first instance.
In 1972 the combined local authorities' spending on educa-

tion was £2349 m., when receipts from rates amounted to
£2777 m., and the total spending of local authorities was
£7162 m.   So the education budget is one of the chief
items which require a government grant to local authorities which in 1972 was £2923 m.   (The above figures have
been obtained from National Income and Expenditure, vols
1946-73, London, Central Statistical Office.)

Now the point I want to make arising from this is that
while it is clearly the case that the social services are
paid for either via insurance contributions or through
direct and indirect taxation, it is clear that a substantial number of persons receive goods and services far in
excess of what they pay into the scheme either via contributions or taxation.   A married man with two children
stands to receive 'in return for' his insurance contributions and taxes, medical care for himself, wife and children, Unemployment Benefit, Maternity Grants for his wife,
Family Allowances, Sickness Benefit etc., as well as education for his children.   Yet he will contribute the same
amount on his stamp and less in taxes than a man earning
the same but with no dependants.   It might be said that
he still has to pay as much in indirect taxes for the
goods he purchases as anyone else; yet just because he is
paying the same he still remains at a comparative 'advantage' over a person who makes less claims on the state.
This point is not, of course, a point only about the
family man.   The same situation is 'enjoyed' by the
person who suffers from more than average ill-health and
receives from the health service more than he contributes,
at the expense of the healthy man who pays his contributions and taxes yet makes few demands on the health service.

So much is common knowledge to many, and the object of
complaint by some.   My object is not to complain about
such a state of affairs, but rather to point out that
these facts entail that the proposed account of the relation between welfare benefits and charity will not do.
It is not at present the case, and it looks as if it never
was the case, that welfare rights in Britain are earned by
being paid for.

It might be argued against such a conclusion that while
some - perhaps many - persons who receive social welfare
benefits do not pay on total more than a nominal contribution towards the cost of these services, this is not inconsistent with the view that their right to such services
is grounded in the fact that they pay something.   After
all, contributions towards Health and Unemployment Benefits are made in Britain through what is still called an
insurance scheme, based originally on the Beveridge Report

mentioned above.   Beveridge argued strongly for a scheme
of social welfare based on each man paying a contribution
to the state insurance scheme.   It was precisely this
feature - that the service or benefit received would be
paid for - that Beveridge claimed would ensure that a man
could feel he was claiming benefits 'not as a charity but
as a right' (Beveridge, 1942, para. 296).   Now the whole
point of an insurance scheme is that an individual may
receive benefits well in excess of the premiums he has
paid.   Thus if I insure my car against accidental damage
and the vehicle is subsequently destroyed in an accident,
I am entitled to receive from my insurers a sum well in
excess of the original premium;   this is what insurance is
all about.   Such a scheme relies for its success, of
course, on comparatively few people making successful
claims on their policy.   Those who do not claim still pay
for their cover and in this sense can be said to 'subsidise' those who do claim.   But the analogy with a
starightforward insurance scheme does not fit the health
and welfare services at all well.   For it is part of any
normally run insurance scheme that any identifiable class
of persons who regularly make higher claims will have to
pay higher premiums.   Thus, if it is found that people
under the age of 25 frequently get involved in expensive
motor accidents, they will pay higher premiums since the
company is faced with higher risks in insuring them.   But
the policy of charging people in accordance with the likelihood of their requiring services is not part of the welfare state.   The original Beveridge proposals insisted on
a 'flat-rate' contribution from all insured persons.   Although this has now been discarded in favour of the graduated pensions system this system charges and provides
future benefits to people according to their ability to
pay and not according to their liability.   If then people
do not pay a realistic proportion of what they receive,
and the total contributions do not cover anything like the
cost of the services provided, the 'insurance model'
breaks down.   So the idea that welfare rights are earned
by being paid for through some kind of state-run insurance
system is a fiction.

In Social Policy and Social Justice (1974) Robert
Pinker argues that the principles on which Beveridge based
his 1942 Report are no longer operating in Britain.
Whereas Beveridge argued for a flat-rate contribution, and
one which would be sufficiently high for a person to be
justified, in Beveridge's opinion, in regarding his benefits as rights based on his having paid his insurance contributions, the graduated pensions system introduced in
1959, when the flat-rate contribution had become too high

for the lowest-paid worker to bear it, marked the beginning of a scheme in which it was more clearly accepted
that the better-paid worker would have to subsidise to
some extent those who were less well paid.   Two of the
points made by Pinker are particularly relevant to the
present issue.   First, he points out that in the 'post-
Beveridge' era, growing poverty was fought by a 'gradual
but massive increase in the use of supplementary forms of
assistance' (Pinker, 1974, p. 7), provided only when it
was shown that work was not available or that a man was
unable to work through ill-health.   Thus, while the gap
between what many paid for social services remained or
even widened, government attitude remained in line with
the basic principles of the Beveridge Report.   As Pinker
says (1974, p. 7), 'At all costs, it seems, the fiction
had to be maintained that a work status, however marginal,
was synonymous with economic independence'.

Second, Pinker points out that the 'egalitarian' aspect
of Beveridge's proposals is further departed from under
the proposed tax-credit system and pensions plan, to such
an extent that we can no longer regard as credible the
principle that 'payment of a substantial part of the cost
of benefit as a contribution is the firm basis of a claim
to benefit' (Beveridge, 1942, para. 21).   This, Pinker
says, is because 'What the new proposals embody is the
view that the just level of obligatory insurance contributions should now be more closely related to individual
means and not to some absolute flat-rate sum' (1974, p.
15).   It is not clear why Pinker thinks that there ever
was a time when it was 'credible' to assume that people
paid 'a substantial part of the cost of benefit'.   Beveridge, as has been said, insisted on a flat-rate basis
for contributions because he thought that only this would
make the scheme an *insurance* scheme.

> The distinction between taxation and insurance contri-
> bution is that taxation is or should be related to
> assured capacity to pay rather than to the volume of
> what the payer may expect to receive, while insurance
> contributions are or should be related to the value of
> the benefits and not to the capacity to pay.   (Bev-
> eridge, 1942, para. 272)

But, I have argued, this is not sufficient to make Beveridge's proposals an insurance scheme.   For it is not
the case under this scheme that payment is in proportion
to the services offered - a fact which curiously enough
Beveridge acknowledged; he seems to have thought that
while 'In voluntary insurance the contribution is a premium which must be adjusted to some extent to the degree
of risk....   In compulsory insurance, the contribution

may vary with the risk but need not do so' (Beveridge,
1942, para. 272).   Just why a scheme's being compulsory
rather than voluntary should make such a difference is not
explained by Beveridge.   And it is not clear what the
'insurance principle' to which he frequently appeals could
be other than the principle I have already quoted from
Beveridge, that 'insurance contributions are or should be
related to the value of the benefits and not to the capacity to pay'.   Yet if this is Beveridge's considered
view, his adherence to the flat-rate contribution seems
to be at odds with it.   He admitted 'it is certain that
the National Exchequer, that is to say the citizen as tax-
payer will continue to meet a substantial part of the
total expenditure ...' (Beveridge, 1942, para. 273), while
also claiming that the individual was paying 'a substantial part ... as a contribution' (para. 296).   It looks
here as if Beveridge was trying to reconcile what could
not be reconciled - the claim that the individual could
credibly be regarded as 'paying his own way' with the acknowledgment that large amounts of government finance would
be required to fund the insurance scheme.   It seems,
then, that not only is it clear from the sums involved
that people in Britain do not now pay a realistic proportion of what they stand to receive as benefits, but also
that it never was realistic to regard the Beveridge proposals as an insurance scheme.

So welfare rights are not paid for in any society in
which they are funded in the way outlined above.   If this
is so, what follows from it?   Clearly, we have to say
either that social welfare benefits are *not* to be regarded
as rights, or we have to find some other basis for 'earning' the right.   I shall assume here that we do want to
regard social welfare benefits as something that people
have a right to.   Now if the criterion of entitlement is
not paying for the benefits, the only plausible alternative candidate is that of *need*;   that is to say, recipients of benefits if they have a right to them enjoy this
right because they need them.   (David Watson discusses in
Chapter 2 of this volume matters relating to the issue of
how needs are identified, for instance by the principle of
respect for human beings.)   But if we say that the criterion of entitlement to welfare benefits is need, what
has happened to the original distinction we drew between
charity and social welfare?   What follows from the view
that payment is not the basis of the right, is that it
becomes problematic to distinguish between charity and
social welfare on the grounds that charity is not a right.
For what we are now saying is that social welfare benefits
are supplied as a right because they are needed;   yet this

is just what would be said by any charitable organisation - its services or benefits are provided because they are needed. So it *looks* as if the distinction implicit in the Beveridge report has collapsed. Both charity and welfare benefits organised by the state meet needs and are provided because they do this. If we want to continue to say that people have a right to social welfare *and* say that need is a sufficient basis for this right, then in principle it is possible that what we presently refer to as charity, thus distinguishing it from what people have a right to, is in fact something that people are entitled to.

It might be replied to this that we can save the distinction between charity and welfare benefits by distinguishing various levels of need, or different levels at which relief is required. After all, the argument would go, a person's requirement for a diet which sustains life is more important in one obvious sense than this requirement for a wheelchair if he cannot walk, desirable as the latter may be. And it may be *nice* for a lonely old person to have a television, but does he *need* it? Since there clearly are these different levels at which we can relieve need, surely we can distinguish between those levels which we consider it to be intolerable that a person should fail to reach, and those levels which it may be desirable that individuals should reach, but which are not necessary. Thus, we might say that everyone has a right to a diet which sustains life, and this is the level which we should insist must be met, but that television sets for the house-bound is a quite different level of relief which is not a right and the giving of this kind of relief is charity. But I do not think that charitable organisations could or should admit that the needs which they meet are less important or basic than at least some of the needs served by a welfare state. Oxfam may be meeting needs far more basic than some welfare benefits when what is involved is, for example, not merely seeing that a family can pay the rent, but that people in some areas survive at all. If it is objected that such relief is not usually required in countries with a developed welfare system, then it can be replied that a charity in Britain such as the Royal National Lifeboat Institute sets out to save lives which clearly would be lost but for their help; it is implausible to say that this kind of service is not as important as many of the services of the welfare state. Some of the services we presently call charity are as important to the recipients as some of the services of the state. If those things are needed, then the argument of this paper is that a

welfare state is committed to regarding them as rights,
though there may also be things which people are considered not to have a right to and which charities might provide.   It is difficult to avoid the latter part of that
conclusion unless one is prepared to commit oneself to
the view that anything we might feel was desirable to give
to another is actually one's duty and that the other
person has a right to it.   In Mill's words, 'to make out
that mankind generally, though not any given individual,
have a right to all the good we can do them' is to say
that 'our utmost exercises are *due* to our fellow creatures, thus assimilating them to a debt' (Mill, 1863, pp.
305-6).   It would be difficult to sustain a case based on
an analysis of the ordinary moral consciousness for saying
that an action is either a duty and that someone has a
right to demand it of us, or else that it can have no
moral worth whatever, and that 'acts of supererogation'
can have no place in a moral scheme.

Two possible objections to such a view of welfare:
first, it is sometimes said that it is conceptually con-
fused to suppose that many of the things we presently
speak of as charity should come under the notion of
rights, since the welfare state is only an instrument of
social *justice*.   But, the argument continues, it cannot
be a matter of justice to make provision, for instance,
for the needs of the handicapped, because justice is concerned with arrangements brought about by human agents,
and most handicapped people are not in this condition as
a result of human agency.   Thus in 'The Morals of Markets' (1971, p. 71) H.B. Acton argued that 'basic welfare
should not be removed from the market and provided for
everyone out of taxation.   Poverty and misfortune are
evils but not injustices, and the moral demand they make
for help is on the ground of humanity'.   In saying this,
Acton gives a clear expression of the kind of argument
mentioned above.   He reasons that:
> the rain that falls upon the just and upon the unjust
> cannot be condemned for its lack of moral distinctions.
> Neither can a social order be condemned as just or
> unjust if no-one has planned or controlled it.   If a
> whole system of social and economic relationships is
> held to be unjust, this must really mean that *if* some-
> one had made the distribution deliberately, then it
> would have been unjust.   But something that merely
> *happens* cannot be just or unjust.   It is not unjust
> for a good man to die in an accident and for a bad man
> to live long and happily.   (Acton, 1971, p. 63)

Although it is not explicitly stated in the passages I
have quoted, it is clear from this that Acton wants to say

that people ought not to be able to claim welfare rights
from the state as a right, since it is not the other's
fault that they require it.   Someone less wedded to the
virtues of the market economy than Acton might be tempted
to make capital out of the comparison drawn here between
the operations of a free market and an accident; but more
relevant to our present purposes is that the view of the
nature of justice presupposed in the passage quoted is far
from unassailable.   We might well question the view that
justice is only concerned with states of affairs deliberately brought about by human agents and not with states of
affairs such as accidents or features of a social order,
which even if not the result of human agency can often
exist only as long as human agents omit to change them.
Furthermore, in order for the arguments of the kind
Acton presents to constitute a serious objection to what
I have suggested, it would need to be shown not only that
there is nothing unjust in poverty and misfortune but also
that all rights which the welfare state might insist upon
are rights derived from the notion of justice.   It does
not follow, without argument at any rate, from what Acton
says that even if the moral demand to redress the inequalities of poverty and misfortune is a demand of humanity
rather than injustice, such a demand may not give rise to
rights on the part of the poor.   It is arguable that not
all rights are derived from notions of the kind Acton has
in mind but might arise, for instance, from the fact that
an individual *needs* something in order to do a particular
job, or to have a tolerable standard of living.   (See
Campbell (1974) for a discussion of the relation between
notions of merit, desert, justice and rights.)

The second possible objection to the argument of this
paper is that the notion of need as a valid criterion of
social welfare policy is inevitably a conservative one
which does not allow scope for the radical social and
economic change which some people argue is necessary for
many present states to be just states.   After all, it is
very easy to restrict the notion of what someone needs in
such a manner that wide inequalities can remain in a
society where nobody is thought of as being 'in need'.   I
have already mentioned the difficulties of spelling out in
detail just what a person can be said to need in order to
live a reasonable and satisfying life.   Does a family
really *need* an income which is sufficient for annual holi-
days, Christmas presents, etc., or are these things not
really luxuries when we consider how many people in the
world survive without them?   But the criterion of need
need not necessarily pre-empt the possibility of radical
change, any more than it necessarily implies it.   For the

claim that society has a duty to relieve need is not inconsistent with a 'liberal' view of what people need to
live well, nor is it inconsistent with attempting, if we
think it right, to argue for change of a sweeping kind in
the way society is organised.

I conclude then that many of the ways we speak about
charity and the welfare state conceal anomalies in our
thinking.   If we retain the distinction as at present,
and I have suggested it does mark some important points,
but carry along with it the assumption that it is only
those things included in state welfare benefits that a
man can be said to have a moral right to, it remains
likely that we will fail to recognise that many of the
services now referred to as 'charity' are as important
as at least some of the services offered by the welfare
state.   And this is especially true when it is assumed
that we can regard benefits such as unemployment insurance
and health services as in some sense directly paid for by
the recipient.   If the principles on which the system are
incoherent to that extent, then it is surely important
that this is recognised, since it is only in the presence
of a coherent framework that reasonable principles can be
drawn up.   The resentment of those who see themselves as
being offered 'charity' by a welfare state is by no means
then the sole difficulty in working out satisfactory
social policies.   By labelling something as 'charity' it
is easy to covertly suggest that there is no duty on the
part of the state to provide it.

5   Non-judgmental attitudes

R. F. Stalley

1

Social workers often stress the importance of adopting
what they call a 'non-judgmental attitude' towards their
clients, but although this notion of a non-judgmental attitude plays an important part in casework theory, the
accounts which are given of it are often very unsatisfactory.   Of course it is easy to see in a very general way
the sort of point which is at issue.   Modern social workers want to make it clear that their whole approach is
very different from that which was taken for granted by
those who administered the old poor laws, and even by some
of the pioneers of social work.   According to the old
approach, the basic distinction which had to be made was
that between the deserving poor, whose plight was due to
sheer misfortune and who therefore deserved to be helped,
and the undeserving who were to be left to endure the consequences of their own wickedness or folly.   Even the
early caseworker, we are told, was often seen as 'an interfering busy-body, an authoritative do-gooder imposing
his own rigid, moralistic, upper-middle-class ways of life
on the helpless poverty-ridden widow' (Hollis, 1963, p.
9).   But although it is relatively easy to describe some
of the undesirable practices which are supposed to be excluded by the non-judgmental attitude of the modern social
worker, it is not nearly so easy to say exactly what this
attitude is.   Indeed I shall argue that there is no one
simple account which can be given of it and that the
demand for a non-judgmental attitude, if it is to be taken
seriously, must be seen as a protest against a number of
different faults which could infect social casework.
Some writers see the doctrine that a caseworker should
adopt a non-judgmental attitude as an application of a
more general moral principle, the principle that we should

refrain from judging our fellow men.   This principle is, of course, a familiar part of Christian ethics, where the underlying idea seems to be that God alone can judge because he alone knows what goes on in men's hearts.   One could cite passages such as Matthew, VII, 1, 'Judge not that ye be not judged', and Romans, XIV, 13, 'Let us not therefore judge one another'.   But it is not difficult to see why people should hold the doctrine that it is wrong to judge our fellow men, even outside a purely Christian framework of morality.   Most of us dislike morally censorious people.   We do not like feeling that our characters are being assessed or that we are being categorised as good or bad people.   Furthermore it is difficult, and perhaps impossible, to understand fully the psychological and environmental pressures to which another person is subject, and such pressures are clearly relevant to the decision whether he is a good or bad man, a praiseworthy or a blameworthy character.   So, if we do endeavour to judge our fellow men, the chances are that our judgments will be not simply unkind but also unjust.   In this way we can see how someone might regard the principle that we should not be judgmental as an important principle in everyday life as well as in social casework.   What is not clear is whether the principle as it applies in casework is the same as the general principle which applies in ordinary life, or whether there is some special sense in which the caseworker should be non-judgmental over and above the sense in which everybody should be non-judgmental.   Some of the literature gives the impression that the non-judgmental attitude is a distinguishing feature of the casework relationship but this could not be so if the requirement that the caseworker should adopt a non-judgmental attitude was simply an application of a principle which should apply to all human relationships.   So another question we might ask is 'Are there any respects in which a caseworker should be non-judgmental and in which an ordinary man need not?'

2

Perhaps the most obvious way of explaining what it would be for a caseworker to adopt a non-judgmental attitude towards a client would be to say that it involves excluding moral judgments from the casework relationship.   To make a moral judgment is to form or express an opinion on a moral issue.   So it may seem that if a caseworker is to be non-judgmental he must make sure that any opinions he has about the morality of the client or of the client's

actions do not affect his own behaviour towards the
client.   It is not difficult to imagine cases which
would appear to support this interpretation of the non-
judgmental attitude.   For example, there must be many
caseworkers who believe that sexual relations outside
marriage are wrong but would feel that this should not
affect their attitude towards unmarried mothers among
their clients.   Although they privately think that the
unmarried mother has done wrong they are not for this
reason any less willing to help her and although they
might try to discourage her from doing the same thing
again this would not be because what she had done was
wrong but because it had caused difficulties for her.   In
other words, whatever the caseworker's private views, in a
case such as this he might well behave as though moral
questions simply did not arise.   One might try to gene-
ralise this model to cover all cases and say that to be
non-judgmental is always, so to speak, to 'leave morality
out of it'.

Although this view is in some ways attractive it has
been rejected by influential writers on casework such as
Florence Hollis and Felix Biestek, neither of whom would
be prepared to exclude moral judgments from casework in
the way suggested.   Biestek offers three reasons for
this (1957, p. 94):

First, the caseworker, because he is a social worker,
has a *social* responsibility; he is an agent of the
community, whether employed in a public or private
agency.

Second, the client will not be helped if he finds
that the caseworker is indifferent to the antisocial
illegal or immoral attitudes or standards that brought
trouble to the client.

Third, to maintain the integrity of his own personality the caseworker cannot remain interiorly indifferent to standards contrary to his own.

It might well be objected that Biestek assumes that casework must take place within a certain framework of moral
judgments without proving that this must be so.   There
must also be many caseworkers who would feel that Biestek
overemphasises the role of moral judgments.   Nevertheless
it can plausibly be argued that there are cases where the
caseworker neither can nor should refrain from making
moral judgments about his clients or their activities and
Biestek's points do indicate what some of these cases
might be.

First, it is sometimes only in the light of a particular moral view that the client could be seen as having a
problem.   For example, it could be argued that one could

only see a woman who neglected her children as having a problem if one thought that there was something wrong with neglecting one's children.   Equally it might be claimed that one could not engage in probation work without accepting that one's clients had done wrong in breaking the law.   Many caseworkers would, no doubt, take exception to these claims.   They would say that in order to see people such as mothers who neglect their children or teenage delinquents as having problems they do not need to regard them as having done something morally wrong but merely as having done something which is against the law and is therefore liable to have unpleasant consequences.   The role of the caseworker is simply to help the client to avoid these consequences in future.   But the trouble with this sort of position is that there are other ways in which the neglectful mother could avoid the penalties of the law besides coming to love and care for her children, and there are other ways in which delinquents could avoid punishment besides becoming law-abiding citizens.   One could help the neglectful mother to avoid the penalties of the law by showing her how to conceal the fact that she was neglecting her children.   One could help delinquents to avoid punishment by teaching them how to escape detection.   Thus a caseworker who took seriously the idea that in cases such as these his concern was primarily to help his clients avoid the unpleasant consequences of breaking the law might find himself using methods which, to put it mildly, would be extremely peculiar.   This shows that the reason why people such as the neglectful mother or the teenage delinquent are seen as having problems is not simply that their conduct has painful consequences.   Part of the problem must be that they have done wrong to other people or to society at large and need help to avoid doing wrong again.

Second, it can be argued that there are cases where the worker could in theory prevent his moral judgments from influencing his approach to his client but where it would be wrong for him to do so.   Such cases might arise if the client proposed to do something which the worker believed was wrong because it would do serious harm to others. For example, if a client indicated that he intended to solve his financial problems by stealing from his neighbours, most people would, I think, agree that it was the caseworker's responsibility to discourage him, even if there was a strong probability that the theft would go undetected and would bring no troublesome consequences to the client.   If one took this view one would presumably be recognising that a reason for discouraging the theft was that it would be wrong.   No doubt it is this kind of

possibility which Biestek has in mind when he talks of
the caseworker having a social responsibility, but Biestek's way of putting the point may be misleading, since it
suggests that this responsibility arises purely out of the
professional role of the social worker.   Quite apart from
anything else, there must be many who would reject Biestek's view of the social worker as the agent of the community.   The important point really seems to be that we all
as human beings have some responsibility to discourage
acts which would be harmful to society or to other people,
although the social worker may also have special responsibilities which arise out of his professional role.

Third, the client may sometimes see himself as having a
moral problem.   He may have difficulty in deciding what
is the right thing for him to do now or he may feel guilty
about what he has done in the past.   A caseworker could
not help such a client by behaving as though there was no
moral problems.   As Biestek points out (1957, p. 94), it
would not help an unmarried mother who felt guilty and expressed this feeling verbally if the caseworker made remarks such as 'Marriage is after all only a social conven-
tion'.   This would do nothing to remove her guilt feelings, and would probably make her feel that the worker did
not understand her problem.   In order to help a client in
this kind of situation the worker would need to recognise
the moral problems and be prepared to discuss them with
the client.   This does not mean that he would have to
tell the client what was right or wrong, but it is difficult to see how he could discuss this issue without to
some extent involving his own moral judgments.

The above points are, I think, implicit in what Biestek
says and seem plausible in themselves.   If they are correct they suggest there may be occasions when a social
worker, simply because of his professional relationship
with his client, has a special obligation to concern himself with the moral issues which arise out of the client's
behaviour.   This in turn suggests a different account of
the non-judgmental attitude, one which writers on casework
may have in mind although it does not usually come to the
surface very clearly.   According to this account the important point about the non-judgmental attitude would be
not so much that the role of the caseworker excludes the
making of moral judgments but that it lays special conditions on what moral judgments may appropriately be made
and how they may be made.   The idea here would be that
the caseworker should only allow his moral judgments to
influence his approach to his client in so far as these
judgments are relevant to the overall aims of casework.
The objective of casework, as I understand it, is not to

improve people's morals, nor to impose society's norms
upon them, but to help them solve their own problems.
Sometimes, as we have seen, the client's problem may be
intimately connected with moral issues, and a caseworker
clearly could not help such a client if he simply ignored
these issues.   He will need to think about them and may
well need to discuss them with the client.   In most
cases, however, although the caseworker may have views
about the morality of his client's behaviour, he will not
need to take these into account in order to help the
client with his problem.   So the important point would
be, not that the caseworker should ignore moral questions
altogether, but that he should only concern himself with
them when they are relevant to the client's problem.
Thus the demand for a non-judgmental attitude would resolve itself first into an insistence that the aim of
casework is not to improve the client's morality, to
reward his virtue or to punish his vice, and second into
the assertion that unnecessary moralising may make the
primary goals of casework impossible of attainment and
that the caseworker should therefore only concern himself
with moral questions to the extent that this is necessary
in order to achieve these primary goals.

Something analogous to this might be true in everyday
life.   I may have views about the morality of the gro-
cer's private life but I do not need to express these
openly unless he asks for my advice or invites me to participate in his misdeeds.   There is a difference between
having a moral code and being a moralistic busybody.   So
I think one thing which might be meant by saying that
someone was judgmental is that he goes in for unnecessary
moralising about other people's behaviour when it is none
of his business.   The difference between casework and
ordinary life might be that the casework relationship is
defined by reference to certain fairly specific goals and
it may, therefore, be relatively easier to say when it is
appropriate for the caseworker to express a moral judgment
and how it should be expressed.   Relationships in ordinary life are not normally defined by reference to such
specific goals and it may therefore be relatively more
difficult to decide what is or is not one's business.
However, this sort of point cannot be all that is at issue
when casework theorists talk of the importance of being
non-judgmental, for even when it is appropriate to express
one's moral views or to allow them to influence one's behaviour it is still possible to do so in a way which could
be criticised as unnecessarily judgmental.   For example,
the relationship between a probation officer and his
client may generally involve a recognition that the client

has in some sense done wrong, but this recognition should
not involve the probation officer's trying to convey to
the client that he is a wicked, irresponsible, worthless,
character.   Thus the demand for a non-judgmental attitude
cannot be merely an assertion that the overt expression of
moral judgments is usually inappropriate in casework.   It
must also be a protest against certain undesirable ways of
moralising and we need an account of what these undesirable ways of moralising are.

If the above points are correct they show that considerations about what is morally right or wrong cannot be
excluded altogether from casework.   There are, however,
other more fundamental philosophical reasons for thinking
that being non-judgmental in casework cannot be a matter
of simply 'leaving morality out of it'.   If someone suggests that moral considerations can be excluded from casework he is implying that it is possible for a caseworker
to reach an understanding of his client's problems and to
use this understanding in helping the client without
thereby committing himself to any moral judgments.   Anyone who wanted to maintain this view would have to show
first that there is a distinction between moral judgments
and those kinds of judgment which are permitted within
casework, and second that making the sort of judgment
which is required in casework does not commit one to
making moral judgments.   To put it briefly, he would have
to show that there is a logical gap between moral judgments and casework judgments.   I think there is only one
way in which one could plausibly argue that such a gap
exists and that is by appealing to the doctrine held by
many philosophers that there is a gap between facts and
values.   According to this doctrine we must distinguish
between judgments of fact which describe how things *are*
and judgments of value (or evaluative judgments) which say
how things *ought to be*, or what would be right or good.
Moral judgments would, of course, be prime examples of
value-judgments, so one might try to explain the non-judgmental attitude by saying that the caseworker should restrict himself to the facts and should avoid making judgments about values.

One problem with this is that it is by no means clear
that a sharp distinction can be drawn between fact and
value.   It is true that many philosophers have held that
there is such a distinction, and that, therefore, a judgment about how things are cannot imply anything about how
things ought to be.   The views of these philosophers have
influenced social scientists who have thought that their
own studies should be 'value-free'.   However, a large
number of philosophers now believe that this conception of

the distinction between fact and value is mistaken.   For
example, some of them would argue that one cannot admit
that an action would damage the interests or happiness of
those affected by it without thereby committing oneself
to the view that, other things being equal, the action
would be morally wrong.   Conversely, they would say that
one could not admit that an action would make people hap-
pier without committing oneself to the view that, other
things being equal, the action would be morally good.
Clearly the caseworker must form some opinions about
whether the client's actions are likely to promote or to
damage the interests or happiness of the client himself
and of those around him.   Thus, if these philosophers are
right, a caseworker can hardly avoid committing himself to
some judgments about the morality of the client's actions.

The situation is no easier if we do allow that there is
a distinction between fact and value.   The trouble here
is that even the most enthusiastic proponents of the fact/
value distinction agree that one cannot in practice draw a
clear line between judgments of fact and judgments of
value.   At one extreme there are judgments which may seem
to be entirely concerned with questions of value.   Examples of such 'purely evaluative' judgments might be 'Eat-
ing people is wrong' and 'St Francis was a good man'.   At
the other extreme there are judgments which may seem to be
purely factual, such as 'A molecule of water contains two
atoms of hydrogen and one of oxygen'.   But in between
these two extremes there is an enormous class of judgments
which seem to be both factual and evaluative.   Most of
the judgments we make in everyday life come into this last
category, for most of the language we use and the concepts
we employ in ordinary interpersonal relations seem to have
both factual and evaluative components.   Some examples of
this kind of term would be 'responsible', 'rational',
'friendly', 'hostile', 'helpful', 'stubborn', 'conside-
rate', 'aggressive', 'loving', 'egocentric', 'immature',
and 'anti-social'.   These terms form a very mixed bag but
they all carry with them implications about the goodness
or badness, the rightness or wrongness of the behaviour
they are used to describe.   It may be possible for the
physical scientist or the technologist to avoid using
terms of this kind, and it may, therefore, be possible for
subjects such as physics, chemistry or engineering to be
value-free.   It may even be possible to make a value-
free study of human beings in psychology or sociology,
though there are reasons for doubting this.   But even if
we do accept that psychologists or sociologists can study
human beings in a value-free way, they could only do this
in so far as they looked on human behaviour in the same

sort of way as a physical scientist looks on the phenomena he studies or as a technologist looks on the mechanisms he manipulates. A caseworker, on the other hand, cannot regard his client in the way in which a scientist or technologist regards the objects of his investigations. The casework relationship, we are told, requires a personal involvement, an ability to see the client's behaviour and that of those around him as it appears to the participants. The caseworker must be able to convey to the client the feeling that he is accepted as a person, that the caseworker is concerned about his interests, his desires, his purposes, his feelings and so on. None of this could happen if the caseworker saw the client purely within the limits of the concepts of science. He must also use what one might call the concepts of personal relations. He must see the client, not as the scientist sees the subject matter of his science, but as human beings see one another and, as we have seen, most of the concepts one uses in doing this have evaluative implications. We cannot therefore base an account of the non-judgmental attitude on a distinction between factual and evaluative judgments.

The conclusion one must draw from this is that being non-judgmental cannot be a matter of refraining from making moral judgments or even from making value-judgments in general. Conversely, those who are criticised as being judgmental do not go wrong simply because they make moral judgments. They must make the wrong kinds of moral judgments or make them at the wrong times or in the wrong kinds of way.

3

One account of the non-judgmental attitude which may be helpful is that given by Florence Hollis (1961, pp. 152-3). She discusses the fundamental attitude of acceptance which the caseworker should adopt and insists that it is not the same as approval. She concedes that 'there are many times when we think our client is in the wrong, that his behaviour is unwise, to put it even more strongly sometimes that his behaviour is truly wicked', but she does not regard this as being inconsistent with an attitude of acceptance. Nor does she think that the attitude of acceptance requires the worker to give up his personal code of ethics. 'It is not by any means a denial of values in behaviour. A sense of values the caseworker must have. Rather it is separation of judgments about values from feelings toward a person.' She goes on to

commend the suggestion of Father Swithun Bowers that the
term 'non-condemnatory' should be substituted for 'non-
judgmental', because she holds that:

> the worker always has an opinion, a judgment, about his
> client's behaviour, but what he must not allow himself
> to do is to have feelings of condemnation toward his
> client because in his judgment the client is in the
> wrong.   This is really a translation into casework
> terms of the age-old religious admonition to 'hate the
> sin but love the fellow sinner'.

This account is rather puzzling.   Hollis identifies
being non-judgmental with being non-condemnatory and then
interprets this as not having feelings of condemnation.
But the idea of 'feelings of condemnation' is a worrying
one because the word 'condemnation' does not normally
refer to a kind of feeling.   Condemnation is the act of
condemning.   The 'Shorter Oxford English Dictionary'
lists three senses of 'condemn' which might be relevant to
our present concerns: '1 To pronounce an adverse judgment
on; to censure, blame.   2 To give judicial sentence
against; to convict.   3 To pronounce guilty.'   Clearly
one can pronounce an adverse verdict on someone, convict
him of a crime or pronounce him guilty without having any
particular kinds of feeling.   Condemnation is primarily a
matter of the judgment one makes, not of the feelings
which one has.   It is true, of course, that when we condemn someone we do often, although not always, have some
kind of hostile feeling towards him, but this does not
mean that condemnation is itself a kind of feeling.   Thus
it is not really clear whether Hollis means that the caseworker should refrain from some kind of judgment which
might be described as condemnation, or whether she means
to say that the caseworker should refrain from the hostile
feelings which are often consequent upon condemnation in
ordinary life.   There is a similar uncertainty in a foot-
note in 'Women in Marital Conflict' in which she describes
what she calls 'the negative aspect of acceptance' by
saying 'the caseworker must not condemn or feel hostile
toward a client because of his behaviour no matter how
greatly it may differ from the behaviour of which he per-
sonally would approve' (Hollis, 1949, p. 197).   Here
again condemnation is linked with hostile feeling as
though they were much the same sort of thing, but, as we
have seen, they are not.   It may therefore be helpful to
consider separately the suggestions that being non-judgmental is a matter of refraining from hostile feelings,
and that it is a matter of refraining from some kind of
adverse judgment or condemnation.

4

Taken literally the claim that the caseworker must not
allow himself to have hostile feelings towards his clients
asks too much, for a person cannot simply choose what
feelings to have.   They are, to a considerable extent at
least, outside his control.   This point is strictly correct but probably over-pedantic.   It may not make sense
to say that someone decides not to have hostile feelings
but he can at least try not to have them.   A caseworker
might do this by trying to see things as far as possible
from the client's point of view, by trying to look on the
client as an individual with a problem rather than as say
a criminal or an alcoholic, and so on.   Moreover, even if
he cannot avoid some feelings of hostility he can do his
best to see that these feelings do not affect his attitude
to his client.   As an individual he may not be able to
choose what feelings to have but he can try to see that
these feelings do not influence his professional attitude.
But if this was all that was meant by the non-judgmental
attitude then what is required of the social worker would
be no more that what is required of many other professions.   Even people such as policemen and judges are supposed to separate their professional attitudes from their
private feelings and it would be paradoxical that their
attitude should be non-judgmental.   This suggests that
being non-judgmental cannot be simply a matter of refraining from hostile feelings or of not allowing these feelings to affect one's professional attitude, but that it
must rather be a matter of refraining from the kind of
judgment which is called condemnatory.   There are other
considerations which point in the same direction:
(a) It is clear that at least some of the reasons offered
for not being judgmental are not simply reasons why the
social worker should not have hostile feelings towards his
clients but reasons why he should refrain from making
moral judgments about them.   This point is made very forcibly by Biestek (1957, pp. 91-3), who goes so far as to
argue that praise is just as much out of place in casework
as blame, because both praise and blame imply an assessment of the client as good or bad.   Even if we do not go
so far as Biestek does in excluding praise as well as
blame I think we must agree that a feeling on the part of
the client that he is being morally assessed is likely to
inhibit successful casework as much as a feeling that the
caseworker has feelings of hostility towards him.   Most
men are as anxious that others should have a good opinion
of them as they are that they should refrain from feelings
of hostility.   We fear that others may think us bad or

stupid just as much as we fear that they may actively dislike us.   This suggests that the caseworker should avoid
not simply hostile feelings but also giving the client the
impression that he is being assessed or judged in some
way.
(b) The charge of being judgmental has been laid against
people such as the early social workers, ministers of religion, voluntary workers, and others who are seen as
'moralistic do-gooders'.   The point cannot be that these
people are actuated by a positive ill-will or feeling of
hostility towards their clients because that would be
transparently false.   The point is that their good will
takes the wrong form.   Their attitudes and behaviour towards their clients are based upon an assessment of them
as deserving or undeserving people.   They are liable to
see their good work as redeeming or reforming a sinner or
scoundrel rather than as assisting an individual in need
of help.   Thus the complaint against these people is not
primarily that they have the wrong kind of feeling but
that their feelings, attitudes and behaviour are based
upon a certain kind of moral judgment.   Being judgmental
is not a matter of having hostile feelings but of seeing
people in a certain kind of moral light or putting them
into certain kinds of moral categories.
    If these arguments are correct then the distinction
between judgmental and non-judgmental attitudes cannot be
primarily a matter of the feelings which one has.   The
judgmental person may have different feelings from the
non-judgmental but these feelings are the result of the
way he assesses other people.   Thus, the primary difference between the judgmental and the non-judgmental person
seems to lie not in the feelings which they have towards
others but in the way in which they assess them.

5

The account of the non-judgmental attitude in social casework which is most commonly given relies on a distinction
between judgments made about a person and judgments made
about his behaviour.   It is said that the caseworker may
make adverse moral judgments about the behaviour of his
client but he may not make such judgments about the client
himself.   In other words, the caseworker may consider
that his client's behaviour is wrong but what he may not
do is to conclude that his client is therefore a bad or
wicked man.   Something like this view seems to be hinted
at in the passage from Florence Hollis which I discussed
above, where she grants that a caseworker may believe that

the client's *behaviour* is unwise or even wicked but insists that he may not therefore condemn the *client*, but as
we saw she rather confuses the issue by treating condemnation as though it were a kind of feeling rather than a
kind of judgment.   We must therefore consider the claim
that the idea of the non-judgmental attitude does rest on
a distinction between judgments made about a person and
judgments made about his acts.

   This account is both attractive and puzzling.   It is
attractive because it would give a very clear explanation
of how we can be non-judgmental without abandoning our
moral views;   it is puzzling because it obviously raises
considerable problems about the relationship between the
judgments which we make about men and the judgments which
we make about their behaviour.   To say that Smith did
something wrong is clearly not the same as to say that
Smith is a bad man, but there is some sort of logical connection between the two judgments.   One might be tempted
to say that a bad man is simply a man who does wrong.   If
this were right then in saying that Smith did wrong we
would be implying that he was to some extent, at least, a
bad man.   We might be able to draw a formal distinction
between judgments about a man and judgments about his
deeds but this would not really give us what we need because in making a judgment about the man's deeds we would
be committing ourselves to a judgment about him.   Thus,
if we are going to base an account of the non-judgmental
attitude on a distinction between judgments made about
people and judgments made about their behaviour, we need
to show that there is a logical gap between the two, that
in making a judgment about the act we are not also committing ourselves to a judgment about the man.

   One way of trying to solve this problem would be to say
that adopting a non-judgmental attitude involves refraining from attributions of responsibility.   Thus, Biestek
(1957, p. 90) writes of the non-judgmental attitude that:
'it is based on the conviction that the casework function
excludes assigning guilt or innocence or degree of client
responsibility for the causation of the problems or needs,
but does include making evaluative judgments about the
attitudes, standards or actions of the client.'   He goes
on: 'The fundamental meaning of "judging" is to determine
whether a person is innocent or guilty of doing wrong.
It is the process of deciding whether or not a person
committed an act with knowledge and intent and, therefore,
is blameable for it.'   Biestek is here making a comparison with what goes on in a court of law and this comparison seems eminently appropriate, for the primary uses of
words like 'judging' and 'condemning' are in connection

with legal processes, but I think one may doubt whether
Biestek has made a correct use of the comparison.   A
criminal trial, at least in the Anglo-American legal
tradition, normally has two distinct stages.   In the
first stage it has to be decided whether the accused did
in fact do something which is against the law and, if so,
whether he did it with what is called 'mens rea' (literally: 'a guilty mind').   Broadly speaking, in order to
establish that someone acted with mens rea one has to show
that he knew what he was doing and intended to do it, and
so the accused may defend himself by bringing forward ex-
cuses such as that he acted through accident or ignorance
and, therefore, did not intend or did not know what he was
doing.   If it is established that the accused did do
something against the law and did it knowingly and with
intent then the jury, if it is a jury trial, has to return
a verdict of 'guilty'.   If it is held that the accused
did not act knowingly and intentionally, then the verdict
is 'not guilty'.   Biestek wants to say that the caseworker may need to judge that his client has done wrong
but should not concern himself with assigning guilt or innocence.   He therefore concludes that the caseworker must
not concern himself with whether the client has acted with
knowledge and intent, but I do not think this can possibly be right.   We cannot properly understand any human
action unless we know whether the agent performed it intentionally and knew what he was doing.   If, for example,
we were concerned with the case of a mother who had harmed
her child, we could not in any sense understand the woman
or her action unless we knew whether she had harmed the
child intentionally and with full knowledge of what she
was doing or whether she had harmed it by accident or
through ignorance of the proper ways of caring for children.   Thus, since a major concern of the caseworker must
be to understand the client's behaviour, he cannot avoid
trying to decide whether he acted with knowledge and
intent.   Indeed, this kind of question would be much more
pressing for the caseworker in his professional role than
it would be in ordinary life.   If one of my acquaintances
in everyday life has done something I believe to be wrong,
it may be good policy for me to behave as though I thought
he had done it unintentionally even though I suspect the
contrary.   But presumably there would be many occasions
when a caseworker simply could not do this, because in
order to help his client he needs to understand his behaviour as much as possible.   Thus, as far as casework is
concerned, it would not seem that the non-judgmental attitude could exclude decisions about whether the client had
acted with knowledge and intent.

It may be that Biestek has been misled by the use of the words 'guilt' and 'innocence'. Although in a criminal trial the fact that a person has knowingly and intentionally broken the law is sufficient to justify a verdict of 'guilty', the word 'guilt' in ordinary usage conveys rather more than this. It may suggest that the guilty person is wicked, that he deserves punishment, that he ought to make amends, and so on. But even in legal contexts it is often recognised that the finding that a person is guilty does not necessarily imply that he deserves any particular degree of punishment. There is in criminal trials a second stage in which the court has to decide how severely the accused is to be punished. The courts often have considerable latitude in this and may even be able to grant a complete discharge. At this stage in the proceedings the court can consider what are known as 'mitigating conditions', that is considerations which tend to show that the person who has been found guilty should be punished less severely than might otherwise be supposed. Points which might be considered here would be that the accused had been subject to particularly severe temptation or provocation, that the crime was an isolated incident in an otherwise blameless life, and so on. It may be that if Biestek wanted to draw an analogy with a criminal trial he would have done better to look at this stage in the proceedings. Neither in casework nor in ordinary life is there usually any question of punishment, but we do recognise that the fact that a person who has, on a particular occasion, knowingly and deliberately done wrong does not necessarily mean that he is a bad or wicked man, and we take into account here considerations which are in many ways parallel to the mitigating conditions in the case of a criminal trial. For example, there are cases where we believe that a person has knowingly and intentionally done wrong but we do not feel that his motives are wholly bad. Suppose the wife of a criminal, acting out of affection for her husband, deliberately misleads the police as to his whereabouts, then we might say that she had done wrong but refuse to blame her for it. Another kind of case would be one where we feel that the person who has done wrong was subject to particularly difficult psychological or environmental pressures. Thus it may be easy for someone from a comfortable middle-class background to resist the temptation to steal; it may not be so easy for someone from a more impoverished background. A girl may become an unmarried mother because she has a need for affection which she can satisfy in no other way. If we are aware that someone is subject to particularly severe pressures of this kind we will be less inclined to blame him.

Even when we feel that a person has done wrong and is
to be blamed for it, that does not mean that we are committed to categorising him as a bad or wicked person.
To say this would be to pass a sweeping judgment on a
whole life, but, just as one swallow does not make a
summer, a few wrongful acts do not make a bad man.   One
can do wrong without being a particularly wicked person.
Indeed it could plausibly be claimed that we never know
enough about a person to be justified in making such
sweeping judgments.

These points make it clear that there is, first, a
distinction between judgments about the rightness and
wrongness of actions and judgments about the goodness or
badness of a person who performed them, and second, a
distinction between the judgment that a person is to be
blamed for a particular act and the judgment that he is a
bad or wicked man.   Thus it would make sense to say that
while the caseworker may think of his client's actions as
being wrong he should not think of the client himself as
being a bad or wicked person.   No doubt a tendency to
think of other people in these terms would be symptomatic
of a judgmental attitude.   Nevertheless, I do not think
that this can be all there is to the judgmental attitude,
for it would in theory at least be possible to be very
judgmental while restricting oneself entirely to judgments
about the rightness or wrongness of actions and saying
nothing about the goodness or badness of people.   If, for
example, the caseworker, when he saw his client, was to
review everything the client had done and to pronounce
whether it was right or wrong, his behaviour would be just
as objectionable and, one would imagine, just as incompatible with successful casework as would the making of judgments about the goodness or badness of the client himself.
It would be just as unpleasant for the client and would
presumably set up exactly the same inhibitions and tensions, for most of us dislike having moral judgments made
about our actions just as much as we dislike having them
made about our characters.   Conversely one could make
moral judgments about the character of a person without
necessarily being very judgmental.   If, for example, I
was to say to someone 'You are a little bit unreliable'
that would hardly indicate a very judgmental attitude on
my part, but I would be making a judgment about the person
I was addressing.   Thus, although a tendency to make
moral judgments about people rather than about their
actions may well be a symptom of an overly judgmental
attitude, I do not think it can be more than a symptom.
We have to look elsewhere for an account of what it really
is to be judgmental and non-judgmental.

6

I believe that the term 'judgmental' is commonly used to
point to a series of faults which might affect one's attitude to moral questions.   Among these one might mention
the following:
(a) One thing which might be meant by calling a person's
attitude judgmental is that he is authoritarian or dogmatic in his moralising.   Some people may talk as though
they know for certain what is right or wrong and have a
duty to proclaim it to their ignorant fellow men.   But
clearly this is wrong.   None of us should assume that we
have a monopoly of moral truth.   We all need to be aware
that we may be mistaken in our moral views or have mis-
understood the situation with which we are concerned.
Although we have to make moral judgments, we need to make
them with a proper humility, to keep our minds open to
discussion, and to be ready to see things in a fresh
light.   Similarly in casework, even when moral issues
come to the fore, it is not the part of the caseworker to
dogmatise about them or to tell his client what is right.
Rather he needs to discuss the issues with him in an open-
minded way and to be ready for the client to adopt a different point of view from his own.   This may in fact be
the most important element in the non-judgmental attitude.
It is the closed mind, the feeling of having pre-judged
the issue and precluded all further discussion, which is
most objectionable.   People often talk as though moralising can only be dogmatic and doctrinaire, but this is
clearly wrong.   Moral questions are open to rational un-
prejudiced discussion.
(b) Writers on casework often stress that the caseworker
should individualise his approach to his client.   The
point here is that he should see the client as an individual with his own unique personality; he should not be
content to put him in some general category and see him
primarily as, say, an alcoholic or a work-shy layabout.
The point applies equally to everyday life.   We can
hardly achieve satisfactory relations with our fellow men
if we continually put them into preconceived categories
and allow this to condition our whole attitude to them.
There is a real danger that this kind of mistake will
infect our moral judgments.   It can do so in two ways.
First, we may put other people into moral categories and
allow these categories to obscure the individual.   I
might, for example, judge that Smith is dishonest and
allow this judgment to condition my whole approach to him
without making any real attempt to see him as an individual.   Second, our moral judgments may themselves be

based upon some prior categorisation of the people with
whom we are dealing rather than on an attempt to know them
as individuals.   So I may classify what Smith has done as
theft and base my moral assessment of Smith on this classification rather than on any attempt to examine the individual features of Smith's case or to understand why he
acted as he did.   In other words our moral judgments may
themselves constitute a barrier to our knowing the individual and may also rest upon a failure to understand the
individual as he really is.   This kind of moralising
might properly be called judgmental, but one can certainly have moral views without being judgmental in this
sense.   One can make an effort to understand the individual, to see the particularity of his situation and
finally come to a conclusion about whether he behaved
rightly or wrongly.

(c) The word 'judgment' with its overtones of the law
courts, suggests the passing of judgment on something
which has already happened.   If we think of moral judgments in this way, we may well conclude that the making
of moral judgments is a rather unprofitable kind of pro-
ceeding.   Is it not better to let bygones be bygones and
concentrate on the future?   This, of course, would be a
misunderstanding.   We talk about moral judgments in connection with decisions about what will be the right or
wrong thing to do in the future just as much as in connection with decisions about whether what has been done in
the past was rightly or wrongly done.   The primary purpose of morality, one would suppose, is to guide action,
not to grade what has happened in the past.   I think one
might well use the word 'judgmental' to characterise the
attitude of one who is too concerned with passing judgment
on what has been done.   One could certainly see why a
caseworker should want to avoid being judgmental in this
sense.   It might well be argued that the caseworker
should not be concerned with what has happened in the past
except in so far as this is indicative of a problem to be
solved in the future.   The caseworker, it might be
claimed, does not need to make an assessment of his
client's actions in the past except in so far as this is
necessary in order to help him now.

(d) My last point is closely connected with the previous
one.   In many people's minds to say that someone has done
wrong implies that he deserves punishment or reproach,
that other people would be right to feel resentment
against him and to withdraw from normal relations with
him.   He himself ought to feel ashamed of what he has
done and if he wishes to be restored to normal relations
with other people he must in some way repent and atone for

what he has done.   This attitude was well expressed by
J.S. Mill (1863) when he wrote 'We do not call anything
wrong unless we mean to imply that a person ought to be
punished in some way or other for doing it; if not by
law, by the opinion of his fellow creatures; if not by
opinion, by the reproaches of his own conscience' (p. 45).
It is an attitude which is far removed from the ideals of
social casework or of any non-judgmental kind of morality.   Although the caseworker may have to recognise that
his client has done wrong, he will see this as a fact like
any other fact.   It may indicate that there is a problem
to be solved, but it does not require retribution, it does
not justify resentment or indignation, it does not cause a
breach in the relationship, and it does not require to be
atoned or repented for.   Thus, if Mill were correct in
suggesting that we do not call something wrong unless we
mean to imply that a person deserves to be punished for
doing it, a caseworker would certainly have to refrain
from judgments about the moral rightness or wrongness of
his client's action, for Mill has defined the notion of a
moral judgment in such a way that one could not make a
moral judgment without being judgmental.   However, Mill
would appear to be mistaken.   There is nothing illogical
or self-contradictory about admitting that Smith has done
wrong, or even that Smith has been immoral, while denying
that he should be punished for what he has done.   Two
quite distinct kinds of moral judgment are in question
here.   On the one hand is the judgment that he has done
wrong.   On the other hand are the judgments that he
ought to be punished or suffer for what he has done, that
other people would be justified in feeling resentment or
indignation against him for it, that he ought to make
amends or atone for his behaviour and so on.   There is no
necessary connection between the two kinds of judgment.
The non-judgmental moralist may sometimes make judgments
of the former kind but he will refrain from the latter
kind of judgment.   For him, wrongdoing does not necessarily justify punishment or any kind of feeling.   It may
well be that Hollis had this kind of point in mind when
she said that the attitude of the caseworker should be
non-condemnatory, but she was mistaken if she supposed
that being non-condemnatory meant refraining from hostile
feelings.   The judgmental moralist need not have any
special feelings.   He merely believes that the wrongdoer
deserves punishment or reproach, that other people would
be justified in having feelings of resentment or indignation against him, and that he ought to feel ashamed of
what he has done.   It is in this sense that the attitude
of the old poor law administrators could be called judg-

mental, for they assumed that if people were poor through
their own fault they did not deserve help.   Similarly,
in spite of their evident goodwill, one might lay the
charge of being judgmental at the door of people such as
the Victorian ladies who went slumming, if they set out
to distinguish the deserving from the undeserving or to
arouse a sense of shame or guilt in the people to whom
they ministered.

6   Aim, skill and role in social work

R. S. Downie and Eileen M. Loudfoot

1

At any stage in his daily work a person may have to think
about the most desirable way of implementing a given policy, or even decide whether or not to carry out a course
of action ordered by another which he himself believes to
be morally wrong.   Problems of this sort, depending on
circumstances, may or may not arise out of anyone's daily
work.   But the work of the social worker is such that by
its very nature it cannot but lead to value-problems, and
this for several reasons.   In the first place, the very
idea of having some form of social work system embodies
value-judgments, for it presupposes that there are certain
categories of people who ought to be given help of certain
kinds, and that there ought to be special occupations to
provide this kind of help.   How best to provide this
help, in terms of both general policy and specific instance, poses a second set of value-problems.   Third,
complex value-judgments are generated by the questions of
whether there are special skills which it is possible for
a social worker to acquire, and, if so, in what manner it
is permissible or desirable for him to exercise them.
Finally, there are questions of value raised by the direction in which social work is or ought to be evolving, and,
in particular, whether it ought to become more or less
'professionalised' or 'institutionalised'.   These questions of value, and many more besides, arise, we said, out
of the very nature of social work.   But what is the
nature of social work?

2

As a start in answering this question we shall introduce a
way of describing or classifying occupations which can
bring out their important conceptual features.   Occupations can be described or classified from three different
points of view, or in terms of three different sets of
concepts: as role-jobs, skill-jobs and aim-jobs.   Let us
begin the analysis of these distinctions by considering
the difference between role-jobs and skill-jobs, or role-
job-descriptions and skill-job-descriptions.

The job of Income Tax Inspector or Lord Mayor is a
role-job, 'role' here being defined in terms of a set of
rights and duties.   In contrast, the job of musician is
defined in terms of a skill, or set of skills - to be a
musician one logically must have certain skills.   This is
not to say that certain skills are not required for the
job of Lord Mayor or Income Tax Inspector to be carried
out successfully, but it is to say that one need not have
the skills to have the job in question.   In general, the
distinction between role-jobs and skill-jobs can be stated
as follows: the connection between a skill-job and the
possession of an ability is a necessary one, whereas the
connection between a role-job and the possession of an
ability is a contingent one.

It would also seem to be the case that a number of occupations are defined in terms of the end at which the
occupant of the position aims.   For example, the job of
'farmer' can be said to be an aim-job, in that to be a
farmer is to aim at the end of cultivation, milk or beef
production or whatever.   It is not necessary that the end
be always attained, and obviously skill in the choosing
and implementing of means will enter here, but before a
person can be described as a farmer, a forester, a game-
keeper, etc. he must see himself as aiming at a certain
end.   It is doubtful if we would apply the term 'farmer'
to someone who never bothered about cultivation, etc. at
all.   We would call him a *bad* farmer if he chose the
wrong means to the end, or was unskilful at implementing
the means, but if he is not pursuing the end at all, then
he is not a farmer.   The same would hold for all who profess occupations which are aim-jobs.   In general, then,
to say that A, B or C is an aim-job, is to say that there
exists some purpose, aim or end which is essentially or
necessarily connected with job A, B or C.   It is to say
that unless a person aims at the end in question, he cannot be counted as a member of the class of those who have
jobs, A, B or C.

We have been speaking as if there were three types of

job, and this is so in the sense that some jobs are to be
defined in terms of one or other of the three categories
of role, aim or skill.   And it is so, irrespective of
the fact that many jobs, while they may be defined in one
of the three ways, clearly involve the other categories
also.   In the case of some jobs, however, it is not so
obvious that they are to be placed in one category rather
than another, and at any rate they certainly involve all
three.   The job of social worker is one example of this.
For 'social worker' cannot be defined exclusively by reference to any one of the three categories, but requires to
be placed in all three.   To bring this out let us consider social work first in terms of its end or aim.   In
discussing this end or aim we are ipso facto discussing
the values inherent in the setting up of a social work
system, for whatever a person pursues as an aim he thinks
good in some sense (not necessarily a moral sense), worth
having from some point of view.   That is to say, our discussion of the aim or end of social work is at the same
time a discussion of the first way in which we stated
problems of value enter into social work.   What then are
the aims or ends of a social worker? (1)

3

It might be said that there is no one aim of a social
worker.   In a child-care case, a given social worker
might be said to aim at visiting a foster family, at im-
proving relationships within a family, at earning his
salary, etc.   The answer to this kind of objection is to
distinguish different kinds of aims or ends which a social
worker will have.   First of all, he will have what we can
call 'personal aims'.   For example, he might aim at earning his living, at expressing his idealism, or at sublima-
ting his deviant sexual tendencies.   These aims he might
fulfil in his social work, but he might fulfil them equally well in certain other jobs.   We call them 'personal
aims', since they are the aims which a person might have
who just happens to be a social worker.   The fact that
social work has the nature it does have may explain why
certain people tend to take it up, and while personal aims
in social work must be distinguished from the intrinsic
aims of social work itself it may be that those who teach
courses on values in social work should consider personal
aims, first, with a view to enabling prospective social
workers to come to terms with their own idealism, motives
etc., and second, to enable them to understand similar
personal aims or values in their clients.

Second, there is what we shall call the intrinsic aim of the social worker, the aim of the social worker qua social worker, or, as we can also put it, the aim inherent in the setting up of a social work system. One view is that the intrinsic aim of the social worker is the good, welfare or interest of the individual client with whom he is dealing at a given time. This view suggests that the special interest of the social worker terminates in his concern for the particular individual there before him. The doctor/patient analogy is clearly involved in this view of the intrinsic aim of the social worker. Another view is that the social worker qua social worker has a much wider concern, a concern for the well-being not simply of the individual client, but of the whole community. This view of the intrinsic aim of the social worker has influenced the development of community work during the last decade. Which, if either, of these alleged aims of the social worker is to be regarded as the intrinsic aim of social workers? The dilemma here is only apparent, however, for presumably the community is valued because it consists of individual persons who are valuable in themselves; apart from the individual persons who make it up, 'the community' is a metaphysical abstraction. To maintain this is quite consistent with allowing that the *methods* of a community worker (say) may differ in important respects from those of a caseworker. Our point is that the *value* inherent in the setting up of a social work system is the individual as such.

It is plausible to suggest that society as a whole has as its basic value that the individual should be free to pursue his own self-realisation to the extent that this does not interfere with a similar pursuit by others. Social work can be regarded as removing impediments to, and as positively fostering, the self-realisation of the individual, either by direct contact with the individual, or by action in the community designed to increase opportunities of self-realisation for the individual. Most statements of the ideals of social work stress a basic value of this general description. We might give some content to the idea of the self-realisation, well-being, or welfare of the individual by saying that it consists in the exercise of the human capacities to choose for oneself and to carry out policies of one's own (the capacity to be self-determining); and to order one's desires in terms of rational policies and to respect the pursuit of similar policies by others.

There is one other kind of aim which we must mention in connection with social work. This kind of aim is what we shall call the extrinsic aim of the social worker.

What do we mean by 'extrinsic aim'?   As a result of his
job a social worker will be made aware of many social
problems.   For example, he may become aware of the hard-
ship caused by a certain piece of legislation or by the
lack of it in some field.   Again, he may be able to point
out to a local authority that, say, some of the problems
in a certain area are caused by the lack of adequate facilities for recreation, or he may come to realise through
his work that a well-informed tenants' association could
do a great deal to ensure that a given Housing Act is im-
plemented, or, he may become involved with political parties or societies, in an effort, perhaps, to have legislation of a certain kind introduced or repealed.   A
social worker, as a result of the special insights and experience which his job gives him, may well be able to provide authoritative advice on a whole range of matters concerning the welfare of the community of which he is a
member, and it might be said that it is his duty as a
citizen to do so.   The extrinsic aim of the social
worker, then, is the general social purposes which he can
pursue *as a result of* being a social worker, but not, it
might be claimed, qua social worker.
    Now some social workers may accept that the distinction
between extrinsic and intrinsic aims can be drawn for some
professions or occupations but deny that the distinction
applies in the case of social work.   This view may be expressed particularly by the community worker, who may
argue as follows:

> The intrinsic aim of social work is the welfare of the
> individual as such.   One way of pursuing this aim is
> by community work, and successful community work may
> well involve the kind of activities which have been
> described as extrinsic aims.   If the pursuit of the
> intrinsic aim requires the undertaking of certain acti-
> vities, how can these activities be described as ex-
> trinsic aims?

There is in fact no one obviously 'correct' answer in
this kind of dispute.   Whether in the case of social work
we can distinguish between activities in terms of intrinsic and extrinsic aims, or whether activities referred to
above as extrinsic aims are to be encompassed by the intrinsic aim of social work will turn on the answers to a
number of questions, for example, on the answer to questions concerning the very nature of the social work profession, such as, 'Is it the task of social workers simply
to implement existing laws and policies, to operate within
existing institutions, or is it part of the task of the
social worker to attempt to bring about change in laws,
policies and institutions?', and, 'Does political involve-

ment have the effect of making the authorities antagonis-
tic to the social work profession, to the detriment of its
clients?'.   It is well known that disputes exist among
social workers on precisely these kinds of issue.   Thus,
whether a distinction is to be drawn in the case of social
work between intrinsic and extrinsic aims may be said to
depend on one's views on, for example, the nature of
social work and the best way of attaining the welfare of
the individual.   Since these are value-problems, there is
no one answer which can be held to be correct.

Value-problems also arise for a social worker when he
is implementing an *agreed* policy or decision.   In order
to see that this is the case, let us draw a comparison
with the medical profession.   A doctor, like a social
worker, will be presupposing general evaluative aims, and
in most cases he will have cut and dried criteria for specific success in the pursuit of his aims.   For example,
in mending a broken leg a doctor is clearly presupposing
some general value concerned with the well-being of the
individual and diagnosis of the trouble and the criteria
for success in removing it are uncontroversial.   But
other medical cases are rather more complex.   These are
cases in which it is not cut and dried that the patient is
suffering from this disorder rather than that, or cases in
which there is difference of opinion about the treatment
in a given case, or a combination of both.   In such
cases, the doctor has to evaluate the facts before him and
come to a decision about the likely nature of the disorder, or he has to decide, on the basis of the evidence
available to him, what treatment is to be preferred in a
given case.   Again, a doctor may find that he has to make
straightforwardly moral judgments, for example, on issues
of birth control or abortion.

The case of the social worker is like the second and
third kinds of medical case in that complex and controversial value-judgments enter in at every stage.   Thus,
two social workers might agree on the factors involved in
a client's case, but differ in their opinions on how the
case should be conducted.   Or, a social worker might
diagnose the social ill of a family as 'deprivation', and
he will then be making a value-judgment.   Moreover, the
criteria for saying that there has been an improvement in
the condition of the deprived family and the steps to be
taken to improve it are unclear and controversial.   What
quality of life has to be attained?   How is it to be
attained?   Again, a social worker may be concerned with a
state which is not in any ordinary sense pathological.
For example, someone may have difficulty in readjusting
his life after a bereavement or in coping with a deformed

child.   Difficulty in managing such situations is no kind
of disease, and the criteria for success in them involve
value-judgments.   Again, a social worker may have to
decide in a given case whether or not to reveal information given him by a client, whether or not to consult
parents or other members of a client's family.   These
judgments will in the end be made in terms of the social
worker's own human values.   Thus we can see that not only
do the aims of social work presuppose the basic values of
our society, but also the specific judgments and decisions
taken by a social worker in his attempts to further these
aims are evaluative in their turn.   Let us now turn to
consideration of social work as a skill job.

4

The possession and exercise of skills of various types is
clearly an essential aspect of the occupation of social
worker.   What these skills are will depend partly on the
branch of social work we are considering.   Thus, the
medical social worker will require a different set of
skills from those of the probation officer.   But, although this is undoubtedly true, there are fundamental
similarities in the skills, and the problems of value in
this aspect of social work arise at the fundamental level.
The basic problems centre on the question of whether the
social worker's skill is thought to approximate to that of
an *expertise* in handling human relationships, or whether
he is simply (although there is nothing *simple* about it)
a particularly patient, tactful person who happens to have
knowledge of the social services and keeps records of his
conversations, etc.   Clearly, questions of value of more
than one kind arise in discussing this issue.   That is to
say, the notion of the skill of the social worker raises
the question of how we are to expand and give some content
to what we have suggested can be regarded as the basic
value presupposed in the setting up of a social work system - the personality of the individual.   For what is it
to be a person?   In particular, is human personality such
that it can be an appropriate object of any sort of skilled expertise, scientific or otherwise?   The answers we
give to this and related questions ought to have a bearing
on the kind of decisions made by the social worker in his
implementation of the aims and policies of the social work
system.   Let us begin our examination of these questions
with a discussion of what kind of skills are possible for
the social worker.
    One sort of skill we might call, unkindly, skill in

filling up forms or, more generally, the skill which enables the social worker to know his way around the relevant welfare legislation.   Skill of this sort is based on
a detailed knowledge *that*, and there seems no doubt that
such knowledge is possible (and necessary) for a social
worker.   The question of its desirability and the problems of value which are associated with it we shall discuss later.

It might be claimed that a social worker ought also to
have skill in human relationships.   Is this possible?
Can there be a special expertise in human relationships?
It is with regard to these questions that the basic problems are raised.   Whether or not we think that there can
be such a skill and the nature of this skill, if indeed
there is one, will depend on what we consider to be the
nature of a human being or person, and the moral value to
be attached to such a skill will depend on how we think
human beings ought to be treated.   Can there be a skill
in human relationships?

It might be thought at first that obviously there can
be, because the basis for such expertise is nowadays supplied by the social sciences.   The argument might be that
the relevant aspects of sociology and psychology can provide a scientific basic for an expertise in human relationships which it is possible for the social worker to
acquire, just as he can acquire knowledge of the social
services or welfare legislation.   There are, however,
serious objections to the idea of a science of human
beings and their relationships.

The first two of these objections are based on views
about the nature of human beings and their actions.   The
first objection is that human actions are free, and there
can be scientific knowledge only of the determined.   An
adequate discussion of the major premise of this objection
raises fundamental philosophical problems, of whether
human actions are free, or of whether, supposing they are,
they might not also be determined.   In view of these complexities, we shall simply concede the major premise but
deny the minor premise that there can be scientific knowledge only of what is determined.   After all, some physi-
cists would say that quantum mechanics is based on an assumption of indeterminacy, and that there can therefore be
knowledge which is scientific although it is no more than
statistical or based on probabilities.   Likewise, there
might be the possibility of statistical knowledge of how
human beings are likely to behave, and this could count as
scientific.

A second objection to the possibility of even a statistical science of human action might be that human action

is meaningful, whereas the objects of science are 'colour-
less'.   In more detail this objection is saying that to
understand a human action we must be, as it were, on the
inside of it, we must be able to see it as part of a way
of life.   Human actions may be events, but they are more
than events, and we cannot understand them if we regard
them simply as events; we must know what they mean to the
persons who performed them.   Statistical knowledge about
human actions does not provide us with this kind of understanding.

This objection is a strong one when it is raised, say,
within social anthropology.   Statistical information
about what groups of natives tend to do tells us nothing
of interest unless we know what the actions mean in the
way of life of the community in question.   In a community
of which we have inside knowledge, however, there seems no
reason why statistical information should not be helpful.
If we know that in a certain percentage of cases maternal
deprivation leads to certain sorts of delinquency we have
useful scientific knowledge because we already understand
from the inside the nature of the social context.

A third objection to the idea of an expertise based on
the social sciences is that the social sciences are themselves based on value-judgments and hence the information
they give us does not have the certainty of the knowledge
to be found in the natural sciences.   The claim is that
the social sciences are not 'value-neutral' but are ideological, in the sense that they are based on certain sorts
of value-judgment.   Thus the social science of a Marxist
will be different from that of a Liberal, and there is no
value-neutral way of sorting out their disagreements.
Hence, they are equally valid, or equally matters of
taste.

There is no doubt that this objection is a serious one
and suggests that the social sciences are perhaps closer
to philosophy than they are to the natural sciences.   It
does not follow, of course, that there is no common ground
among the alternative ways of looking at social life, nor
that a social worker has nothing to learn from the different possible systems.   It does follow, however, that
the possibility of a science of human relationships with
the *certainty of the natural sciences* does not exist, and
hence that there is serious doubt about the reality of a
social work expertise based exclusively on it.

Let us now consider the questions which arise when we
ask whether the use of expertise is desirable in social
work, even supposing it were to a minimum degree possible.
It might be said that obviously it is desirable for social
workers to have the first sort of expertise we mentioned -

an expertise in social services.   We agree with this, but
it is important to mention certain problems of value which
arise over even this sort of expertise.   First of all, it
might be claimed that a social worker who acquires a detailed knowledge of welfare legislation, etc. will be reluctant to encourage any changes in it.   He will become
identified with 'the system' and his attitude will as a
result become rigid.   Consequently, he may accept uncri-
tically policies which are not the best ones to further
the aims of the social work system, and he may make judgments and decisions on specific occasions which are not in
the best interests of his clients.   Sometimes this objection can be pressed in a radical direction, when it is
said that merely by learning how welfare services operate
a social worker is becoming ideologically contaminated.
Such an extreme view must be rejected.   Apart from anything else, it is based on misleading biological analogies
of disease-catching - to know something is not necessarily
to agree with it.   A more plausible way of developing the
objection is to base it on the familiar phenomenon of
human inertia.   Just as an accountant who has mastered
tax law will be reluctant to see it changed, so, it might
be said, a social worker will be reluctant to see changes
in the social services of which he has a grasp.   Even in
this form the objection is not serious.   To have a good
critical approach to something it is first necessary to
have knowledge of it, and the more knowledge the more
effective the criticism is likely to be.   Hence, while
recognising the dangers of complacency and rigidity, we
do not see them as objections to the view that a social
worker ought to acquire as much knowledge as he can of the
social services.

Another danger arising from undue emphasis on such
knowledge is that it can become a substitute for dealing
with the client's real problems.   If the social worker
concentrates too much on suggesting the claims which a
client can make for various benefits he may ignore the
root cause of the client's difficulties.   Once again,
however, we have an argument against 'undue emphasis' on
form-filling, but not an argument against the view that it
is highly desirable that a social worker should acquire an
expert knowledge of the branch of the social services
relevant to his kind of social work.

Let us turn to that side of a social worker's skills
which are concerned with human relationships.   How far is
it morally desirable, or methodologically helpful, for a
social worker to use on his clients such expertise as is
possible?   One argument against the use of such expertise
is that it is unhelpful because it requires detachment

from the client, whereas identification with the client is what is most needed. But before we can answer this we must know what is meant by 'identification'. If 'identification' is to mean 'emotional involvement' then it is not necessarily helpful, and if it is to mean 'agreement with the ends and aims of the client', granted that these may, on some occasions at least, be anti-social or illegal, then it may show irresponsibility on the part of the social worker. But 'identification' need not mean either of these things, but can mean 'sympathetic awareness'. But if this is what it means it is not necessarily incompatible with the detachment of a social worker. Of course, if the 'detachment' is to mean the detachment of a natural scientist looking at a specimen under a microscope, then this is morally undesirable, showing a lack of respect for persons: and no doubt some mechanistic psychologies encourage this attitude. But there is no need for detachment to involve this.

A second argument against the use of expertise in human relationships is that it involves manipulation, and manipulation is wrong. Now there is no doubt that manipulation is a fact of life in social work, but it is also a fact of ordinary life. The girl who dresses carefully to impress an interviewing committee is in a sense using a manipulative technique. Manipulation makes up a continuum, with morally acceptable everyday practices at one point and social work techniques at another. Of course, at a further point on the continuum we have something which is morally wrong, but social work need not involve manipulation of that sort; and there is nothing in the idea of applying such expert knowledge of human beings as there is to imply that morally wrong uses of manipulation will take place. One might in fact want to say that skill in human relationships might well be a guard against the use of undesirable manipulative techniques; the person who has expert knowledge of human relationships will be less likely to ignore the root cause of the client's problems and attempt to find an apparent solution by persuasive means.

We have suggested that there is a limited possibility of an expertise in human relationships which a social worker can acquire, and that such techniques are morally permissible or desirable, at least up to a point. The skills of a social worker can never be reduced to such expertise, however, for the following reason. Knowledge of the social services is one kind of knowledge *that*, and the same is true of social science. Techniques which follow from such knowledge we might call knowledge *how*. But no amount of knowledge *that* or *how* can be any substitute for

the social worker's *practical judgment* as to how he *ought*
to act in a given situation.   That is to say, even granted that he has certain special skills, the social worker
still has to decide how and when he ought to use these
skills.   The possession of skills does not remove the
necessity of making evaluative judgments and decisions,
and indeed it can be said that the possession of skills
gives rise to value-judgments and decisions as to how and
when to use the skills.   The hankering for an expertise
in human relationships is often a hankering to have the
necessity for such practical judgments removed.   Thus it
is sometimes said that if only we had enough knowledge of
human behaviour, then, granted we can establish the para-
meters of a given situation, we can hope to read off from
our computer what we ought to do.   Such a belief is il-
lusory.   No amount of knowledge of what is the case can
ever establish for us what we ought to do about it.   The
need for practical judgment of what we ought to do, granted our knowledge, is inescapable; and therefore there
are radical limitations to the possibility of expertise.

In cultivating the latter the social worker is cultivating what is his as an ordinary moral agent.   There is
a continuity between the nature of the problems which the
social worker encounters in ordinary life and those he encounters in his professional life.   Likewise there is a
continuity between the problems which he himself faces as
an ordinary person and those which he will find in his
client.   It is on the connection between his own everyday
problems and those of his client, rather than on any
doubtful connection between the natural and the social
sciences, that social work education should concentrate.
In short, expertise is not a substitute for value-judgments.   Let us now turn to social work as a role-job.

5

Social work is not only an aim-job and a skill-job but
also a role-job.   It is in the context of social work regarded as a role-job that our third kind of value-problems
are most clearly seen.   These are the problems generated
by the increasing 'professionalisation' or 'institutionalisation' of social work.   But before we go on to discuss these problems, we must make clear what we mean by
saying that social work is a role-job.

The concept of a social role is used in many different
and indeed conflicting senses in sociology and related
disciplines, and we therefore ought to make it clear that
we are here using it to mean a set of institutional rights

and duties.   Why must social work be a role-job in this
sense of role, or why is it important for social work to
have an institutional framework?   The first reason is
that social workers, by the nature of their job, intervene
in the lives of others.   This is a serious matter and its
consequences for a client can be enormous.   It is, therefore, in the interests of clients that the social worker
should have some sort of professional entitlement to intervene.   If he is not simply to be a busybody he must
have the *right to intervene*, and if he has the right to
intervene he must have duties and responsibilities; the
concept of social role encapsulates these ideas of rights,
duties and responsibilities.   A second reason is that
social workers necessarily find out many intimate details
of people's lives, to do with their marriages, finances or
health.   It is important that the social worker should
know these details and the client must therefore be able
to feel sure that no untoward use will be made of this
information, that it will not be passed on to neighbours,
etc.   The idea of a social role entails that of rules,
and the rules can impose *confidentiality* on the social
worker and provide security for the client.   Third, the
social worker can himself derive *security* from working in
an institutional framework.   For example, he can fall
back on his official position to give him guidance on
proper procedures with a client in case of legal action
against him.   These then are some arguments in favour of
the view that social workers should operate within institutional roles and lay down clearly defined rights and
duties for their professional activities.   What are the
rights and duties of the social worker, or what is the
nature of the normative framework in which he furthers his
aims?   Putting the question in another way we might ask
what is the nature of the responsibilities of the social
worker, and what powers or authority can he assume in
order to fulfil his responsibilities?
     First of all he will have various legal rights and
duties, to his employers and his clients, and to others,
such as local government officers, involved in the whole
social work situation.   Second, he will have duties and
rights which stem from the fact that he is a member of a
particular profession with its own standards of conduct.
For example, he has a duty of confidentiality.   This is
the area of what we might call 'professional ethics'.
Third, he will have moral duties which arise from the fact
that he is dealing with specific individuals in specific
situations.   Finally, although a social worker he remains
a citizen, and, moreover, one who has opportunities to do
more civil good than many.   Thus, as we said in section

2, his work may make him aware of areas in which society
needs to be reformed, and although he may not always be
able to do this as a social worker there may, nevertheless, be actions he can perform and they are also what we
might call his social duties.   But is the institutionalisation of social work to be regarded as entirely a good
thing?

There are two connected arguments against emphasising
the institutional structure of social work.   The first is
that the idea of rights and duties suggests limits to the
scope of social work activity, whereas social workers,
particularly those involved in the new movement of community work, do not want to be restricted in this way.
Similar issues arise when it is said, secondly, that a
stress on the institutional structure of social work will
tend to make social workers resistant to the need for
change in methods and general outlook, whereas social workers in particular ought to be alive to the need for
change.   There is no simple answer to the conflicts which
arise from these different judgments about the direction
in which social work ought to develop as a profession.
All that can be done is to put in a plea for flexibility,
as against rigidity and a doctrinaire approach.   Third,
there is a danger that what from a formal point of view
are the rights and duties of a role will, from the point
of view of an actual social worker, become undue concern
about his status, his advancement in the profession, his
equality with other professions, etc.   Such factors represent the pathology of institutionalisation and do not
work for the interests of clients.   Finally, an institutional structure suggests exclusiveness and the mystique
that goes with it, as in the medical profession.   Now
whereas this may be to the advantage of the patients of
the medical profession similar considerations do not obtain in social work, where much excellent work is done by
non-official bodies, such as the Salvation Army.

It is clear, then, that many social workers will have
valid points to make against the view that they should be
moving as a profession towards increased institutionalisation.   Our point is that such disagreements are disagreements of value which are important to the future development of social work, and not simply the internal wrangling
to which most occupations are liable.

It is also easy to see how value-problems of a different kind can arise for the social worker acting in a
social role.   We have said that the social worker is subject to normative demands of four different kinds: he
will have legal rights and duties to those involved in the
social work situation, he will have rights and duties

stemming from his membership of a particular profession,
he will have moral duties which arise from his dealings
with particular individuals and he will have moral demands
made on him in his capacity as citizen.   Problems of
value may arise from possible conflicts between these
different normative demands.   For example, the duty to
show sympathy with the predicament of a particular client
may, as we have mentioned, conflict with legal duties as
laid down by the employer or the law of the land.   Again,
the desire to help a person as an individual may conflict
with the duties of the professional ethic.   That is to
say, in so far as a social worker is a person acting in a
role with rights and duties he is not acting as a person
simpliciter.   He certainly ought to show personal qualities - tact, patience etc. - in his enactment of his role,
but his relationship with his client logically cannot be a
truly personal relationship.   Of course, as we have said,
some critics might argue that the aims of social work
would be better attained if the social worker were not
operating in an institutional framework.   And there is no
doubt that much good can be done by individuals operating
voluntarily in a private capacity (and sometimes much harm
too).   Be that as it may, the social worker in the
modern state is acting in an institutional framework and
this fact restricts his personal involvement.   Clearly,
then, there are important problems of value in the tensions between the rights and duties of the role and the
personal qualities which may be required in the enactment
of the role.

6

We have suggested that because of the nature of their job
and the present state of development of the profession,
problems of value can arise for the social worker in at
least three different contexts.   We have argued that the
mere setting up of a social work system presupposes value-
judgments, that the social worker has to make value-judgments when he is deciding how to implement a policy or
decision and that there is a set of value-problems generated by the 'professionalisation' or 'institutionalisation' of social work.   These three different kinds of
problems are theoretically distinct, but in practice they
may well overlap.   Thus, the social worker who is trying
to decide how to implement a particular policy or trying
to judge what it is best to do in a particular situation
may find himself coming to question the fundamental values
of the social work system.   For example, he may wonder

how far social work is simply propping up a bad social
system.   Again, in trying to help a particular client he
may be forced to assess the value of the increasing professionalisation of his job.   For example, he might
wonder whether he ought to show anger rather than maintain
a 'professional' coolness.   It has not been part of our
aim in this paper to give solutions to specific questions
of value: rather, we have attempted to show that such
questions must exist for every practising social worker,
and we have tried to indicate general considerations which
are relevant in discussion of them.   It should be clear
that an adequate analysis of these questions raises the
central problems of philosophy in a form which is relevant
to social workers with theoretical interests.   Moreover,
since social work more than most occupations involves
close connections between theory and practice, the questions we have raised, if not our suggested answers, are
worth raising with all trainee social workers.

NOTE

1   The conceptual distinctions we have drawn in this sec-
    tion are discussed in more detail in Downie, Loudfoot
    and Telfer (1974), ch. 1.

7   The morality of law and the politics of probation

Barry Wilkins

1

The work of the probation officer may seem to be largely
or even wholly a straightforward matter of applying various specialist skills, methods and techniques in dealing
with clients.   For example, Phyllida Parsloe spends a
great deal of her book, 'The Work of the Probation and
After-Care Officer' (1967), setting out the social and
legal role of the probation officer and the methods and
ways of working which he has available to him.   She hardly even touches upon any important theoretical issues
raised by probation work.   (On the occasions that she
does discuss theoretical issues, her treatment is unsatisfactory as, for example, in her few remarks on the responsibility or otherwise of offenders on p. 89.)   Probation
work is taken to be theoretically (though not, of course,
practically) straightforward and unproblematic.
   In this paper I want to raise some questions about the
aims and objectives of probation work, and I want to suggest that there are more problematic issues here than
might immediately meet the eye.   These problematic issues
involve very wide-ranging considerations of morality, law
and politics.   Within the confines of the present paper
I can hope to do no more than explore a few of the problems and begin to sketch out what I hold to be the correct
responses to them.   An adequate defence of my claims
would have to go far beyond what I have the space to say
in this paper.   However, I hope that my approach will
serve the purpose of stimulating the reader to explore the
problems for himself and, in so doing, to assess the
claims which I make.

2

As a lead into the question of aims and objectives I want
to return to the idea of the skills, methods and techniques of probation work which I mentioned above.   Now a
skill, method or technique is necessarily a skill, method
or technique of doing something, and of bringing something
about.   In exercising a skill one has a goal or an end in
mind, and the skill provides the means for achieving the
end.   A skill is necessarily goal-directed; it necessarily requires an end, goal or purpose.

So what are the ends and purposes of probation work
which its skills, methods and techniques are aimed at
achieving?   It will be helpful to set them out as clearly
and explicitly as possible.

In the literature there is a fair amount of agreement
as to how this question should be answered.   In his book,
'Crime in a Changing Society' (1971), Howard Jones has
this to say: 'probation is by far the most important element in our present programme of *correction* outside
institutions' (p. 9, my emphasis); and the duty of the
probation officer 'is on the one hand to keep the court
informed of the offender's progress, and on the other hand
to help him *to make good* - in the words of the law on this
matter "to advise, assist and befriend" him' (p. 77, my
emphasis).   And most explicitly of all, Jones writes that
the probation officer should have 'the kind of influence
which will *change the individual's life* to the extent that
is required to turn him from a criminal into a law-abiding
citizen' (p. 131, my emphasis).

In discussing the nature of the probation officer's
authority Phyllida Parsloe writes that 'authority is given
for the purpose of re-establishing the offender in the
community and preventing further offences' (1967, p. 28).
She further states that in probation work 'the ultimate
task is the rehabilitation of the offender in society'
(1967, p. 31).   I think it is fair to say that these
goals of probation work are taken more or less for granted
by Parsloe, and she discusses neither their meaning nor
their justification.

The Report of the Morison Committee on probation work
(1962) provides some fairly clear statements about the
aims and objectives of probation work.   The following
quotation is taken from paragraph 54 (my emphasis):

> To-day, the probation officer must be seen, essential-
> ly, as a professional caseworker, employing, in a
> specialised field, skill which he holds in common with
> other social workers....   It must be added that while,
> as a caseworker, the probation officer's prime concern

is with the well-being of an individual, he is also the
agent of a system concerned with the protection of society and as such must, to a degree which varies from
case to case, and during the course of supervision,
seek to regulate the probationer's behaviour.   He must
also be prepared, when necessary, to assert the interests of society by initiating proceedings for breach of
the requirements of the probation order.   This dicho-
tomy of duties should not be over-stressed: the offender cannot realise his own potential for contented
living while he is at odds with society, and one of the
probation officer's tasks is to help him to perceive
that, in this sense, *his interests and those of society
are identical*.

Finally, I will refer to two passages from the Home
Office booklet, 'The Probation and After-Care Service in
England and Wales' (1973).   The probation officer, we are
told, has an obligation

to 'advise, assist and befriend' the probationer.
Nevertheless, coupled with this helping role, there is
also an element of control.   Probation is not a soft
option;   it is a form of professional treatment within
the community.   It serves to protect society as well
as to help the offender.   (p. 5)

And:

Most probation officers would not be content with
simple authoritative restraint, although this may play
a part.   A deeper purpose, through social casework and
with the use of community resources, is to help the
probationer to develop qualities which will enable him
to adjust to the demands of society and to become and
remain a happy and useful citizen.   (p. 6)

From the above brief survey of the literature there
emerge two of the main purposes of probation work.   The
first of these main pusposes is *the prevention of further
offences*.   Although, as I shall argue, this purpose is
not free of problems, at least its *meaning* is clear and
straightforward.   Much less clear and straightforward is
the meaning of the second main purpose, *helping the offender to lead a better life*.   There does, however, seem to
be a fairly strong implication in the literature that
helping the offender to lead a better life will involve
re-establishing or rehabilitating him in society.   I will
now discuss these two main purposes in turn.

3

The general idea of preventing further offences against
the law is, I have suggested, fairly clear and straightforward.   It implies that the probation officer is, at
least in part, an agent of law enforcement.   He must try
to persuade his clients to remain within the law.   Now
this raises at least two important questions: first,
should all laws in fact be enforced?, and second, what
moral status do particular laws have?   For agents of law
enforcement these might well seem rather heretical questions to ask.   But I hope to show their relevance and
importance.

I will take the second question first.   Law varies a
great deal from time to time and place to place.   Laws
are constantly being amended, added to or deleted.   And
changes in the law are often motivated by considerations
of morality.   The almost but not quite complete abolition
of capital punishment (in English law capital punishment
is still available for piracy and treason), the legalisation of homosexual behaviour between consenting males over
the age of twenty-one, and the legalisation of abortions
performed under certain defined conditions are all reforms
of English law which were initiated, at least in part, by
moral reasoning.   The reader may disagree with some of
the moral reasoning involved in the examples I have mentioned, but my general point stands, that the law can be
reformed in the light of moral considerations.

If this is admitted, the next point is obvious enough.
Some existing legislation may be morally unworthy, and if
so, should be changed.   To substantiate this point some
examples of existing legislation need to be examined in
order to raise moral doubts about them.

The first example I want to mention is the compulsory
admission of mentally disordered persons to psychiatric
hospitals for the purposes of treatment.   There are, of
course, safeguards attached to this procedure - nevertheless the procedure is, I think, morally disturbing.   For
certain forms of psychiatric treatment can have far-reaching effects upon the mind and personality of the recipient.   In particular I am thinking of things like elec-
troconvulsive therapy, brain operations like leukotomy,
and the administration of some very powerful drugs.   It
seems to me to be very disturbing indeed that such serious
steps can be taken in the complete absence of the free
consent of the recipient.

There is a connection here with the work of the probation officer.   For probation orders may require the probationer to submit to psychiatric treatment.   Now al-

though submitting to a probation order is voluntary, it is well known that an element of coercion is involved in the sense that if the offender refuses probation he will probably get something worse (e.g., imprisonment).   So in the context of the probation order it is possible for there to be coercion upon the offender to submit to psychiatric treatment.   Add to this the fact that most people do not have very much understanding of the far-reaching effects of some forms of psychiatric treatment (and the fact that psychiatrists rarely think it is worthwhile to explain such matters to their patients), and I think it may reasonably be concluded that the legal situation is considerably less than morally satisfactory.

My second example of morally questionable legislation concerns the anomalous legal status of homosexuality in English law.   Homosexual behaviour between consenting males is only legal in specially defined circumstances, e.g., they must be aged twenty-one or over.   But the age of consent for heterosexual practices (at any rate, those of them which the law is good enough to allow) is sixteen; and furthermore, lesbianism has no special legal control at all.   Here the legal discrimination against homosexuals seems completely unjustifiable, and on grounds of fairness and justice *alone* I would argue that homosexual behaviour should have the same legal status as any other kind of legal sexual behaviour.   In Scottish law homosexual behaviour between even consenting adults is, in fact, still illegal.   This raises a dilemma for the Scottish equivalent of the probation officer - should he try to dissuade a homosexual client from committing further offences against Scottish law, or should he advise him to move south of the border?   And since Scottish and English criminal law differ on a number of points of detail, this kind of problem may also arise in connection with other types of acts which are offences under only one of these two systems of law.

In introducing my third example of moral criticism of law I would like the reader to consider the following situation.   Suppose that one evening at his local pub a man (let's call him Jones) gets into conversation with an off-duty soldier, home on leave from Northern Ireland (or Hong Kong, or wherever he happens to be posted).   Suppose Jones has some objections to what British troops are doing in that part of the world, and explains these objections to the soldier as clearly and convincingly as he can. Closing time interrupts the discussion and the two men agree to continue it the next evening.

Jones has a friend, Davies, and the two men hold very similar views.   The following evening Davies accompanies

Jones to the pub.   On the way there they decide that in
that evening's discussion they will press their objections to the British military activity where the soldier
is based to the point of arguing that he ought not to take
further part in it.

Under the Incitement to Disaffection Act 1934 such
behaviour constitutes a crime punishable by a maximum of
two years' imprisonment.   Furthermore, Jones and Davies
will also be guilty of conspiracy to incite disaffection.
(They would, in fact, be guilty of such conspiracy even
if the soldier had not turned up that evening to continue
the discussion.)   The maximum punishment for conspiracy
is life imprisonment.   In 1967 the House of Lords ruled
that only in very exceptional cases should the punishment
for conspiracy exceed the maximum penalty for the substantive offence (Verrier v. Director of Public Prosecutions,
1967, 2 A.C. 195).   However, the comments made in the
course of the ruling as to what may count as an exceptional case for the purposes of punishment seem capable of
fairly wide interpretation and application.   It seems
possible, at the very least, that conspiracy to incite
disaffection would be regarded as exceptionally serious by
the judiciary.

It is worth raising the question what the criminal
offences committed by Jones and Davies amount to.   Their
acts consisted, first, in discussing with an off-duty
soldier objections to the military activity in which he
is involved, and in arguing their case to the point of
claiming that he should take no further part in that military activity;   and second, in agreeing to do this prior
to meeting the soldier on the second occasion.   It seems
to me entirely deplorable that such free discussion should
be prohibited by a government.   What reason can the government have for placing such an intolerable restriction
upon the free interchange of ideas and arguments?   Surely
the only reason can be that the government does not have
sufficient confidence in its soldiers' belief in the jus-
tifiability of particular instances of military activity
in order to allow them to be exposed to contrary arguments
and opinions on the matter.   This, in my view, is no justification for the legal provisions I have been criticis-
ing. (1)

In my brief discussion of these examples I have tried
to illustrate the possibilities which there are for the
moral assessment of particular laws.   And I have suggested that sometimes the law will come off rather badly from
this moral assessment - although, of course, in other
cases the law will no doubt be morally upheld (e.g., the
laws prohibiting such offences against the person as caus-
ing grievous bodily harm, or false imprisonment).

At this point I will return to the first of the two
questions I raised, namely, should all laws in fact be enforced?   My response to this question is: in order to
determine whether or not a particular law should be enforced, the law in question needs to be assessed, both
morally, and as to how it fits in with other legislation.
After such an examination we might well come to the conclusion that a particular law is not reasonably enforceable, on the grounds, perhaps, that it is clearly morally
unjustifiable.   In other words, I am suggesting that an
answer to the second question as to the moral status of a
particular law is directly relevant to answering the first
question as to whether or not that law should be upheld.
And if we do come to the conclusion that a particular law
should not be upheld, this will have a direct bearing on
the first main aim of probation work, i.e., the prevention
of further offences.   For it suggests that there is a
class of exceptions to this aim, namely those acts (defined as offences by the legislation under criticism)
which in fact should not be prevented.

In order to illustrate this point I will take the example of soliciting, a crime under the Street Offences
Act 1959.   In English law prostitution is not an offence,
so why is it that soliciting custom, *in itself*, is criminal?   If someone on the street invites the passer-by to
purchase, say a bunch of flowers, or the publication of
some religious or political sect, he acts within the
law. (2)   Yet if a woman invites the passer-by to purchase sexual intercourse, she will be committing a criminal offence.   But why should this be so?   It will not do
to argue that the simple invitation to purchase sexual
intercourse is, in itself, offensive to passers-by.   It
may be, but it may not,be, depending to a large extent
upon the manner and the context of the invitation.   It is
worth remembering that the invitation to purchase a bunch
of flowers, or a religious or political publication, may
be offensive if pressed too far.   And, if so, there
exists adequate legal provision for dealing with this.
Equally, if invitations to purchase sexual intercourse are
pressed so far as to constitute offensive behaviour, adequate legal provision already exists.   In both cases, the
invitation, pressed to the point of being offensive,
would constitute a public nuisance;   additionally, there
are independent legal provisions prohibiting invitations
to purchase sexual intercourse which are delivered in an
obscene way.

I would argue that the prohibition of soliciting *as
such* is quite unjustifiable.   Other legal provisions
exist which are sufficient to prohibit offensive or

obscene soliciting, and to protect the sensibilities of
the innocent passer-by.   Yet a large number of women are
fined, put on probation, and even imprisoned, for the
criminal offence of soliciting - for performing an act
which after all may have been only slightly offensive, or
in fact not offensive at all, to those to whom the invitations to purchase were addressed.   In addition, as many
probation officers will know, the state of the law at the
present time in effect discriminates against working-class
prostitutes.   Unlike their more socially elevated
counterparts, working-class prostitutes have no elaborate
network of contacts in middle- and upper-class social
circles, and sometimes need to be able publicly to offer
their wares in order to stay in business.   Often the
street is the only place in which the working-class pros-
titute is able to bring supply into contact with demand,
though obviously more private places are necessary in
order for the business to be transacted. (3)

In view of the above sorts of considerations my argument would be that the prohibition of soliciting as such
is not reasonably enforceable and should not be enforced.
I use this simply as an illustration of my general argument that when the question arises as to whether a particular law should be enforced, considerations other than
purely legal ones (e.g., moral considerations) are relevant.   In the long term, the most satisfactory way of
dealing with a bad law is clearly for it to be amended or
deleted.   But such reform is very often a long time
coming.   In the meantime the problem remains: to enforce
or not to enforce bad laws?   I have been making the
fairly modest claim that it is sometimes justifiable not
to enforce bad laws.   Whether or not a particular law is
sufficiently bad to justify its non-enforcement is something which would obviously need to be argued out at
length.   My brief idscussion of the prohibition of soliciting provides a sketch of how I think the argument
should go on that particular issue.

A fairly common response to this line of argument runs
as follows.   All law should be upheld, enforced and
obeyed.   The morality of it is irrelevant - law should
be enforced simply because it is the law.   This view is
often supported by the argument that the law as a whole
would be brought into disrepute if a blind eye were to be
turned towards breaches of some laws - for example, those
laws which some people regard as being morally unjustifiable and in need of change.   The authority of a legal
system as a whole would be undermined by the failure to
enforce some particular elements of it.

I do not find such a response as this very convincing.

To take the last part first, it is a fact that some laws
are already not properly enforced.   As well as the obvious minor examples (e.g., many speed limits) there are
more important cases.   A recent interview in the 'Lis-
tener' with an ex-Factory Inspector revealed that the laws
governing safety regulations in factories are nowhere near
properly enforced (The Right to Know - an Investigation
into Secrecy, especially p. 561).   Again, many local
authorities do not properly fulfil their statutory obligations to provide certain social services, and often the
(legally obligatory) provision of education for the children of gypsies living in the area is well known to be
deficient.   And third, the police often exceed their
powers (as defined by the Judges' Rules) to investigate
suspected crime, by detaining people for questioning without formally arresting them on suspicion of having committed an offence.   The Judges' Rules do not have the force
of law, but it seems clear that such detention will sometimes amount to the common-law offence of false imprisonment.
    I would argue that these omissions in the enforcement
of the law do not bring disrepute to the law in general.
If they bring disrepute, they bring it upon the factory
inspectorate, the offending local authorities, and certain
members of the police force, for failing to implement and
enforce the reasonable legislation which is involved in my
three examples.   This leads on to a more general point
which I would like to make.   Reasonable legislation, or
morally justifiable law, does not lose its force simply
because other, unreasonable or morally unjustifiable laws
are flouted.   As far as I can see homosexual behaviour
between consenting sixteen-year-olds, or arguing with a
soldier about the legitimacy of the military activity in
which he is involved, do not in any way undermine respect
for, say, the laws prohibiting murder, grievous bodily
harm, dangerous or drunken driving, and racial discrimination.   And this is because proper respect for the law
does not depend upon its simply being the law of the land,
it depends upon the law being reasonable and morally justifiable law.   And laws prohibiting murder, grievous
bodily harm, dangerous or drunken driving, and racial discrimination are clearly reasonable and morally justifiable
and hence deserving of proper respect. (4)
    As against this, it is sometimes argued that if people
see that certain laws are being broken, because not properly enforced, their resistance to breaking other (perhaps
quite reasonable and justifiable) laws will be lessened,
and in the long run the authority of these other laws, and
indeed the legal system as a whole, will be undermined.

Briefly, my answer to this objection is that it under-
estimates the ability which people have to differentiate
between reasonable and unreasonable legislation.   If
this distinction is perceived, then publicly known
breaches of unjustifiable legislation will not seriously
diminish the authority of reasonable and justifiable law.

4

At this point I will move on to discuss the second main
aim or purpose of probation work which I earlier distinguished, namely helping the offender to lead a better life,
with the strong implication that this will involve re-
establishing or rehabilitating the offender in society.
I will begin by discussing re-establishing and rehabilitating the offender, and will then move on to discuss what
is supposed to imply this, namely the more general aim of
helping the offender to lead a better life.
     The main point which I want to try to make about the
objective of rehabilitation is that it is, at least in
part, an overtly *political* aim.   For it involves attempting to reconcile the offender to the existing economic,
social and political system.   This emerges quite clearly
from the passages I quoted early on in this paper, particularly the passage from the Morison Report (1962).   The
underlying assumption here, as so often in social work
(especially casework), is that in the conflict between
society and the client, it is the client who is the real
problem. (5)   The client does not fit into society and
therefore he must be *fitted in*, re-established or rehabilitated into society.   The view is rarely considered
seriously that there might be some fault in the structure
of society which is the real root of the problem - that
there might be some fundamental deficiency or inadequacy
in society which requires modification or reform.
     This general point requires two brief explanatory com-
ments.   First, the client's immediate social background
is very often considered in trying to understand his frame
of mind and personality.   His offence may be partially
explicable in terms of the social background from which he
comes.   Thus, the client's immediate social circumstances
(e.g., a particularly rough housing estate, or a gang of
delinquent friends) may be identified as deficient, and an
attempt may be made to remove the client from that particular social background.   But, generally, the deficiency
will be seen as lying in that particular social background
rather than as a deficiency in society as a whole.   The
particular housing estate or delinquent gang will seem to

be the root of the problem, as against the backcloth of
the existing social and political system which will be
taken largely for granted.   The aim will be to rehabilitate the offender in the existing social and political
system, even if that means taking him away from his immediate social background.

Second, since caseworkers and probation officers often
(or usually) work with individual clients who are, in some
way, at odds with society, it is quite understandable that
their attention should be concentrated upon the individual
client and that they should attempt to reconcile him with
society as it is.   For the caseworker or probation officer can hope for at least some small degree of success in
changing the behaviour of individuals.   Whereas, even if
they thought that some deficiency in society itself was
partly (or largely) responsible for the behaviour of many
offenders, as *individual* social workers or probation officers they could have no significant influence in reforming society to rid it of this deficiency. (6)

With the addition of those two explanatory points my
general point does, I think, stand.   I am claiming that
the general theoretical perspective which lies behind a
great deal of probation work (and casework) is that the
existing economic, social and political system is more or
less acceptable, and that in the conflict between society
and the offender it is the offender who is the real problem requiring attention.

But whether or not the existing economic, social and
political system is acceptable is an issue which depends
very much upon the social and political viewpoint to which
one is committed.   It is, in fact, an explicitly political issue.   The following considerations may help to
bring out the force of this point.   In Britain (and very
many other countries) two very important features of a
person's life depend to a great extent upon that person's
abilities.   The more able a person is, then, generally
speaking, the greater the chance that person has, first,
of working in a relatively satisfying job, and second, of
earning sufficient money to secure a tolerable standard
of living.   The abilities I am referring to are usually
intellectual ones, but physical skills and abilities can
occasionally provide these things. (7)   To some people
this will seem a perfectly reasonable way of running society - to others it will seem thoroughly unjust, and un-
fair to those who, through no fault of their own, possess
low ability.   (For a general discussion of this issue see
Feinberg, 1973, ch. 7, especially pp. 107-17.)

Now I want to take a hypothetical example of a man, not
very intelligent or skilful, nor very articulate, who

works in a rather tedious job with very few prospects of
advancement and very few opportunities for enjoying his
work.   He commits a crime, either for material reward,
or in search of excitement to relieve his boredom, or with
a combination of these motives.   He is discovered, con-
victed and put on probation.   (Although my example is a
hypothetical one probation officers, I am sure, will be
able to recognise more or less similar cases among their
clients.)   The probation officer's job is to prevent the
occurrence of further offences and to rehabilitate the
offender, to reconcile him with society (in the course of
helping him to lead a better life).   Now what does this
latter aim, of rehabilitation, amount to in the present
case?   I have no doubt that probation officers differ in
their interpretation of the aim of rehabilitation and
these differences are due, I think, to the lack of clarity
of the overall aim, helping the client to lead a better
life, upon which I have already remarked.   In spite of
these differences of interpretation, I think that for a
large number of probation officers rehabilitation in the
present case would mean trying to make the offender more
contented with his lot in life.   In the words of the
Morison Report (1962) they may help him to realise that
'his interests and those of society are identical'.   And
seeking guidance from the Home Office booklet they may
decide that they should 'help the probationer to develop
qualities which will enable him to adjust to the demands
of society and become and to remain a happy and useful
citizen'.
      Now let us look at this from the point of view of the
man in my hypothetical example.   Why on earth should he
be more contented with his lot in life?   He gets little
satisfaction from either his job, or probably even his
life in general.   He is discontented, but probably cannot
articulate his discontent.   This may make him frustrated,
and can only add to his unhappiness.   But though he does
not understand his discontent, he does know that he has no
desire to be reconciled to his humdrum existence.   Yet
because of his limitations he is unable to obtain a more
satisfying job and to lead a more fulfilling way of life.
For he is not one of the people who benefit most from the
way in which our society is organised.
      In general terms I would claim that our society does
little to secure satisfying and fulfilling jobs and lives
for people of below-average abilities.   That such people
often try to break out of their situation should cause us
no surprise.   But rather than try to reconcile the individual with the society which, he feels, has little to
offer him (and which, in effect, discriminates against

him) would it not be better to improve those aspects of
society which give rise to these problems in the first
place?   This would, of course, involve economic, social
and political change - it would be an explicitly political aim.   But what the probation officer is committed to
is equally political, except that here it is the individual client who is subject to the process of change rather
than society.   The obligation of the probation officer
to 'advise, assist and befriend' the client is interpreted
as helping him to adjust to society, and to lead a more
contented and 'useful' life.

But *how else* might the idea of helping the client be
understood?   Must helping the client necessarily be taken
to imply re-establishing and rehabilitating him in society, helping him to adjust to society as it is and to
become more contented with his lot in life?   I do not
think that the notion of helping the client need be interpreted in this way.   In the example I sketched out
earlier the probation officer could help the client to
articulate and understand his discontent with society.
No doubt some probation officers do this in their relationship with their clients, but I do not think it is
orthodox practice.   For helping the probationer to understand his own discontent would be unlikely to make him
more contented with his lot in life.   On the contrary, by
helping him to see the connections with unsatisfactory
aspects of society, it might, if anything, make him more
discontented.

Nevertheless, the probation officer could help the
client to come to terms with his discontent - for since
society is unlikely to be rapidly reformed, the client may
have to live with his own discontent for some considerable
time.   But helping the client in *this* way does not defuse
his discontent.   The client remains at odds with society.
He might well be prepared to live within the law, but
having understood that the main source of his problems
lies within society he will want to see society changed in
the relevant respects.   In contrast, a man who has been
successfully re-established or rehabilitated in society
will not want to see it changed.   He will be happy with
it as it is; again, in the words of the Morison Report
(1962), he will have come to believe that 'his interests
and those of society are identical'.

In helping the client to come to terms with his discontent the probation officer may be fulfilling the first
main aim of probation work, namely, the prevention of
further offences.   (But an important qualification to
this, as I explain below, is that clients may decide to
pursue more constructive responses to their social condi-

tion than they have hitherto attempted, and that these
more constructive responses may involve illegal acts.)
For the probation officer may consider it to be in the
client's own interests to live within the law, and the
client may come to agree with this point when the likely
punishments for further offences are explained to him.
My point is that the fulfilment of the first aim of probation work is quite separate from rehabilitating the
offender in society and making him more contented with his
lot in life.   An offender turned law-abiding citizen may
well remain acutely aware of his socially disadvantaged
position.

The outcome of my argument is that there is a certain
ambiguity in the notion of helping the client to lead a
better life.   It can be understood in different ways, and
does not necessarily imply attempting to re-establish the
client in society.   I am claiming that the economic,
social and political perspective of the probation officer
will unavoidably influence his interpretation of the idea
of helping the client.   In the example I discussed it
will be natural to see the client as the basic problem if
society is taken to be acceptably organised and basically
fair.   However, if one regards society as unacceptably
organised and as containing major structural deficiencies
which give rise to many human problems, one will be far
less willing to regard the client as the fundamental problem in the context of his conflict with society. (8)   Instead, one will think that it is society which is in most
need of urgent reform.   And if the client is helped to
articulate his discontent he may well come to agree.   If
he does, then he may decide to pursue courses of action
which he hopes will be a more constructive way of responding to his socially disadvantaged position; more constructive, that is, in the sense of attempting to provide
a more stable and long-term solution than simply committing criminal acts with a motive of immediate advantage.

Adopting this more constructive response to a socially
disadvantaged position may, however, still involve the
client in committing criminal acts.   But here the motive
will not so much be the immediate advantage (though this
may be a contributory element) as a desire for a long-term
solution.   I have in mind such things as squatters' cam-
paigns, designed to draw public attention to inadequate
housing provision (and the large number of properties
kept vacant for months, and even years); and the occupation of factories due for closure, designed to highlight
the prospects for unemployment, or to try to continue production on a workers' co-operative basis.   There are
those who believe that such acts of civil disobedience

cannot be justified in a parliamentary democracy such as that in Britain, where legal channels of protest and change are available. Though I cannot argue it here I am not convinced by such a view, and for discussion of this issue I would refer the reader to Cohen (1971), Singer (1973a) and Wasserstrom (1963).

5

Finally, I want briefly to raise one further problem which is relevant to the themes of this paper. Some of the literature implies that part of the job of the probation officer and caseworker is to attempt to bring about changes in the client's personality (cf. Pollak, 1967; Grossbard, 1967). Some of the probation officers that I have met certainly take this view. This view of the probation officer's job may indeed underlie the aim of rehabilitation in probation work - the client, it may be thought, is adapted to society by having changes brought about in his personality. There is clearly a very strong connection here with psychoanalytic theory, and on this view of the probation officer's job he is clearly expected to perform a psychoanalytic function.

This raises two issues. First, if probation officers attempt this, they depart from the principle of client self-determination. For they and not the client are trying to determine what the client should become and how he should behave. This point seems to me to be worth making, despite the fact that the principle of client self-determination has come in for a good deal of criticism in recent years (cf. some of the papers in McDermott, 1975; though it should be said that other papers in the same collection are concerned to defend the principle). For the principle of client self-determination, at the very least, provides protection for the client from the possible excesses of a psychoanalytically oriented probation officer (or caseworker).

I can best elaborate this danger by making my second point. If probation officers attempt to change the personality of the client they may be involved in infringing his autonomy and dignity at its deepest level. For the client may be being treated as an object to be manipulated into a more socially acceptable, adaptive role.

If the client freely consents to such change, and fully understands what is going on, then there can be no moral objections. He may be unhappy with who he is; he may want to change as a person and he may welcome any help in this direction which the probation officer can provide.

(Such help, if it is freely accepted, may even contribute towards increasing the self-determination of the client.) But the client may not want to be changed in this way. If the attempts to change his personality are overt and explicit, then he can resist them. But if he does not fully understand the probation officer's techniques, or if he is not fully aware of the techniques being used, then he is being manipulated against his will in a way which he cannot effectively resist. Such an infringement of the autonomy, and, indeed, the very self-identity of the client is morally objectionable in the extreme. It does not, of course, follow from this that it is *never* morally justifiable. But it does follow that the onus is upon those who wish to practise such methods to provide an especially strong and convincing justification for doing so in connection with each case which they propose to deal with in this way.

The type of treatment of clients which I have just outlined should be clearly distinguished from the process of helping the client to grow and develop into an autonomous, mature person, able to take responsibility for his own actions. This again may involve the use of methods of which the client is not fully aware. For example, the probation officer (or caseworker) may aim to build up the client's self-confidence by keeping up a steady flow of encouragement for his efforts and praise for his achievements. The client is, of course, aware of the encouragement and praise, but he is not aware of the objective towards which the encouragement and praise are directed. Indeed, if he were aware that the encouragement and praise were being used (partly, at least) as a method to reach an objective, it is possible that this awareness would undermine the effectiveness of the method. (I can best explain this point in the following way. My self-confidence can be boosted by your praise and encouragement when I think that your praise and encouragement are appropriate to my achievements and efforts. But if I come to be aware that your praise and encouragement are given for a rather different reason, i.e., mainly to build up my self-confidence in the long term, I may start to think that your praise and encouragement are excessive, and not really earned by my achievements and efforts so far. Thus, your praise and encouragement may fail to have their intended effects by my becoming aware of your long-term objective.) It follows, then, that sometimes (though not always) the probation officer or caseworker cannot be entirely open about the methods being used to encourage the client to develop into an autonomous and mature person.

The point which I want to emphasise is that although

this approach and the type of psychoanalytic approach discussed above may share a common feature, namely, the use
of methods of which the client is not fully aware, in the
case of the present approach the *goal* of such methods is
quite different.   Rather than aiming to produce a socially adapted and adjusted person (as is the case with the
type of psychoanalytic approach discussed above) the goal
is now to assist in the development of a human being who
is sufficiently mature and self-confident to decide upon
his own courses of action and to take responsibility for
those decisions.   And this is far from adjusting the individual to fit society for one very simple reason.   The
mature and self-confident person will take upon himself
the responsibility for deciding what his relationship with
society is to be. (9)

NOTES

1   In the present paper I do not have the space to deve-
    lop criticisms of the law of conspiracy, though I hope
    that my few brief remarks in the above paragraphs il-
    lustrate some of the dangers involved.   For a general
    critical appraisal of conspiracy law I would refer the
    reader to Abbate (1974) and Robertson (1974).
2   In order to be lawful certain types of street trading
    require a licence.   This presents no problem to my
    argument since there are no good reasons why prosti-
    tutes should not be licensed.   There are, in fact,
    good reasons why they *should* be licensed.   For ex-
    ample, this would make it possible to check regularly
    for venereal disease, a procedure which would be of
    benefit to prostitutes as well as to their customers.
3   It is, of course, regrettable when sexual intercourse
    takes on the status of a saleable commodity;   this is
    indeed a sad comment on the quality of human relation-
    ships.   But such issues are not satisfactorily tack-
    led by legal prohibition.   In a society in which most
    people have to sell their abilities in order to make
    their way through life (or 'prostitute their talents'
    - a phrase which, significantly, we often use in non-
    sexual contexts) it should occasion no great surprise
    that some will wish to sell their sexual abilities.
4   In making this point I am assuming an 'objectivist'
    account of morality, i.e., that certain moral views
    are correct and that other moral views are incorrect.
    This account is disputed by, e.g., those who hold
    either relativist or subjectivist theories of moral-
    ity.   I have no space here to defend the objectivist

view but I would refer the reader to Nielsen (1968) and Warnock (1971), each of whom, in his own way, upholds moral objectivism.   Moral objectivists do not always agree about *which* moral views they hold to be correct.   The point is that moral objectivism gives sense to the idea of a correct moral view, and hence gives a point to moral argument, construed as an enquiry into the most adequate answer to a particular moral question or problem.

5   For further discussion of this point see Plant (1970). I do not by any means accept all that Plant says in this book, but he does, I think, succeed in highlighting the political dimension of casework.

6   However, it is worth remembering that social workers and probation officers *collectively organised* as a political pressure group almost certainly would be a significant influence on questions of social and economic reform.

7   However, when physical skill enables a person to earn sufficient money to secure a tolerable standard of living, often the job is unpleasant (e.g., assembly-line car production) and sometimes even dangerous as well (e.g., coal-mining).   And when physical skill is applied to relatively enjoyable and satisfying jobs (e.g., furniture-making, nursing) the material rewards are often meagre.   In order to secure both a relatively enjoyable job and a tolerable standard of living, typically one needs intellectual rather than physical skills.   In a highly bureaucratised and administratively complex market-society the possessor of intellectual ability is a valued commodity and is in a relatively strong position in the market.

8   I have, of course, simplified matters greatly here by referring to only two of the many possible economic, social and political perspectives which it is possible to adopt.   And in the present paper I do not have the space to argue about which of these many perspectives is the right one to adopt, though it is probably clear where my sympathies lie.

9   I would like to thank Jeremy Hazell, Vernon Pratt, Helen Slyomovics, David Watson and Robert Young for their helpful comments on an earlier draft of this paper.

8   Authority and the social caseworker

Alexander Broadie

1

The question with which this paper deals concerns the
nature of the social caseworker's authority. I am not
concerned, except illustratively, to develop an inventory
of the kinds of things a social caseworker has the authority to do, but rather to isolate those features of the
social caseworker's job that constitute his authority.
I want, in short, to say what it means to speak of the
social caseworker's authority.

The term 'authority' occurs characteristically in a
small group of phrases, in particular 'an authority on'
and 'in authority over'. Much light is thrown upon the
second of these phrases by taking account of its conceptual relationship to the expression 'an authority on'. I
shall therefore begin by examining 'an authority on' in
order to secure an area of reference by means of which a
conceptual cross-reference between the two relations can
be established.

2

Just as human authority must always be understood as authority in respect of specific powers only, and plainly
carries restrictions with it, so also being 'an authority
on' is understood to be restricted to specific, and certainly a limited number of topics - usually less than the
authority willingly admits, for the authority a person
gains as a result of convincing others that he has mastered a particular field of enquiry may result in his acquiring authority on topics bearing little or no relation
to the one topic over which he has proved his mastery.
In any case, there must be at least one topic upon which

the authority is taken to be able to speak with authority, and for our purposes there is no need to suppose more than is necessary for conceptual accuracy.

To be an authority on a given topic one must be taken to know considerably more about that topic than do most other people.   Hence the existence of authorities implies a recognised uneven distribution of knowledge;   for while it is possible for there to be a social group in which each member recognises all the others as authorities on some topic or other (some senior common rooms and social service departments may have this feature), there cannot be a social group in which each member recognises all the others as authorities on the same topic - unless, of course, that recognition is based on a comparison between the members of that social group and the members of another, larger group.

Recognition is essential to authority, in the sense that if there are not others for whom a person is an authority, i.e., others who take him to be, or recognise him as, an authority, then he is not an authority.   Hence, being an authority on a topic has an essential social aspect.   It follows that a person can first become and then cease to be an authority though there is no change in the amount he knows about the topic on which for a time he was an authority, for what may change is the way others regard him.

Since the social aspect of authority is conceptually essential, it follows that to be an authority one must not merely have an exceptional amount of knowledge on a topic, one must also, at least to some extent, be able to articulate it.   If this were not the case then others would not become aware of the knowledge one possesses by virtue of which one would become an authority for them.

In the sense of 'authority' just outlined, a social caseworker is an authority.   Over a range of matters he is recognised as able to speak authoritatively.   In particular, he is taken to have a much deeper knowledge than most on the topic of the kinds of things that have to be done if people are to surmount obstacles to their well-functioning.   This matter is, however, greatly complicated by the fact that even though social recognition is accorded to social caseworkers it is by no means obvious that different social groups recognise quite the same thing.   Thus the answer to the question: on what does the public at large recognise the social caseworker to be an authority? may well be different from the answer to the question: on what do informed colleagues (informed in the law, medicine and police matters, say) recognise the social caseworker to be an authority?   And furthermore,

the caseworker may himself profess special competence in
still other matters.   Thus an empirical study may well
show that the public at large regard the social caseworkers primarily as authorities on mechanisms for the
distribution of public money, or on procedures relating
to social service benefits.   The informed colleagues may
agree with this picture, while augmenting it, but the
caseworkers themselves may stress their knowledge of human
relationships.   Hence it is possible that caseworkers are
in the position where they profess expert knowledge of X,
but are recognised on Y.   Or at best, they profess expert
knowledge on X and Y, but are recognised as authorities on
only one of these.   But it must be stressed that public
recognition of their competence in some aspect of social
casework is vital.   A client will not willingly take the
advice of a social caseworker unless he takes the caseworker to be speaking authoritatively.   Thus, the effectiveness of a caseworker is to a significant degree based
on the acceptance by others of the professional guarantee
that a social casework agency bestows on its workers.
What exactly the guarantee guarantees is of course a
matter that is open to miscalculation.   A client who
takes the caseworker to have less knowledge than he in
fact has is liable to disadvantage himself for that very
reason, since he is less likely to follow the professional
advice he is given, distrusting as he does the competence
of the donor.

But the opposite miscalculation can also be made, in so
far as the caseworker's authority may be taken to involve
a far greater range and depth of knowledge than he in fact
could reasonably be expected to possess.   Such a miscalculation by a client could clearly lead to disillusionment
when the caseworker is judged incompetent through being
less knowledgeable than it is - wrongly - thought he ought
to be.   In such circumstances the client would not derive
from the caseworker the sense of security that is commonly
thought to be necessary in a wide range of cases if the
caseworker is to be of help.

The social caseworker is, naturally, faced with a
number of problems concerning his knowledge, such as how
much he should acquire from, and how much he should divulge to the client.   A caseworker must, of course, have
some knowledge of the client if he is to help him.   He
must, after all, know what the client's problem is.   But
a caseworker may have no less difficulty in identifying
the client's true problem than in identifying the appropriate solution, and indeed the solution may occasionally
be a comparatively simple matter as compared with the
question of the identity of the cause that has to be

tackled.   For it is well known that a client's own
account of his problem may be seriously misleading, and
not necessarily through a determination to mislead the
social caseworker.   Of course a client may lie about his
situation in order to avoid having to divulge to the caseworker information that he would prefer the caseworker not
to have.   But the misleadingness of the client's own
report may be due to the client's own failure to realise
what his problem is.   A client may fail to identify the
cause perhaps because he prefers not to think of one
aspect of his life, say his relationship with a relative,
as the cause of his troubles, and settles for regarding
something else, less close to the bone, say genuine
enough economic difficulties, as the cause.   The possibility cannot indeed be ruled out that the client, in an
act of self-deception, has created a source of worry for
himself in order precisely to avoid having to look the
truth in the face.   Peering at a financial imbalance may
be a severely uncomfortable experience, but for many
people vastly easier an experience to live with than is
peering at a cracking marriage.   Consequently a social
caseworker's authority must involve a knowledge of how to
identify a pseudo-problem for what it is.   It is a
pseudo-problem in the sense that resolving the problem
expounded by the client may leave him not only with the
original and real problem, but also with the need to
create another pseudo-problem whose job is to mask the
main one or at least to distract attention from the main
one.
      The fact that a client's report of his difficulties can
be (though of course not always is) so misleading leads to
the social caseworker often having to pursue his investigation of the client in areas that seem quite irrelevant
to the client, and that in consequence seem to the client
to involve gratuitous probing and hence a misuse of authority.   It is, of course, often necessary for the caseworker to engage in such probing.   But the manifest
danger is that it will create a build up of resentment in
the client, whose feeling that the privacy to which he is
entitled is being needlessly invaded will damage the quality of the encounter between himself and the caseworker.
Thus, although the social caseworker must have knowledge
if he is to work effectively, the very gleaning of the
knowledge he needs can itself be counter-productive.   The
caseworker, thus, has to be able to make a very fine calculation concerning how far he dare go with his client in
his search for knowledge.   If he seeks too little he will
have insufficient to work with, but if he seeks too much
he may lose his client's co-operation.

A further complication for the social caseworker is
that he must not only tread warily in seeking knowledge
from the client, he must tread no less warily in giving
knowledge to him.   A social caseworker can, by virtue of
his knowledge, skills and privileged position, come to
have insights into a client that the client himself lacks.
And, what is more, the social caseworker's picture of the
client may at certain points be inconsistent with the
client's own picture of himself.   The client's image of
himself no doubt, as with most of us, has a certain survival value.   He needs to think as he does of himself
just in order to make life at all bearable.   If in this
situation the social caseworker tells the client some
truths that the client is bound to accept as true but that
wreck the client's image of himself the caseworker may
thereby have succeeded only in damaging the client, no
good at all emerging from that exercise in honesty.   If
the client simply loses his self-respect, if he loses all
value in his own eyes, on being presented with some home
truths by the caseworker, the relationship between the two
will needlessly have been destroyed.   The client's condition may indeed have deteriorated.

Nevertheless there are grounds for saying that the
social caseworker ought, in the interests of efficiency,
to disclose to the client insights that he has into the
client.   For such disclosures can have a therapeutic
effect.   It is commonly held that the best results are
often achieved where the client acts for himself on the
basis of his own understanding and appreciation of the
situation.   No doubt that understanding and appreciation
have to be guided by the social caseworker on the basis of
the latter's own knowledge and understanding of the situation.   But on the principle that 'the soundest growth
comes from within', the outcome of the social caseworker's
activities on behalf of his client will often be less
ephemeral where the client acts, not simply on instruc-
tions from the caseworker, but rather on the basis of his
own knowledge, authoritatively guided, of his predicament.
No doubt the client's progress is slower where he has to
be made to see for himself what his situation is and why
some ways of dealing with it are better than others.   But
the slowness of progress is adequately compensated by the
greater permanence of the outcome.

One reason why the slowness of the therapeutic method
just outlined is advantageous is based on the aforemen-
tioned consideration that abruptly undermining a person's
image of himself, an image he may need in order to maintain his self-respect, can be very damaging indeed.   If
the social caseworker engages in a process of education

of the client, gradually changing the client's view of himself and his predicament, the period of time inevitably involved in this process will naturally also allow more time for the client to accommodate himself to a new, and in some ways far less pleasant picture of himself.   The caseworker's greater knowledge of the situation would allow him to guage how much knowledge he can afford to make available to the client.   The calculation is a delicate one.   There may be very little difference between the amount of knowledge that would raise the client's spirit and set him on the right path and the amount that would depress the client's spirit even further.   It is clear from all this that the caseworker's authoritative knowledge serves to render him a potential danger to at least some of his clients - a fact that will merely increase the wariness of the more insightful client, counter-productive though such wariness may be.

3

Having discussed the relation 'an authority on' and shown that the social caseworker must have the kind of authority expressed by that relational phrase, I turn now to the second relational phrase, 'in authority over', mentioned earlier.   First certain points about the conceptual relation between the two phrases must be made.

Just as a person cannot be an authority on a topic unless others regard him as such, so also a person cannot be said to have authority over anyone unless others regard him as having it.   That he has authority does not, however, mean that he exercises it well, any more than a person's being accepted as an authority on a topic means that he is a good authority - for experts can be bad experts.

While a person cannot give an account which is regarded as authoritative without himself being regarded as an authority, a person can be authoritarian without having authority, though it is possible that our concept of 'authoritarian' would not be what it is were it not for the fact that in general those with an authoritarian personality do have authority.   Furthermore, while it is not possible to be an authority on a topic yet not be regarded as able to give an authoritative account of that topic, it is possible to have authority over others and yet not be authoritarian.   An authoritarian authority must not merely have authority, he must exercise it in a way characterised by his tendency to override or ignore the wishes, opinions and feelings of his subordinates.

(Where the authority is authoritarian we express this fact by saying that he wields, rather than simply has, authority.)   Hence, 'authoritarian' is less closely related to 'has authority over' than 'authoritative' is to 'is an authority on'.

A distinction must be drawn here between the concept of 'authoritarian' discussed above, and 'authoritarian' as a technical psychological concept.   'Authoritarian personality', as a term in psychology and American sociology, is applied to individuals who achieve scores of a certain kind on a special projective test.   The technically authoritarian personality certainly need not occupy a position of authority.   The technical term is, however, derivatively related to the non-technical term, since the projective tests tend to reveal those who would be (non-technically) authoritarian if in a position of authority, and who are likely to be in, or to achieve such a position.

But what is it to be in such a position?   The first point that needs to be made is that not only does possession of authority not imply ability to exercise it well, it does not logically imply ability to exercise it at all. For a person with authority might be unable to exercise it, though it does not diminish in consequence - in special circumstances it might even increase.   This is not to say that there is no logical link between 'possession of authority' and 'exercise of authority', since our concept of authority would not be what it is if those who have authority are not in general able to perform certain types of action that are recognised as constituting the exercise of it.   Thus, despite the empirical fact that it is possible to have authority while not able to exercise it, it remains true that the nature of authority cannot be understood if no attention is paid to those features that would be said to characterise the exercise of it.   It does indeed seem that actions performed in the exercise of authority do have features distinguishing them from other types of action.   And hence an examination of them can be expected to shed light on the concept of 'authority' itself.

4

One kind of action that, not surprisingly, characterises the exercise of authority is authorisation.   But what is it to authorise?   In answering this question I shall take roughly the line developed on this matter by Thomas Hobbes in his 'Leviathan' (1651).   If A authorises B to do $\underline{X}$

then logically the most basic aspect of this action is
that he has made B his representative.   Having authorised
B to do X, B, in doing X, is acting for, or on behalf of,
or in the name of, A.   But to the extent that B, in doing
X, is representing A, it follows that it was really A who
did X.   Of course, if B did X as authorised, then *he* did
X.   But on one level of analysis the performance of X was
at least no less A's action than B's, and was in a sense
A's action but not B's.   If I, as a client, were to
authorise a social caseworker to represent me before, say,
a rent tribunal, and he duly performs certain actions in
my name and with my authority, then not only can I correctly be said to have performed those actions but, further, the caseworker would mislead if he said that he had.
For this would imply that he was acting for himself rather
than for me.   Thus the real agent of an authorised
action is taken to be the authoriser rather than the
person authorised.

   The obvious point has already been made that if a given
person does X as authorised then that person has done X.
But a question arises here concerning the description of
the action symbolised here by 'X'.   If I, as a client,
authorise my social caseworker to do X for me and he does
as authorised, then we might say that what I did was X,
and what he did was help me to do X, or more precisely he
was the instrument I used in my performance of X.   Hence
the authorised person can be regarded as an extension of
the authoriser's agency, and thus a little like the
agent's body.   If I kick someone, then a movement of my
leg was part of the causal chain that resulted in a kick
being landed.   But under normal circumstances if accused
of kicking someone I could not truthfully reply 'It was
not I that did it but my leg', for it clearly was me,
using, we might say, my leg.   Similarly, if a social
caseworker, while acting on my authorisation, does X for
me, I cannot truthfully claim that it was not I who did
X, but the caseworker.   Consequently, an authorised
action can be regarded as an example of what is known
metaphorically speaking as 'action at a distance'.
Through the mechanism of authorisation I can do X though
in one sense I am not present when I do it, for my body
may not be present.   In another sense I am present, at
least to the extent that the authorised action constitutes
an embodiment of my will.

   A consequence of the account of authorisation I have
been developing is that all authorised actions bind the
authority rather than whomever he has authorised.   If,
for example, the authorised person makes a promise in the
name of the authority, that promise binds the authority

but not the authority's representative (assuming, of
course, that the promise was authorised).   For promises
bind their maker, and in the case here envisaged the maker
was the authority who acted through some other person whom
he chose to represent, or act for him.   Equally, if the
representative does what he has been authorised to do, the
authority cannot complain, for his representative's
actions are really his own, i.e. the authority's; and if
he thought the action worthy of complaint it was up to him
not to perform it.   It follows from this that it would be
unjust of the authority to punish his representative for
performing an authorised action, since this would be to
punish someone else for an action that he himself had performed.   Sometimes, of course, we are angry with ourselves for an action we have performed (with our own
bodies).   And sometimes indeed as a consequence of that
anger we inflict suffering on ourselves.   But it does not
follow that we are ever morally entitled to inflict suffering on another person for performing an action we have
authorised.

5

I wish to return now to a consideration of the similarity
outlined earlier between, on the one hand, the relation
between an agent and his body, and on the other, the relation between an authority and his representative.   For
it could easily seem that this account of the matter has
unacceptable moral implications.

   We do not consider a part of a person's body morally
assessable if it is involved in the performance of an
action.   But we do consider a person morally assessable
if he performs an authorised action.   However, in view
of what I have been saying about the nature of authorisation this must be seen to give rise to a problem.   For if
A does X as authorised we ought not to be able to consider
him morally assessable for doing X, since it was not he
who did it but the person who authorised him.   And
indeed, the fact that something wicked that was done was
done in obedience to an authority's command (and therefore was authorised) is generally seen as mitigatory for
the person who carried out the command.   Yet it does not
always absolve.   But my account of authorisation seems
to imply that for logical reasons it should.

   Now, if I obey a command to do X, the authoriser of the
action, not myself, is morally assessable for doing X.
But I, as his representative, was responsible for being
instrumental in his performance of X.   Certainly we may

be willing to admit that once X is done I can divert certain criticisms from myself by pointing out that I was
'only' obeying orders.   The point that has to be made,
however, is that it does not follow that I played no part
in the authority's performance.   For it was as a result
of my allowing him to make use of my services that he was
enabled to do X.

If I try to escape responsibility of any sort for being
instrumental in the performance of a specific action by
saying that I pursue a policy of absolute obedience to
authority, my adoption of that policy is itself open to
moral assessment.   Certainly from a Kantian point of view
pursuit of such a policy is immoral, for it entails a be-
trayal of myself.   I allow myself to be used entirely as
a means to another person's end, and have no regard for
the value of my own agency (any more than I would, in this
situation, have regard for the value of other people - the
authority excepted).

The policy of absolute obedience is entailed by the
notion of obedience to authority as an absolute obligation, one that overrides all others.   And indeed, if we
regard some being, say God, as possessing absolute authority we must regard ourselves as having an absolute obligation to obey Him.   But this is not in general how we
regard authorities.   As was said earlier, 'human authority must always be understood as authority in respect of
specific powers only, and plainly carries restrictions
with it'.   Hence, though we have a prima facie obligation to obey authority, it is possible for this obligation to clash with another one.   In that case our solution to the conflict can be made the material for a moral
assessment of ourselves.   And it may be concluded that
though we had a prima facie obligation to obey the authority, in the case in question a decision to obey would
have been morally reprehensible.   For example, there are
many things I could ask my lawyer to do for me which he
would be morally unjustified in doing, even though he
could correctly claim that he was acting in my name and,
hence, was himself not really performing the actions in
question.   The moral objection in such a case would have
been to his willingness to be my representative in the
performance of such actions.

I conclude from this that though a person can be said
to have performed an action he authorised it does not
follow that whomever the authority uses as his representative in the performance of the authorised action is
thereby assured of an infallible escape route from the
charge of moral culpability for the part he played in the
performance of that action.

6

Let us now suppose that A authorises B to do X. As a
result of this authorisation B has the authority to do X.
But A must also in some sense have authority, since in
doing X, B acts on A's authority.   However, though in the
sense outlined both A and B have authority, neither has,
or more precisely need have, authority over the other.
If the client authorises the social caseworker to act for
him before a rent tribunal, and he duly acts on the
client's authority, the caseworker no more has authority
over the client than the client has over the caseworker.
    Let us say, therefore, that having authority *to do* does
not imply having authority *over*.   On the other hand
having authority over does imply having authority to do.
And what in particular the authority over has the authority to do is command.   This point provides us with a clue
to the difference between 'authority over' and 'authority
to do'.   For a command can be issued only to someone in a
subordinate position.   Thus if A has authority over B, A
must stand to B in the relation of superordinate to subordinate.   It is clear that the relation between a social
caseworker and his client who has authorised him is not of
this nature.   A client's ability to authorise a caseworker in no way implies that he stands in a superordinate
position to the caseworker.
    Perhaps the clearest type of case of authority *to do*
that is not also authority *over* concerns the relation between a parent and his infant.   A parent cannot be said
to have authority over his infant, for authority over
logically implies entitlement to command and corresponding obligations to obey, and an infant is too young to
have such (or any other) obligations.   But this does not
imply that the parent has no authority vis-à-vis his
child, since he clearly has a good deal.   This authority
is due to his recognised entitlement to act for the child
or in the child's name.   That someone has to do this is a
consequence of the infant's own incapacity to do anything
for himself; if he cannot act for himself then someone
else must act for him.   And whoever does, and is accepted
as having a right to, has authority.
    It is not necessary to think of the parent's authority
as due to a specific act of authorisation (though it may
be that as soon as a person achieves parenthood the law
grants him authority to act for the child).   For even in
a community lacking a formal legal system the parent would
have authority vis-à-vis his children.   The obligation to
act in the child's name can be regarded as devolving naturally on him, since someone must act for the child until

he is capable of acting for himself, and what more natural than that the parent should fulfil this role?   Thus, although the parent's authority may be enshrined in the law it is not created by it.

As the child develops and becomes capable of speaking for himself the parent's role as the child's representative diminishes in scope.   However, simultaneously with this diminution in the parent's authority *to do* there may come an increase in his authority *over*.   For it is only when the child acquires the capacity to speak for himself, to be his own representative, that he can be judged to have acquired the competence to shoulder obligations - including obligations that stem from a recognition of someone as having authority over him.

In certain situations a social caseworker has authority over his client, sometimes on a statutory basis.   But where this is so the authority must be exercised with particular tact and discretion.   Much is made, in theoretical writings on social casework, of the need for the relationship between the caseworker and his client to be a personal relationship characterised by the caseworker's sympathetic understanding and treatment of his client. But if the caseworker's attitude to the client must be one of caring and concern and friendliness then the caseworker would be engaging in a mistaken exercise of authority if his normal way of securing responses from his clients was to threaten them.   One of the chief problems at issue here concerns the client's autonomy.   Authority expressing itself as coercion, and hence constituting a threat to the client's autonomy, may promote an immediate surface co-operativeness if only as a delaying tactic by the client.   But co-operativeness of that kind may be doing nothing whatsoever for the real problems that eventually brought the client to the caseworker.   The co-operativeness here is merely a matter of the client concealing the symptoms of his problems from the caseworker.

There are, however, cases where the fact that a client sees an exercise of authority by the caseworker as a threat to his independence must be disregarded.   Sometimes a client has to be protected from himself, where for example his problems have so eaten into him that he may damage himself to no good effect if a measure of coercion is not used on him.   But the existence of such cases does not constitute an argument for the claim that the coercive exercise of authority should be the norm.   Indeed, the whole tenor of this paper has been to suggest that as much weight as possible should be thrown behind the idea of the client being enabled to help himself to cope with his difficulties rather than have solutions imposed from outside.

For only in certain special cases, where the client is in-
sufficiently responsible, can a solution that is not in-
ternally imposed have a real chance of anything more than
a merely ephemeral success.

The need to respect the autonomy of the client is not
the only limiting factor bounding the authority of the
social caseworker.   Another such factor is set by the resources that his agency makes available to him.   The
agency may have funds for the immediate use of clients in
serious debt.   But the fund is limited, and a caseworker
can provide from it no more than is made available to him
for such use.   Likewise the agency dispenses through its
caseworkers a variety of services that express in their
various ways the particular goals of that agency - for
different agencies are biased towards, or we might say
tend to specialise in, particular problem areas.   And in
consequence a social caseworker's authority within one
agency may extend to areas of activity that would be
beyond the range of his authorisation were he working in
another agency.   One agency may specialise in adoption
problems and another in housing problems.   And naturally
what a caseworker in the one agency has the authority to
do cannot be expected to coincide with the area of authorisation of a caseworker in the other agency.

A further limitation on the authority of the social
caseworker is set by the limits of his knowledge.   He is
expected to have an authoritative grasp of a range of
matters.   But his knowledge will not normally be equally
authoritative in all the relevant departments.   Consequently, when faced with an unfamiliar or a particularly
complicated problem he will exercise his authority by
delegating all, or part of the responsibility for the
case to others within or without the agency who can handle
it in a more authoritative manner.   In social casework,
as elsewhere, the good authority knows when to delegate
authority and to whom.

SUMMARY

What I have attempted to show is that the social caseworker may have authority in several distinct, though not
unrelated ways.   In the first place, he is taken to be
able to speak authoritatively on various topics.   Second,
the caseworker has authority in the sense that he is entitled to act as his client's representative.   He has the
authority to speak on his client's behalf.   And third, he
may in special circumstances have authority over his
client.   Of these three forms of authority, the first and

third in particular require especially judicious exercise.
The caseworker requires information from his client and
must impart information to him.   I have tried to show how
the caseworker, both in gathering and in imparting information, may run the risk of damaging his relationship with
his client.   For in gathering information he must avoid
giving to his client the impression of gratuitous probing,
while in imparting information he must avoid inflicting
needless damage on the client's assessment of his own
worth.   Regarding the exercise of authority *over* the
client, especial tact is demanded by the need to avoid
giving the client the impression that his autonomy is at
risk.   No doubt on occasion the encroachment on the
client's area of freedom is justified.   But only as a
last resort.

9   Medicine and the marketplace

P. D. Shaw

1

In most industrial societies the market is the chief means
of promoting social welfare.   Not the sole means;   governments raise money in taxes to relieve poverty and to
provide goods which cannot, or cannot so easily, be supplied by the market: such goods as defence and water
supply.   How far should the market extend, and what
principles should guide us in determining whether a good
should or should not be produced in the market?
    By a market system I understand a system having these
properties:
 (a)   people earn income from selling their labour;
 (b)   goods are privately owned and consumed;
 (c)   production of goods is determined by the hopes of
        profit of those controlling the means of production.
This third condition would be fulfilled either by the private ownership of the means of production, or where the
government owns investment capital and directs it to where
the rate of return is highest.   Criticism of the market
should be distinguished from criticism of capitalism.
    To try to determine the limits of the market by a
direct approach would be unhelpful.   But in recent years
there has been debate on whether or not medical welfare in
general and blood in particular should be bought and sold.
In Britain blood for transfusions and other medical uses
has always been freely given, and for many years there has
been a general presumption in this country that medical
care should be taken out of the market, for the most part,
if not entirely.   So the suggestion that blood should
bear a price-tag, running counter to received opinion, led
to a reconsideration of the principles involved.   I shall
outline some of the main moves in the debate, trying to
assess the arguments, point out conflicting value-judg-

ments, and draw some lessons.   I conclude that there is a
very strong case against a market in medicine, but that
what holds for medical care does not necessarily hold for
the provision of welfare in general.   There are implications for the provision of other goods, and some of these
I discuss, but without reaching firm conclusions.

2

The debate about blood was sparked off by M.H. Cooper and
A.J. Culyer (1968) with a trenchant defence of the market.
Their argument was that blood is an economic good in the
sense that there is a demand for it and its supply is
limited;   that supply and demand must be brought reasonably into line;   and that pricing is an effective way of
bringing this about.   As the authors point out, it is not
the only way.   In Britain supply and demand are equated
by collecting freely donated blood and assigning hospitals
with a quota based on previous estimations of their needs.
An alternative method, partly or wholly adopted in other
countries, is to pay the suppliers of blood and sell the
blood to hospitals.   (This may, but need not, involve
passing on the costs to patients.)
      Under a system of pricing, hospitals would have a cash
incentive not to waste blood.   Under a quota system the
constraints would be less clear.   Cooper and Culyer attempt to show (1968, p. 23) that pricing would decrease
the demand for blood, since a quota system encourages its
unnecessary use.   The argument is that economic rationality consists in balancing benefits and apparent costs at
the margin.   A commodity will be consumed until the point
comes when the benefit from using the last small unit of
it no longer outweighs the cost of that last small unit.
Now to society at large blood has a real cost, that of
collection and distribution.   But to the hospital there
is no charge.   Hence blood appears to the hospital to be
a free good.   And since the apparent cost of blood is
zero, *any* benefit, however slight, warrants the use of
blood.   Therefore blood will be used unnecessarily and
carelessly, leading to a continuing upward pressure to increase supplies.
      This seems to me wrong.   Blood has an apparently zero
money cost, but every time the hospital uses blood within
its quota it faces an associated *opportunity* cost;   every
pint used for one purpose now is a pint less for some
other purpose later.   So long as the quota is limited,
blood will not appear to a hospital to be so abundant as
to be a free good like air, so abundant as to be value-

less.   It will not be economically rational to use blood
carelessly within a fixed quota.

It may be that there will be a continuing pressure to
increase quotas.   But the pressure from hospitals to
revise quotas upwards will be met by a pressure from the
National Blood Transfusion Service to keep quotas down.
Cooper and Culyer admit what they call (p. 14) 'the costs
of negotiating additional supplies', with the implication
that these are trivial.   But this whole notion is suspect.   For while one can cost time, ink and paper in arguing one's case for an increase, whether one gets it will
depend in part on how good one's case is.   And you can
buy a good advocate but not a good case.

So much having been said in defence of quotas, at least
one problem must be recognised.   There is a danger of
waste in so far as it makes economic sense to use up a
quota, having once negotiated it.   Any waste would be
constrained within the quota, so the potential waste is
not all that great.   Moreover, it can be minimised by
appeals for careful use.   Nevertheless, there is this
danger, and it should be noted.

In addition to their more-or-less a priori arguments,
Cooper and Culyer do maintain that there are 'major problems' (p. 37) of waste and also shortage in the supply of
blood under the National Health Service.   Their evidence
(pp. 18-19) simply does not support the claim.   It der-
ives from a survey conducted amongst 640 consultants to
the National Blood Transfusion Service.   Of these 55 per
cent considered blood supplies excellent, 41 per cent adequate, and 4 per cent poor.   This does not suggest that
there are major problems.   The authors quote the figure
of 36 per cent who have sometimes postponed operations for
lack of blood as if this were a damaging criticism.   But
since 63 per cent claimed never to have postponed an operation for this reason, and only 1 per cent claimed often
to have done so, this cannot be taken too much to heart.
The scale 'never ... sometimes ... often' is bound to
elicit a fairly large response to 'sometimes'.   Far from
showing that there are major problems, the survey gives
the impression that the National Blood Transfusion Service
is working rather well.

3

Partly in response to Cooper and Culyer, the late R.M.
Titmuss wrote 'The Gift Relationship' (1970).   He sub-
titled the book 'From Human Blood to Social Policy', and
advanced it as his 'social philosophy': a detailed fac-

tual study of how blood is collected and supplied in Britain and abroad is interspersed with speculative sociology and value-judgments.   The argument is intuitive and stimulating, rather than rigorous and controlled.   Titmuss sets himself the question, 'What are the consequences, national and international, of treating human blood as a commercial commodity?' (p. 12).   He tries to show that the consequences would be disastrous.   Market values would infiltrate the social services and inevitably 'All policy would become in the end economic policy and the only values that would count are those that can be measured in terms of money and pursued in the dialectic of hedonism' (p. 12).   In short, advocating self-interest, we would be likely to get a society dominated by what we advocate.

Titmuss treats the blood donor and transfusion services as an indicator of the quality of human relations in a society.   And he is particularly critical of the USA, which he sees as dominated in its medical services by commercialism.

The USA has no central collecting and distributing agency for blood.   Instead there are several thousand institutions of different sorts to which people give or sell their blood.   Titmuss (pp. 54-8) argues that the absence of central co-ordination and planning itself causes waste, in that increasing amounts of blood are collected and not used either for transfusion or for conversion into plasma.

Moreover, there is greater variety in the way blood is supplied.   Titmuss divided 'donors' (that is, paid or unpaid suppliers) into several categories, not all of which need be distinguished here.   He finds that only about 9 per cent of blood donated comes from truly voluntary donors.   Those who receive direct payment for their blood supply 33 per cent of blood donated, while over half comes from schemes involving payment or insurance in kind. Those who receive blood transfusions incur a debt, which can often be repaid in kind.   Arising out of this comes the possibility of donating blood regularly as an insurance for oneself and one's family (pp. 75-89).   While not overtly commercial, these schemes are essentially so. Long-term self-interest replaces altruistic giving; or if there *is* altruism, it is confined within the economic unit, the family, rather than between units.

Paid donors who do not give blood on a regular basis cause problems because of the danger of infection.   Serum hepatitis can be transmitted by those who have had jaundice, malaria, or certain types of venereal disease.   The collectors of blood rely at present upon the truthfulness

of the donor to eliminate such risks, and the paid donor
has a cash incentive to lie.   Hence there is widespread
alarm about 'skid row' donors especially, and a considerable problem of post-transfusion hepatitis.   In Britain,
by contrast, the risk of receiving infected blood is neg-
ligible.

There is, Titmuss shows, a history of legislation to
protect commercial, profit-making blood-banks in the USA
(pp. 159-64).   Hospitals cannot collectively decide not
to buy commercial blood despite the greater risk of infection from it, without falling foul of 'anti-trust' laws.
Somewhat more controversially, he connects the commercialism of medical care with a breakdown of trust between
doctor and patient.   In the USA perhaps one in five of
all physicians has been sued for malpractice.   Premiums
to insure against malpractice are rising, and doctors are
increasingly turning to 'defensive medicine' - unnecessary
precautions taken in case of future litigation rather
than in accordance with professional judgment.   Titmuss
claims (pp. 165-6) that many of these lawsuits are frivolous, and judgment biased against the doctor.   It is not
obvious that 'legalized and legitimated doctor-patient
hostility' (p. 170) should be a consequence of commercialism, but it may not be surprising either.   It is clear to
the patient that he is paying, and paying well.   It is
not so clear that he is getting what he pays for;   only
an expert can estimate that.

This does not, I think, commit Titmuss (or me) to the
view that a legal framework is undesirable, or that doctors should not be answerable in law, as Kenneth Arrow
(1972, pp. 359ff.) suggests.   The claim is that *commercialism* may generate hostility, not the legal framework,
which could exist with or without doctor-patient hostility.   Titmuss admires the trust between doctor and
patient in Britain but not the system whereby complaints
against doctors are investigated by the British Medical
Association.   Arrow suspects that one cannot have it both
ways;   that the trust could not coexist with a decent complaints procedure.   This is to suppose that doctor-
patient attitudes are largely determined by complaints
procedures, and this seems to me unlikely.   However, even
if commercialism leads to hostility and litigation, it is
hard to explain why doctors do *badly* in American courts.
Arrow suggests that court decisions may not be unreasonable, and implies that doctors may deserve all the hostility they get.   Yet Titmuss (1970, pp. 165-6) reports
decisions which *do* seem unreasonable.   In particular,
that a doctor must specify to a patient every known complication which *might* arise from the treatment he is pre-
scribing.

Titmuss concludes (p. 205) that in terms of administrative efficiency, matching supply to demand, cost per unit to the patient (or to the community) and safety, the voluntary system scores heavily.   In addition, the value of a sense of community, the value of altruism, although it cannot be costed, is likely to be pervasive and important.

Woven into this description there are reflections on the nature of giving.   The gift of blood is seen as an example of non-reciprocal and impersonal altruism (p. 121).   There may be benefit to the giver, but it is uncertain and unsought for.   Often, indeed, non-reciprocal gifts are demanded by society.   For example, patients are treated by student doctors, and the willingness of the patient to be taught on is taken for granted.   Students benefit more-or-less directly by gaining experience. Patients make no obvious gains from being treated by students rather than by fully qualified doctors;   yet there is a gain to a future generation of patients.   As we have benefited from the gifts of past generations, so we are expected to give in turn.   This expectation is not the result of any contract, formal or informal.   If anyone wants to say, 'Why should I do this for posterity, what's posterity ever done for me?', we must concede that there is no reciprocity involved.   If I help others because others have helped me, I am not repaying a debt, for the 'others' are different in each case.   Titmuss reproduces a survey (pp. 226-36, 315) offering some clues to donor motivation in Britain.   Altruism, the desire to help other people in need, is frequently given as the reason for first deciding to donate blood;   sometimes a feeling of obligation, having received blood.   Donors sometimes indicated that the fact that blood is not bought and sold was an important consideration in their decision to give; and this raises the possibility that pricing blood might positively deter some people from giving, even as it attracts others.

Finally, there is speculation that a commercial attitude to medical welfare leads to treating groups such as prisoners and the mentally retarded as guinea pigs in human experiments.   Those who give are 'poor people: the indigent, the deprived, the socially handicapped, the socially inadequate ...' (pp. 219-20).   Apart from the costs in health and welfare to the unlucky, what, asks Titmuss, are the effects on society as a whole of this attitude to the 'inept'?   Here again the connection between a market in medical care and this attitude to the disadvantaged is not spelled out.   But one can see connections.   In a society where everyone is expected to make his contribution, where anyone can be the guinea pig,

those on whom risks are taken will include the wealthy and
articulate.   Simply, prudence, would be a powerful cau-
tionary check.   If the human guinea pigs are solely drawn
from the disadvantaged, less caution is needed.   And in
any commercial system it is bound to be the poor who get
the poorest treatment.   They cannot afford better.   Here
is a way in which fully socialised medicine asserts that
all people are equal;   where health and life itself are
involved, wealth will not be permitted to confer advantages.   I am not suggesting that Britain is in this
state;   but it obviously approximates closer to it than
the USA.

4

Titmuss leaves his critics plenty of ammunition.
    Sometimes he is tempted into overstatement.   For ex-
ample, he claims that a market in blood would 'deprive men
of their power to give or not to give' (p. 239).   Not so;
the argument presented is rather that a market in blood is
likely to make people less willing to give, which is not
the same at all.
    Again, Titmuss treats the USA as a paradigm case of a
commercial system for supplying blood, and seems to assume
that the chaos and waste he discerns in America is the inevitable result of the commercialism.   Perhaps the fault
lies not in having a market in blood, but in having a
badly organised market.   This possibility will not commend itself to those who think the profit motive in itself
produces efficiency, but perhaps it should have been more
closely considered.
    A more serious difficulty is this.   Titmuss seems to
regard the method of supplying blood as both indicative of
the relations existing within a society and as having important consequences for social attitudes and relations.
Many of his critics are simply sceptical, but I think
they miss the point.   The discussion focuses largely on
the USA and Britain.   In each of these countries the
methods of providing blood are typical of the methods of
providing medical care in general;   in Britain the cash
nexus is played down, and in the USA it is fairly promi-
nent.   That the method of providing medical care in general in a society has spillover effects into other areas
of social life seems plausible.   That the method of blood
collection must be typical of the country's medical system - that, in particular, the payment of donors would inevitably lead to the billing of patients - seems to me implausible.   If Britain decided to introduce a system of

payment for donors, for example, I imagine that the National Health Service would pick up the bill.   So that
whether *on its own* a voluntary system of blood donation
would significantly alter people's attitudes to their
fellows is open to doubt.   However, if treated in the
context of a system where medical care is given without
direct cost to the patient, the case may well be different.   For it is likely that many will want to give so as
to strengthen and preserve a system which embodies the
ideal of equality.

5

Some of the criticisms of 'The Gift Relationship' seem to
be not just unimaginative but reveal a conceptual malaise
in economics.
    A.J. Culyer (1974, p. 709) writes, in an appraisal of
the book:
    On the ethical dilemma, granted that to give may be
    more noble than to 'sell' (though this view oversimpli-
    fies a complex of motives and emotions, and cannot
    really be accepted on its face value) it is also noble
    to have a health service that cares effectively for
    the sick.
And Kenneth Arrow writes of the book in similar vein
(1972, pp. 354-5):
    I should add that, like many economists, I do not want
    to rely too heavily on substituting ethics for self-
    interest.   I think it best on the whole that the re-
    quirement of ethical behaviour be confined to those
    circumstances where the price system breaks down....
    Wholesale usage of ethical standards is apt to have un-
    desirable consequences.   We do not wish to use up
    recklessly the scarce resources of altruistic motiva-
    tion, and in any case ethically motivated behaviour may
    even have a negative value to others if the agent acts
    without sufficient knowledge of the situation.   In the
    case of medical practice and elsewhere, it might plaus-
    ibly be argued that ethical codes serve as an instru-
    ment for increasing the economic advantage of one seg-
    ment of the population at the expense of the rest.
    Granted that a giver's motives may sometimes be sus-
pect, granted that well-intentioned acts can sometimes be
damaging, granted that codes of behaviour can sometimes be
used as a cover for self-interest, it seems to me, nevertheless, that these writers are being pathologically suspicious of anything but the cash nexus.   If a non-econo-
mist were to write in this way we would regard him as a

suitable case for treatment! It is just not plausible, as Peter Singer (1973b) points out, to treat altruism as a scarce resource like, say, oil. Quite the contrary. In a society where altruism is expected and inculcated, it is likely to grow (p. 319). Nor is it reasonable to cast so suspicious an eye on those who want to give, who want to help others.

It is implausible to suppose that economists are, as a profession, emotionally disturbed. They are simply in the grip of a bad theoretical model.

Thomas Hobbes (1651) left philosophers with a problem which the economists have picked up: the problem of benevolence. He took it as axiomatic that everyone seeks his own benefit. But if so, what about actions which are done supposedly for the benefit of others, actions motivated by altruism? Either benevolent actions will be irrational, or - despite any protestations - not benevolent at all, but aimed at the agent's own self-interest.

Alfred Marshall laid the foundations of marginalist economics, whose structure of concepts still largely dominates economic thought. Marshall's attempt to resolve this problem is instructive. He maintained that all incentives to action may be spoken of as desires for the 'satisfaction' of the agent: 'it may perhaps be well to use this word instead of "pleasure" when occasion arises for referring to the aims of all desires, whether appertaining to man's higher or lower nature' (1966, p. 14). Despite some passages where he speaks as if genuine altruism is possible (notably p. 20), Marshall's more consistent line of thought appears in the following passage:

> For suppose that the person, whom we saw doubting between several little gratifications for himself, had thought after a while of a poor invalid whom he would pass on the way home; and had spent some time in making up his mind whether he would choose a physical gratification for himself, or would do a kindly act and *rejoice in another's pleasure*.   (pp. 13-14; my emphasis)

If the satisfaction of seeing the beggar's smile will outweigh the satisfaction of a packet of cigarettes, then the charitable act will be performed.

This general method of dealing with altruism has persisted, with modifications in two directions. The distinction between man's higher and lower motives was felt to involve value-judgments, and to have no place in a scientific study of economics. The distinction was dropped; thus collapsing Marshall's position into that of the Hobbesians.

The second change has been an attempt to rule out by

fiat any questions about the relations between people's choices and their welfare (benefit, satisfaction, pleasure or utility: catch-all expressions which are effectively interchangeable).   Thus J. deV. Graaff writes (1957, p. 5): 'To say that his welfare would be higher in [condition] A than in B is thus no more than to say that he would choose A rather than B, if he were allowed to make the choice.'   D.M. Winch writes (1971, p. 25) in similar vein:

When we assume that individuals behave rationally and endeavour to maximize utility, there is no indication that such behaviour is good or bad, desirable or undesirable....   We assume that individuals attempt to maximize utility, and define utility as that which individuals attempt to maximize.

The result of redefining welfare (utility, etc.) as what someone would choose, or what someone aims to increase by choosing, is to make important questions trivial.   Do people always choose to promote their own welfare?   Do they always succeed?   Well, says the economist, what you're really asking is 'Do people choose what they choose?'   And, of course, they do.   The only reply to this is to insist that when we asked these questions we were asking about welfare in the ordinary sense, not the new one.

So economists have either conceded, or tried to avoid, the problem of benevolence.   Their terminology suggests that people always seek something for themselves, be it welfare, satisfaction, or whatever.   This runs counter to the ordinary view that giving *costs* us, that we deprive ourselves of benefit to increase the benefit of others.   For the economist this is impossible, at least for a rational agent.   So we can see why Titmuss regards economic values as selfish values.   And we can see why Arrow, in the article cited above, attempts to 'rationalise' giving, either in terms of deriving satisfaction from an increase in another's satisfaction, or in terms of an insurance - 'giving blood in the vague expectation that one may need it later on' (1972, p. 349).

The hostility of the economists towards altruism is largely the result of conceptual confusion.   First they must get straight about the philosophy.

Consider the claim that people always act to promote their own benefit.   This could be (a) a psychological truth about people, (b) a logical truth showing a link between the notions of choice and benefit, or (c) a statement about what it is rational for people to do.   Its power is largely a consequence of not disentangling the three.

The first is a false generalisation.   Apart from the
case in dispute, altruism, people sometimes act hastily,
sometimes in the grip of self-destructive passion.   Only
a man with a theory would refuse to admit, or try to re-
interpret, such behaviour.

The theory might be provided by (b), the logical interpretation.   Here is the thinking behind it: 'If I freely
choose to do A then I do A because I want to.   If I do A
because I want to, then I do A in order to get something
which I want.   So if I freely choose A then I do A in
order to get something which I want.'   Both premisses are
suspect.   The first invites the protest that people sometimes freely do, not what they want to, but they feel they
ought to.   Well, perhaps there is a *wide* sense of 'want'
in which people *want* to do what they feel they ought to
do, but there's a narrow one in which they don't.   The
second premiss seems to me more vulnerable.   Doing A because one wants to is doing A in order to get something
one wants: this seems to make all actions instrumental,
but aren't there also actions done simply for the joy of
doing them?   For example, a man may beat his wife not in
order to still her nagging tongue, but just because he
enjoys beating her.   The premiss can be saved only by introducing artificial 'ends' of such actions.   The man
beats his wife in order to get an increase in benefit
(utility, satisfaction) for himself.   In general, if any
action is done with no obvious end in mind, we can always
say that the agent had in mind his own benefit.   First we
invent a gap by supposing that all actions are instrumental, done in order to ..., then we invent a universal gap-
filler, benefit, which has to be the *agent's own* benefit.
And this is the major implausibility.   If A is wanted *by*
me, it does not follow that is wanted *for me*.   I can want
someone else's benefit.

Finally there is (c), the claim that it is rational to
aim at one's own benefit, irrational to do otherwise.
Now actions are adjudged relative to the wants and beliefs
of the agent: if someone wants to poison himself and believes that yew berries are a swift and painless poison,
it is rational to eat yew berries.   But sometimes we want
to judge actions irrational, not simply when wants and beliefs don't match, but when a belief is fantastic or a
want bizarre.   So it is irrational to keep books in
cages, even if one does believe they bite; and masochism
is irrational because it is bizarre to want pain.   The
latter is obviously more relevant to the   problem of benevolent actions.   Is it bizarre to want others to be
happy?   Surely not, for it is not uncommon and does not
seem inexplicable.   In terms of evolution, it would be

advantageous for any gregarious species of animal to be
strongly motivated to co-operate with and help others of
that species.

The way is now clear for a more adequate analysis of
altruism.

A gift is a transfer of benefit: an agent deprives
himself of benefit in order to increase that of another.
It is unlike an exchange or purchase, which is undertaken
in the hope of increasing one's own benefit. Sometimes
reciprocal gifts are aimed to cement bonds of affection;
sometimes they are simply expressions of affection which
may in fact have this effect. The latter are gifts; the
former are not. In any act of giving the giver gets some
benefit, but in many cases this will not offset the loss
of benefit to himself (i.e., giving has a cost).

Economists can accept these truisms. Their suspicions
of benevolence are groundless. But philosophical stumbl-
ing-blocks cast long shadows.

6

Arrow's critique of Titmuss contains another passage in
defence of a market in medicine which is worth close examination. This concentrates on expanding choice:

> Economists typically take for granted that since the
> creation of a market increases the individual's area of
> choice it therefore leads to higher benefits. Thus,
> if to a voluntary blood donor system we add the possi-
> bility of selling blood, we have only expanded the in-
> dividual's range of alternatives. If he derives sat-
> isfaction from giving, it is argued, he can still give,
> and nothing has been done to impair that right.
> (1972, pp. 349-50)

The suggestion seems to be that a monopoly of altruism
is prima facie a bad thing. For it restricts choice, and
the wider the choice the greater the benefit. But if
this is the argument then it is back to front. Economists typically take for granted that a market increases
consumer choice, and hence net social welfare. There
isn't any obligation to increase the choice of the supplier. A farmer, for example, is faced with a going
market price for cabbages. He can choose whether to
supply cabbages at all, and if so how many, at that price.
But no market mechanism provides a variety of prices
allowing the farmer to elect to sell at whichever price
he chooses; rather the market irons out differences in
price. If an adequate supply can be obtained by offering
suppliers 2 pence per cabbage, they will not have the

choice of selling at 3 pence.   In the same way, in Britain a mercenary supplier of blood must face the fact that an adequate supply can be obtained at zero price to the supplier.   He has the choice, open to any supplier, in any market, of providing at that price or not.   So long as enough people choose to give blood, nobody operating economic principles would buy it.

Arrow has permitted his suspicion of benevolence to lead him astray.   This is partly, as we saw, the result of conceptual confusion;   partly it shows ideological bias.

Underpinning the ideology is a myth, a justificatory history or quasi-history.   The myth is that in the beginning were independent producers, each exploiting the resources of nature and making a portion of them his own. The independent producers began to exchange their produce. Exchanges occurred on terms favourable to both parties to the exchange, and continued just so long as both parties found it beneficial.   Out of such barter grew the price-mechanism.

Sophisticated defenders of the myth would disown it as history but see it as embodying truth.   First, there is no compulsion in the market;   every contract is freely entered.   In addition, there are no favours given or asked;   everyone seeks his own advantage.   Finally, the myth shows that in a market all can improve on their original positions;   there is no conflict because there are no losers.

The freedom of the market is commonly contrasted with the conflict or deference-relations to be found outside. For example, Arrow tries to show that Titmuss was an elitist: 'What is disturbing, in this case as in many others, is that an appeal against the marketplace and its coldness has a way of slipping into a defense of privilege....   It is very easy indeed for "community" to slip over into "status"' (p. 359).

The case against Titmuss strikes me as tenuous, but the terms in which it is   made are interesting.   Outside the market Arrow *expects* to find elitism.

Cooper and Culyer, in the discussion with which we began, make a similar sort of complaint about going outside the market.   In Britain, the techniques for increasing the supply of blood 'have varied from appeals to conscience and other forms of suasion or cajolery to coercion of service-men' (1968, p. 32).   And they conclude that 'the individual's decision whether or not to supply at a variety of prices is ... preferable to (in the extreme case) coercion' (p. 32).

Coercion, exhortation and deference-relations go

together because all three are examples of pressure, or
attempted pressure, by one individual upon another.   Exhortation is an attempt to coerce by the power to make
others feel uncomfortable.   Deference-relations signify
a sort of congealed coercion, a power whose exercise is
widely seen as right and natural.   In contrast, in the
market there is perfect freedom.   One man's coin is as
good as another's;   one does not have to justify oneself.

Yet this belief in freedom is suspect.   In a market
people are not free from 'suasion or cajolery'.   The existence of an advertising industry, and the large amount
of 'fashion-spending' testify to that.   The assumption
that exhorting people to give blood is an assault on their
freedom, while exhorting them to buy lurex underwear is
giving them what they really want, is not plausible.
Only in textbooks are consumers free from the influence of
others;   and it is unrealistic to treat attempts at persuasion as if they diminish freedom of choice.   Exhortations are not threats.

Moreover, there is power in the market.   If it is
sometimes not noticed, that only shows how securely established it is.   Wealth is the legally sanctioned power to
control a disproportionate share of scarce resources, with
the result that the whims of a rich man count for more
than the needs of a poor one.   This power can coerce.
For example, the desire of the wealthy city-dweller for a
weekend cottage away from it all can outweigh the desire
of the poorer country dweller for a home of his own in his
own neighbourhood.   Again, if there are external costs of
industry - dirt, smoke, visual ugliness - to be borne then
the poor bear them;   they cannot afford to escape them.
It may well be that the power of the market is in the long
run benign, that the net benefits to the poor outweigh the
dirt, the smoke and the ugliness.   Nevertheless, there is
no effective choice in the matter;   the poor must bear
such costs if they want jobs and houses at all.   And, of
course, the rich are not just consumers, but investors and
employers too.   Associated with this power is status and
due deference.   In these circumstances the freedom of the
market is a somewhat formal affair, like the famous freedom to dine at the Ritz.

The following passage by the late H.B. Acton   (1971,
pp. 40-1) brings out very clearly the power-structure
underpinning the market:

I suggest that competition between consumers is not
emulative when they think of their budgets in terms of
their resources.   It tends to become so when they take
seriously the idea of expenditure beyond the limits of
their present income.   In the nineteenth century and

earlier twentieth, those who had such ambitions aimed
first to acquire the money necessary to satisfy them.
They tried to get better paid jobs and they saved.
But many consumers now hope for these results by collective measures exerted through trade unions and political parties.

In other words, now they want to change the rules!
Acton deplores this, but he surely cannot be surprised.
So long as large groups of people feel that the present
laws of ownership and inheritance do not serve their interests there will be the likelihood of pressure for
change; unless, perhaps, these present laws are widely
regarded either as fair or as unalterable. An ideological stress upon the freedom of the market, rather than
upon the property relations underlying it, is conservative
in effect, if not in intent. There is widespread agreement that freedom is desirable, and some disagreement
about how wealth should be distributed. To stress the
former is to focus on the harmonious aspect of a functioning market. To ignore the latter is, or is apparently,
to condone already existing patterns of ownership.

7

There *is* freedom, a limited freedom, in the market in so
far as people make their own choices within their income,
and to this extent take control of their own lives. Despite the fact that people sometimes buy on impulse, make
mistakes, order their priorities badly, there is a presumption that on balance this is for the best; that
people know what is best for them. There is, then, a
prima facie case for making the market as wide as possible, given a fair distribution of income. Yet, so far
as medical care is concerned, the case for a market seems
to me a thin one. This is partly because of the nature
of the commodity and partly because of the medical ignorance of the man in the street.

The important features involved in the 'purchase' of
medical care seem to me these:
 (a) the consumer (the patient) is largely ignorant;
 (b) the commodity is universally desired;
 (c) the commodity has spillover effects.
To take these points in turn:
    (a) If medical knowledge was widespread, if children
left school with the expertise of a graduating medical
student, then it might make sense to choose our own medi-
cines, hire x-ray machines, and so on. Given our ignorance, and the possibly disastrous consequences of ignor-

ance, any market would have to be indirect. We would
hire a possessor of expertise, provide him with the necessary information, and rely on his honesty and ability.
This kind of thing happens when we hire a plumber or an
electrician.   Now in terms of freedom of choice, consumer
sovereignty, it is difficult to defend this kind of
market.   How valuable is the power to choose for oneself
between people whose competence one is not competent to
assess?

(b) Health is universally valued, and there is a clear
idea of *what* is valued.   Notoriously, happiness means
different things to different people; physical health is
an altogether more precise concept.   Now normally financ-
ing a good from taxes will involve some people in paying
for commodities they do not much value; but where physical health is involved objections on this ground are
likely to be at a minimum.

(c) Health is a commodity with spillover effects.   One
person's untreated tuberculosis can affect his neighbour.
For this reason any scheme of private medical care would
have to include compulsory insurance or risk a deteriora-
tion in public health.   And insurance for many of those
with bad health would be prohibitively expensive.   It is
generally accepted that any good with large spillover
effects on the community is one whose consumption cannot
safely be left to the market.   Social welfare might
demand in some cases its promotion and in others its restriction.

Some of these features can be illustrated, taking as a
starting point a remark by H.B. Acton who, while defending
a market in medical care, admits that a doctor working in
private practice would, in an epidemic, 'be expected to
treat those who needed treatment most, as far as he could
find this out' (1971, p. 23).   He would not, that is to
say, be expected to go where his fee was highest.   No
doubt Acton would argue that although a market in medical
care, like a market in food, might have to be suspended in
times of extreme need, nevertheless it should be upheld
where possible.   The trouble with this is that the positive advantages of a market in medical care do not seem
very great.   In the case of grain, or foodstuffs generally, welfare consists in the consumption of suitable quan-
tities of carbohydrates, vitamins, and so on.   Left to
themselves most people promote their welfare (nutritional
welfare) reasonably well.   (They do it naturally, not
because they are less ignorant of nutritional than of
medical science.)   In addition, there are lots of different ways of obtaining the elements of a balanced diet and
people enjoy variety and have strong preferences in food-

stuffs. A nutritional expert might be able to assign
each individual a diet, varied at frequent intervals, and
food might be distributed to fit the diet-sheets. This
would be clumsy, very expensive, and has no advantages
over consumer choice. (One could not look forward with
confidence to higher nutritional standards as a result of
such a scheme; if people wanted strongly to overeat or
eat unwisely then there would be a tendency for a black
market to arise in food.) There is no corresponding case
to be made out for a market in medical care. Some
people, it is true, have a taste for variety in medicine;
but this is not in general medically beneficial, as tastes
in food are *in general* nutritionally beneficial. This
broad fact about human nature underpins the case against a
market in medicine.

   Acton argues against socialised medicine that:
   Since the resources for supplying medical services are
   limited, it can be said that in general there is competition for those services between all those entitled to
   them, so that the mildly ill compete with the seriously
   ill. This is to some extent concealed because not
   everyone competes for the services of the brain surgeon
   or the 'heart machine'. But the services of nurses
   and non-specialist doctors are, so to say, *diluted* between those who are seriously ill and those who are
   hardly ill at all.... Furthermore, in a comprehensive
   scheme of this sort, the selfish, the demanding and the
   well-connected can gain attention at the expense of
   others. (p. 70)
   This seems to me not enough. In a market, too, there
will be competition, for medical care is a scarce commodity which will command a price. In the market there is
rationing by price; the price mechanism chokes off excess
demand and one gets what one wishes, or can afford, to
pay for. Those who are hardly ill at all, if they are
comfortably off, can command resources at the expense of
the seriously ill who are poor. Unless the rich are un-
selfish and undemanding the introduction of a market will
not eliminate the abuse of medical resources. Primarily,
abuse can be eliminated only by doctors' judgments of
medical need.
   Moreover, it is wrong to think that the alternative to
rationing by price is an unchecked succession of frivolous
demands. For apart from price, *waiting time* also acts as
a deterrent. As demand increases and resources come
under pressure, people have to spend longer in surgeries,
accept delays before treatment, and so on. Indeed, this
may well be more effective than price in choking off frivolous demands. Waiting around may have less glamour than
handing over cash.

However, there is a danger in putting too much emphasis
on the avoidance of waste.   People do not always know if
their demands are trivial.   A recurring chest pain might
be indigestion or something more serious.   One would not
want the cost of a consultation to be an important factor
in deciding whether or not to seek treatment.   Yet if it
is not an important factor it cannot deter.   The same
applies to waiting time, of course.   It must, impossibly,
deter frivolous demands without being *too* good a deterrent.   But the best plan is to rely on and appeal to the
good sense of the general public;   to rely on education
and appeal to a sense of responsibility.   If there is a
cash nexus such appeals may be less effective;   willingness and ability to pay for treatment may be seen as leg-
itimating the demand for treatment.

There are other problems for socialised medicine.   On
a practical level, it may be that people resent payment
from taxes more than payment over the counter.   If so
there would be a tendency for any National Health Service
to be starved of funds.   Well, practical problems are
there to be solved.   Perhaps even so simple a device as
listing separately the medical contribution on the pay
slip would increase willingness to support health expenditure.

A more theoretical problem is that the notion of medical welfare may not be so distinct from the notion of
general welfare as I have tended to suppose.   They shade
into one another via the concept of mental health.   The
concept of mental health has rightly come under suspicion
as incorporating social norms and expectations.   Curing
the mentally ill can often be seen as adjusting their behaviour to the values which predominate in their society.
But general practitioners often say that an increasing
proportion of their cases concern such things as depres-
sion and tension.   Clearly this does involve difficulties for the claim that health is a clearly defined concept of biology.   But in the case of mental as of physical health, the ordinary person relies on the expert to
bring about the end he desires, and there are sometimes
continuities in the techniques and expertise involved.
One can, therefore, move outwards from the central cases
of medical need, more cautiously as the needs become more
subjective.   This involves making difficult decisions;
for example, is plastic surgery sought because the
patient's mental health is suffering (surgery given free
on the National Health Service) or purely for cosmetic
purposes (not given free)?   The fact that it can be difficult in some cases to draw a line does not show that
there is no valid distinction to be made between a genuine
medical need and a socially determined desire.

8

In other areas of welfare it is hard to argue that people
do not know themselves what is best for them.   The case
prima facie for a market is a strong one.   In conclusion
I shall simply identify areas which seem to me problematic.

In Britain certain basic goods are provided free or
subsidised - health, education, school meals, legal aid,
certain forms of housing.   (Whether these are provided
from centrally or locally raised taxes is beside the
point.)   Sometimes money is provided earmarked for specific purposes - for example, the 'exceptional needs' al-
lowance for clothing, bedding, household repairs and so
on, for those receiving Supplementary Benefit.   If choice
is strongly linked to welfare, and perhaps valuable on its
own account as well, then we might regard cash payments to
those in need as in general preferable to the provision of
payments in kind, or tied payments.

We can sharpen the issue by considering what E.J.
Mishan writes about subsidised housing (1969, p. 38):

> For one thing, if we subscribe to the doctrine that, in
> the choice of material goods at least, each person
> knows his own interest best, then it would be better to
> give these subsidies *direct* to the poor to spend as
> they wish.   After all, any person will consider him-
> self better off if he is given an annual sum of money
> to spend freely than if the sum is given to him contin-
> gent upon his spending it in a certain way.
>
> For another, the subsidy which is tied to house-room
> has the disadvantage that those who receive it have
> less incentive to economize on scarce housing than they
> would have if, instead, they received a direct, or un-
> conditional, subsidy. (1)

The points are obviously closely related.   If people
choose to spend part of their subsidy on other items then
perforce there must be economy in living space.

A complication which arises here is that the economic
individual is choosing not just for himself, but very
often for his children also.   It is all very well for
someone to suffer the consequences of his own mistakes,
but should children be left to suffer the consequences of
bad decisions by their parents?   The answer to this, I
think, is to concede that there are some choices so bad
that nobody should be permitted to make them.   Society
limits choices by law.   A parent cannot choose not to
educate or house his children.   But then, within the
legally permitted area of choice, parents should be free
to make choices for their children.   Net beneficiaries of

a progressive taxation policy, as well as the relatively
affluent, should be treated as responsible until they show
themselves otherwise.   So the issue raises itself anew:
granted that choices must be circumscribed by law, isn't
there a prima facie case for the non-market provision of
welfare through cash payments in general, thus increasing
individual choice, rather than the direct provision of
benefits?

I think there is a prima facie case, although I would
not accept a common extension of the position.   This is
that a government should accept its people, wants and all;
that to try to tamper with people's choices by means of
taxes, subsidies and 'tied' welfare provision is elitist,
for it is to assume that the government knows best what
people want.   This, too, complacently assumes that the
wants which manifest themselves in our society are natural.   It overlooks, for example, the present attempts of
industry to inculcate wants, and change attitudes through
advertising.   If it is true that wants are socially
determined, at least in part, then any government seeking
to change society will if successful, change consequently
the wants, attitudes and values prevailing in society.
Any government, for example, which considerably increased
the real income of the poor, would change their situation
and, inevitably, their attitudes, tastes and wants.
This would be the case whether goods were supplied direct,
or whether cash was given.   Elitism does not seem to me
a serious problem because *any* form of government intervention can, on this way of defining elitism, be construed
as elitist.

NOTE

1 There are, inevitably, difficulties in Mishan's (1969)
approach to welfare benefits.   On a practical level, it
may be that across-the-board provision of certain basic
goods and services appears to be more acceptable to the
poor than a cash payment with the stigma of poverty
attached to it.   Or it may be that the general public
would resent large cash handouts to those in need.   If
this is so, then the effective choice may be between
benefits in kind and a much smaller cash benefit.   The
hope may be that some device such as negative income tax
could solve this problem; if it did, it would be by dis-
guising the fact that transfer payments were taking place.
A more general difficulty associated with this approach
is that so long as taxation is seen as taking what belongs to one individual to give it to another individual,

there will be resentment.   The market is such that property - what is earned - does not at the moment correspond
with a just distribution of that income.   In trying to
right this by taxation policy one has to disturb the
notion prevalent today that what is legally earned is
also justly earned.   This is not an easy task.

10 Affirmation and sacrifice in everyday life and in social work

Donald Houston

INTRODUCTION

This article is concerned to shed some light on a commonly
observed phenomenon: the absence of conviction displayed
by social workers that the work they do has any real
value.   This lack of conviction displays itself in many
ways.   Amongst the most notable is a tendency to give
apologetic accounts of social work practice, to concep-
tualise the theoretical base of social work at a level of
generality which makes valid virtually any favourable interpretation of what the theorist means, and to visualise
the development of social work in terms of acquiring more
ability to cope with the world as it is and more resources
relevant to such modes of coping.   Critics of social work
- and this includes those who are well disposed - frequently protest that they cannot grasp what social workers
are aiming to do: they can neither get a sense of the intended destination, nor can they tell when the destination
has been reached.
   The argument here proposed is that social work is subject to contradictions inherent in the value-base of contemporary society itself and that certain fundamental dimensions of the uncertainty and disenchantment experienced
and displayed by social workers cannot be understood,
still less worked with, until the influence of these contradictions on social work has been explored and mapped
out.   In what follows, the nature of the contradictions
will first be explored, after which all appropriate findings will be applied to the practice of social work.

BEING WHO I AM IN INTERPERSONAL RELATIONS

When men and women come together for any purpose, the task
which first confronts them is who will speak or act first
and what will the others do in consequence.   Whoever
speaks or acts begins to set a direction for who speaks or
acts subsequently.   The subsequent speaker or actor does
not necessarily have to follow his predecessor, but if he
does not then he finds himself in a relationship which is
still without direction, and he, by his own intervention,
becomes the member who proposes the direction it will
take.

Unless people in contact can arrive at a direction for
that part of their lives which they share, they are unlikely to remain together for long.   Direction may be
given by one or more members who are especially strong in
the way they affirm their position.   It may arise naturally out of the purpose of the coming together, certain
directions being readily perceived as more appropriate
than others.   Formal relations may be established with
certain people identified as those who set certain types
of direction, and other people identified as those who
follow the direction set.   At all times we may expect to
find situations in which there are degrees of uncertainty
and disagreement over which direction to take, and that
these are dealt with by various strategies and forms of
organisation.   When people begin to resist the several
sources of direction to which they are subject, their contact must come to an end if alternative sources cannot be
found.

When a man takes up a direction in relation to another
he experiences himself according to a certain pattern.
Some features of himself can be openly expressed, some can
be legitimately held to as possible within the relationship though at another time, and some features have no
place in the relationship.   Every relationship with
another person serves as an opportunity to be 'Who he is',
but it is an opportunity with limits.

The man who sets direction for another can do so in
ways which give him more opportunity to be 'Who he is'
than they give to the other.   To be moved by one's own
experience is a readily arrived at condition which will be
quickly strengthened by repetition.   To be moved by the
state of another requires learning to stand back from the
immediacy of our own experience.   It requires that we
become conscious of what he is revealing about what he
notices and the sense he makes of what he notices.   It
requires that we build into our way of relating to him due
recognition of our consciousness of what it is like to be

'Who he is', at least in respect of these dimensions of
his 'being' which he brings to his relationship with us.
   We develop our ways of being 'Who I am' in relation to
other people.   Our personal histories of relating to
others coupled, perhaps, with certain natural aptitudes
encourage us to repeat certain styles of being.   We approach situations ready to notice certain features and to
make sense of them in certain ways.   Our sense of self
receives sustenance when other people play into our way
of noticing and acting.   On the other hand, we are dimi-
nished by the failure or refusal of others to notice the
things we notice, to act according to the principles which
inform our patterns of action.   Not surprisingly we tend
to seek out relationships which confirm our style of
being, and when we cannot readily find them we strive to
change those we can find into shapes more amenable to our
natures.

PATTERNS OF BEING WHO I AM IN INTERPERSONAL RELATIONS

It is useful to distinguish four overall styles of 'being
who I am in relation to others'.   The *first* entails experiencing myself through the recognition of others, and
acting in continuing awareness that others are noticing
what I am doing.   I exist through their recognition of
me and they exist for me in order to afford me that recognition.   In its most common form I expect others to
notice me and to act towards me in ways which accord with
what I notice and how I act.   This means that in my presence they have to struggle for recognition of their ways
of noticing and acting.   This is true even when their
ways are similar to mine, for their ways remain *their*
ways, and what I am seeking is recognition of *my* ways.
(The actual way I notice and act may not matter all that
much to me.   What does matter to me is that it is *me* who
is noticing and acting.)   Struggles of this nature are
resolved in various ways.   The end state is that either
my style of being dominates that of the other, or his
style of being dominates mine.   One of us must give up a
measure, and often a considerable measure, of personal
recognition in order that the other may experience and
express 'Who he is'.   One of us loses himself in order
that the other may win himself.
   The *second* way of 'being who I am' is a variant on the
first.   It involves my giving up seeking recognition of
how I notice and act in order that one or more others can
be afforded greater recognition than they would otherwise
receive.   They get the attention I otherwise might have

competed for.   In my turn I get satisfaction from experiencing the attention they receive.   This attention
can allow me to argue that their version of how to 'be who
I am' is preferable to my own.   Essentially I am passing
a vote of 'no confidence' in the authenticity and ade-
quacy of my own experience and action.

  The *third* way of 'being who I am' is also grounded on
the recognition which others afford me.   However, on this
occasion the recognition is experienced through my achieving a standard in my ways of noticing and acting.   My
achievement offers me two sources of self-affirmation.   I
may experience myself as affirmed by virtue of the patterns which inform my noticing and acting.   The exercise
of skill in ways which bring order into my relations with
the world provides me with a well-supported sense of self.
In addition, I may experience others as affording me recognition for having achieved success with regard to a
standard.   In contrast to 'being who I am through the
recognition of others' however, we should note that 'being
who I am in relation to a standard' does not depend on
being recognised by others who are disadvantaged relative
to me.   Indeed I may gain most affirmation of self from
people who are equally or more successful than I am.

  A *fourth* way of 'being who I am in relation to others'
is based on quite different ways of giving recognition to
what others notice and do about what they notice.   What
is involved here is a reciprocal enterprise in which all
participants together arrive at ways of noticing and
acting which are compatible with one another.   When
others present me with information about what they notice,
I take care to hear as best I can what they say, and to
indicate that I have heard.   When they act on what they
notice, I strive to understand the experience to which
their actions are giving expression, and to indicate what
I understand.   By displaying to them my openness to their
presentation of self I acknowledge tne value to me of that
presentation.   Through my expression of concern I offer
the possibility to another of enriching his display, and
indeed of discovering more of himself to display.

  Relating reciprocally thus involves giving the other
back to himself, with concern for his nature.   It also
involves giving myself to him by a truthful display of the
effects he has on the person I am.   I show him 'who I
am', 'who he allows me to be', and 'what I do about who he
allows me to be'.   In so displaying myself I challenge
him to value the person I am.   I ask him to give myself
back to me with due concern for my nature, whilst yet displaying a true account of the effects I have on him.   Together we strive to develop a mutuality of experience and

action in which neither participant's version of a situation 'takes over' the version of the other, unless the second participant freely acknowledges that the alternative version offers him a richer range of experience and self expression.

AFFIRMATION AND SACRIFICE IN INTERPERSONAL RELATIONS

In any relationship it is possible for one or more members to engage in experiences and actions at the expense of the experiences and actions of one or more other members.   A great many, and possibly the majority, of relationships in everyday life give expressions to styles of living which entail that some participants must sacrifice aspects of their experience and action in order that other participants can affirm theirs (as in many relations between parents and children, teachers and pupils, employers and employees, experts and laymen).

We may speak of patterns of affirmation/sacrifice as being either *unilateral* or *reciprocal*.   In *unilateral* affirmation/sacrifice, the member who affirms his 'being who I am in relation to you', sets the direction of the relationship which he is currently having with others. He exercises substantial influence over what others notice and what they do about what is noticed.   By affirming himself through 'drawing recognition from others' he leads others to experience him as demanding that they constrain their self-expression within boundaries which he defines (because within these boundaries his way of being is confirmed, and perhaps enriched).   That is, they must sacrifice an area of their being that he may live in and through their presence.

Although unilateral relationships may display a shifting locus for affirmation, so that different members affirm themselves or sacrifice themselves at different points in the history of the relationship, it frequently happens that certain members develop a self and/or public image of being an 'affirmer' or a 'sacrificer'.   It is then very difficult for any experience or action they engage in to be given a different meaning from the socially established one.

In unilateral affirmation/sacrifice each given member is 'who he is' without much regard to the experience and enactment of being on the part of each other member.   The form awareness of others takes in such relationships is (i) to be aware of others as a source of frustration to our own self expression, or as a source of demand for experience and action which is not compatible with the way

we wish to live, and (ii) to find ways of acting which
maximise our ability to get others to conform to the way
we want them to follow us, and which minimise their presentation of demands for us to experience and act in ways
out of line with the life-style we are seeking to pursue.

In *reciprocal* affirmation/sacrifice each member experiences himself in the light of an awareness of how each
other member is experiencing himself. For this to be
possible each member must be given the opportunity to
reveal his experience as it really is. This means first
that *authenticity* in self-expression must be the norm of
the relationship, and that all expressions of self must be
treated *respectfully*. Each member must acknowledge the
meaning to the speaker of what he says or does. Each
member must genuinely relate what the speaker says or does
to his own 'following' expression of self.

Reciprocal affirmation must be associated with reciprocal sacrifice. In order for a member to affirm his experience other members must withhold aspects of their experience which go beyond the material offered by the
member for their immediate attention. In order to follow
up his material in a way which respects its nature other
members may have to 'hold in abeyance' certain things they
notice and certain lines of action they are ready to take,
until the member in question is ready to take up in his
turn their particular experiences and expressions of self.

Reciprocal affirmation/sacrifice can only continue for
as long as all engaged in it can freely take up each
others affirmation of self. As soon as a member affirms
himself without regard for the being of another the other
is hard pressed to continue to treat the first member reciprocally. The relationship quickly takes on the form
of unilateral affirmation/sacrifice.

Reciprocal affirmation/sacrifice in contemporary society must necessarily be open to misunderstanding. The
individual who relates to others according to its principles is likely to have his actions interpreted as if he
were giving expression to unilateral affirmation/sacri-
fice. He will, therefore, be seen as either demanding
the (enforced) sacrifice of others or as being ready to
submit to their demands for (enforced) sacrifice on his
part. His attempt to 'give others to themselves' will be
experienced as a confidence trick, as indeed it is for as
long as the others cannot use what is offered as it is intended to be used. The use of reciprocal affirmation/
sacrifice must be learned and the learning must be expected to entail many experiences of failure.

PATTERNS OF AFFIRMATION AND SACRIFICE IN EVERYDAY LIFE

Within the framework of unilateral affirmation/sacrifice
we may distinguish the following generalised patterns:
(i) Simple affirmation/sacrifice
Relationships in this form consist of initiating and following.   Participants experience themselves primarily as
initiators or followers in any given instance of relating.
They may develop a style of life or a self or public
image which accentuates one pole or the other.
(ii) Normative affirmation/sacrifice
Relationships are experienced and expressed in relation to
identifiable standards.   Standards entail the possibility
of experiencing and expressing oneself in terms of successfully thinking, feeling, or acting according to the
standard in question.   They equally entail the possibility of experiencing and expressing oneself as failing.
Anyone who consistently fails, or who fails in respect of
certain socially fundamental performances may develop a
self and/or public image of being 'a failure'.   His every
action may thereafter be treated as a manifestation of a
'failed' life-style.
    Experiencing oneself in terms of successfully observing
a standard, depends upon innate and learned capacity coupled with the opportunity to exercise that capacity.   The
standards of performance required of participants in a
given situation may reflect the complexity of the work to
be done.   They may also be functioning to allow the more
well-endowed to give relatively unfettered range to their
capacities and opportunities.   They can also be used to
enable the more well-endowed to allocate relatively limited resources to themselves (using the 'high standards'
they observe to justify for example high financial
rewards).
    Every time an individual initiates movement in relation
to others he thereby introduces a standard for their
thinking, feeling and acting.   They may more or less conform to the complexity of his contribution to their experience.   The individual who initiates does so in the
light of previously established standards.   The one who
follows always makes some contribution of his own.
    If a standard is to be experienced as a source of per-
sonal success or failure, it must arise within a relationship where certain participants not only initiate standards but also have the power or the right to set standards for others to observe.   The identity of the other
is affirmed or denied by the experience of observing the
standards set.   Any substantial measure of deviation from
the standards in question is experienced as personal fail-

ure and not as an affirmation of one's alternative style
of life.

(iii) Competitive affirmation/sacrifice

The success/failure pattern of normatively oriented relationships may assume the form of competition for the opportunity to experience and express 'who I am'.   In such
relationships an individual can achieve acknowledged affirmation only at the expense of other people being positively deprived of a similar opportunity.   'Being who I
am' in the context of competition means 'being at your
expense'.   Here the basic relationship is based on winning and losing.   A winning self is one which is accen-
tuated by the existence of losing selves - I am because
you are not.   A losing self is one which is wholly deprived of any opportunity to experience the 'approved
style of being through winning'.   This style of relating
creates the division of men between winners and losers.
The development of a self/public image of winner entails
ensuring that losers continue to be available.   The development of a self/public image of loser means that one
experiences and expresses ones 'being' as 'less than' the
being of the winner.   It is essentially a state of de-
pression and hopelessness.

All unilateral relationships are necessarily grounded
as simple affirmation/sacrifice.   In contemporary Britain
the majority of relationships are of a unilateral form:
at the level of general social norms we may argue that
they are all of a unilateral form.   We are brought up to
expect that 'being who I am' means formulating our
thoughts, feelings and actions of our fellowmen.   When
our fellowmen, in relating to us, express their thoughts,
feelings and actions we experience a threat to our way of
'being who we are'.   If we follow through on their style
of being we will lose out on our own.   We fear that they
will use us to confirm and enrich their own experience and
action.   Given the underlying expectations which all hold
of each other, there arises plenty of evidence to illustrate the soundness of our fears.

Society encourages us to look to ourselves for our experience and expression of self.   We must take the initiative, we must succeed, we must win.   The untold side
of this story is that no one can initiate unless someone
else follows, success is not possible for some unless
failure occurs for others, for one person to win, at least
one other must lose.   Thus, although society's traditions
assure winners that it is they who win, succeed, initiate,
reflection also shows that it is others, freely or under
coercion, who allow winners to be 'who they are' in relation to them, the losers.

Society ensures that certain of its members will experience confirmation and enrichment of self by relating to
others in terms of norms which they can achieve but which
others cannot.   Britain today is full of people whose experience and expression of self is defined in terms of
succeeding where others fail - and of failing where others
succeed.   Successful people experience themselves as
being affirmed by virtue of experiencing other people as
being unsuccessful in affirming themselves.   A great many
political and professional relationships tend to be based
on relating to others as 'unsuccessful'.   The unsuccessful are treated by the successful as 'losers' with all
that means in terms of the denial of the value of their
experience and of their capacity to give expression to it
in relationships.

The basic irony of all win/lose relationships is that
in the final analysis all participants lose.   We have already considered the losers experience of losing.   The
way the winner loses is, of course, less easy to discern,
otherwise winners would be less satisfied with their condition.   The winner loses by virtue of the limits inherent in the experiences he allows into his world.   He
draws a boundary to 'who he is' which leaves out 'who he
might be' if he were to open himself to the world of the
loser.   He opens himself only to other winners.   He may
relate to them either as competitor or as peer.   In
either case an element of repetition enters his life.   As
a competitor he experiences repetition unless he can rise
to ever greater challenges.   Almost inevitably he must
one day experience himself as a loser, a condition for
which he is ill-prepared, and one which will increasingly
press on him unless he can assume more accommodating
values.   As a peer amongst peers he experiences only his
own world in the presence of others.   The sameness of his
experience eventually makes of each tomorrow a repetition
of today.   In due course, sameness in experience and
action leads to loss of differentiation.   Tomorrow becomes less varied than today.   The passage of time is
accompanied by the denuding of self.   Finally, his lack
of openness to the experiences and actions of losers may
persuade him into picturing his relationship with them in
very different terms from how they experience their relationship with him.   In his naive self-affirmation he may
demand that the losers sacrifice more of their being than
they can bear.   They may revolt and out of their revolt
may come changes in the 'rules for winning', one consequence of which may be that the winners become the losers
and the losers become the winners.

MODIFYING PATTERNS OF AFFIRMATION AND SACRIFICE IN EVERY-
DAY LIFE

Certain people who are in a position to affirm themselves
within the context of unilateral relationships may, however, become troubled at the effects which the condition
of sacrifice has on the life-styles of others. They may
seek ways of relating which permit those to whom they
relate to experience and express themselves more affir-
matively than has hitherto been the case.

Typically, they seek these changes within a continuing
framework of unilateral relationships. People working in
roles or work-systems which express the formalised relationships of a society based on unilateral affirmation/
sacrifice can hardly do otherwise. Inevitably in due
course they find their endeavours frustrated by the ubi-
quitous values of society.

The *first approach* to a wider distribution of experiences of self-affirmation is simply to claim that in any
given relationship there are more opportunities for self-
affirmation than have been taken up. This may be true up
to a point, but often it is not. In any case it does not
alter the fact that in normative relationships some
members must experience failure, and in competitive relationships some members must experience losing. It also
fails to give due weight to social forces which are geared
to ensuring that there are sufficient incidents of failure
and losing, and that these incidents are treated with sufficient seriousness, to ensure that established ways of
affirming 'who I am' are maintained and extended. (Only
thus can such a society as ours continue to have members
who give it direction and form.)

The *second approach* is to diversify the relationships
available to people. Due recognition is given to the
fact that within the framework of any given relationship
only some members can initiate, succeed, or win. However, it is argued that it is possible to set up *first*,
relationships which give to people not used to initiating
experience and action for others the opportunity to do so,
second, relationships which are built around norms which
are compatible with their interests and abilities and
which therefore allow them to experience success, and
third, a wide enough range of competitive relationships to
give everyone the opportunity to win in one relationship
or another.

This second approach clearly does promise to extend and
enrich the experience and action of people who remain essentially committed to relationships of unilateral affir-
mation/sacrifice. What it does not do is to change the

continuing experience of following, failing and losing
which certain people have in certain central areas of
social living.   On the other hand, what does happen is
that by giving these people the experience of initiating,
succeeding, winning in other areas of daily living, it
alerts them to the attraction of also initiating, succeeding and winning in the areas where they traditionally
follow, fail and lose.   The seeds of demands for radical
social change are thereby planted.

The *third approach* to extending and enriching experience and enactment of self in a society committed to unilateral affirmation/sacrifice is to attempt to reorganise
relationships within those areas of daily living where
traditional patterns of initiating/following, succeeding/
failing, and winning/losing are being challenged.   The
dilemma here lies in the very nature of the relationships
which are to be realigned.   There cannot be such relationships unless someone follows, someone fails, someone
loses.   There can, of course, be a change in the locus of
affirmation/sacrifice.   The followers can become initiators and vice versa.   The failures can become succeeders
and vice versa.   The losers can become winners and vice
versa.   What cannot happen is that all can become initiators, succeeders, winners, within a single relationship.

For this to happen the relationships in question must
be lifted out of the scheme of unilateral affirmation/
sacrifice.   This can be done either by denuding them of
interpersonal meaning, or by taking them into the realm
of reciprocal affirmation/sacrifice.

If an opportunity to experience and express oneself is
made universally available within a society which is essentially based on unilateral affirmation/sacrifice then,
if it is not to challenge the way the society 'gives
being' to its members the opportunity in question must be
denuded of interpersonal meaning.   Thus access to the
public water supply in Britain does not normally depend
upon being successful at another person's expense.   The
use of public water does not enhance or diminish 'who I
am in relation to others'.   However, we might imagine a
state of affairs in which people began to use the public
water supply in order to experience themselves as winners
in relation to their neighbours.   The use of public water
would have to become competitive.   For this to occur
three conditions would have to hold: first, there would
have to be agreement amongst the competitors that the use
of water was a value to compete over; second, some individuals would have to be seen as using more water than
others; and third, some individuals would have to be seen
as 'giving up' the possibility of using as much water as

the winners.   These conditions are most likely to occur
if a limit existed or could be set to the availability of
water.

It is hard to see how a society grounded on unilateral
affirmation/sacrifice can provide universal services in
any area of living which involves the use of limited resources.   The question is not how do we organise with
some measure of justice the availability of education,
medicine, housing.   It is how do we avoid these resources
being used as means by which some people can experience
themselves as winners in relation to others.   No matter
how much effort is put into universalising them, education, medicine, housing will continue to display relationships of initiating/following, succeeding/failing, win-
ning/losing.   They all constitute areas of being for contemporary man too central to be denuded of interpersonal
meaning.

To take these areas of 'being who I am in relation to
others' into the realm of reciprocal affirmation/sacrifice
is of course to approach them with a sense of 'being who I
am' which is very different from those we have referred to
whilst examining the nature of unilateral affirmation/sac-
rifice.   Although the difference cannot be explored in
detail here, what can be stated is that essentially it
lies in learning to live with and for other people as contrasted to living by using, or being used by, them.

WHO IS IT POSSIBLE FOR A SOCIAL WORK CLIENT TO BE?

Can we apply the above ideas to help us understand some of
the doubts and uncertainties which inform social work
today?   The following discussion will concentrate on the
susceptibility of social work clients to competitive forms
of affirmation/sacrifice.   Not only are social work clients subject to the competitive relationships to which all
citizens are subject, they also find themselves treated as
competitors in respect of issues which other citizens experience as involving more the processes of success/fail-
ure or even initiating/following.   Thus the clients of
social workers must compete for a basic survival wage (and
must be seen to lose in respect of those whose income is
slightly larger), they must compete for recognition by
officials, the professions, policy makers (and must be
seen to lose in relation to other members of society whose
experience of self affirmation depends as much on what the
losers don't receive as on what they themselves do), some
of them must even compete to remain at liberty (some must
lose their access to open society in order that others experience the 'freedom' that they have as an achievement).

Society does not encourage us to look too far into the
personal world of the other, especially when the other is
a 'loser' (or a failure, or a follower).   If we look only
at experiences and expressions of self which are geared to
winning (or to success, or to initiating), then we can
follow them through until we encounter other people whose
experiences and expressions of self can win over those
which have hitherto been dominant.   These in their turn
can be followed until they are defeated.   Winners set a
readily accessible direction for society.

Once we become aware of the personal world of the
loser we may begin to feel uneasy at the consequences for
his life style of competitive affirmation/sacrifice.
This unease makes it difficult for us to commit ourselves
to the strategies and activities of winning.   It introduces stress into our experiences of 'being who I am in
relation to winners', whether we ourselves are a winner or
a loser.   We are likely to find ourselves increasingly at
odds with society, and if we remain largely committed to
society's everyday values, at odds with ourselves.   This
would seem to be the condition of a great many social
workers.

The social worker finds himself having to decide to
what extent he will direct his work towards assisting his
client to experience some form of 'winning'.   He is
likely to make such decisions in the press of everyday
life, without much reflection on the underlying implications of what he decides.   As a result is is almost inevitable that he conducts his endeavours in terms of unilateral relations.   By so doing he presents his client
with two sources of conflict whenever he seeks to inform
their experience and expression of self with the quality
of winning.   First, they may find that whilst he expects
them to 'win' in direct relation to himself, in the sense
that they experience and express their authentic selves in
his presence, he also expects to experience and express
himself as a 'winner' in the process.   That is, he expects to continue to be the main source of direction in
the relationships which he has with his clients.   Using
his status of social worker he places pressure on them to
display the characteristics of a winner.   He thereby
gives himself the experience of having successfully func-
tioned as a social worker.

Second, his clients will almost certainly find that he
expects them to experience and express themselves as
'winners' within a basically unchanging context of social
values.   They must somehow learn to win in relation to
officials, institutions and the generality of their fellow
men, all of whom observe a unilateral approach to affir-

mation/sacrifice in terms of which they, the clients, are
not only expected to be losers, but are so placed in relations to these others that they cannot stop being losers
without a radical restructuring of their relationships
with them.

At this unreflective level the social worker may be
persuaded in two directions.   On the one hand, he may
recognise the immediately noticeable constraints on his
client experiencing and expressing himself as a winner.
He may concentrate on the 'reality of the situation' as
it thus appears, either working firmly in terms of his
client being a loser, or working to obtain for his client
what limited experiences of winning can be snatched from
everyday life.   On the other hand, he may fail to recognise these constraints, or refuse to acknowledge that they
are final.   He, therefore, presses on in search of opportunities for his client to be a 'winner' in areas of
living which are central to 'who his client is'.

In many ways the social worker who accepts that his
client is a loser is the easiest to live with.   By his
every word and action he confirms the reality of the
social world which his client knows.   A client who is excluded by others from many avenues of experience and
action, and who lacks the self-image to see himself in
other terms, may find it a great comfort to be recognised
for 'who he is'.   The social worker who seeks to relate
to him as a potential winner may not only be a source of
acute discomfort as he demands a change in life-style, he
may actually be a source of further diminution of self as
he presses his client into experiences and actions which
his client cannot win, and which must lead eventually to
yet another round of incidents in which his client is a
loser.

The social worker who works in terms of the sacrificial quality of his client's life-style may be far more
helpful when material aids are sought than the social
worker who is troubled by his client's social status.   He
can focus his energies on getting his client access to
whatever opportunities for rewarding experience and action
society will allow.   He is unlikely to be diverted by an
undue concern that the opportunities he can draw on are
socially marginal, and that by concentrating his endeavours on them he is by default failing to examine the central areas of his client's life-style.   By not directing
his endeavours towards such central aspects of everyday
life as education, housing employment and quality of service received, the social worker implicitly, if not explicitly, confirms his client's self-image as a person who
is neither expected nor allowed to win when the issues
become socially important.

THE SOCIAL WORK CLIENT AS A 'WINNER'

The social work client in contemporary Britain can win in
relation to others, but only under clearly defined circumstances. One circumstance we have just noted, that he
can receive 'support services' which by their very nature
confirm his essential subjection to socially enforced sacrifice in the central areas of daily living. A second
circumstance arises in areas of living which are so organised that they contain 'social space' within which the
socially identified loser can break contact with society's
definition of him, and experience and express himself 'out
of sight'.
   Many forms of organised living can only continue because they allow an 'underground life' to those who are
subject to them. In the underground world the socially
identified loser may exercise substantial initiative, experience real success, and win in relation to many others,
including those who in the 'formal organisation' are defined as 'winners' in relation to him. Opportunities for
underground winning are essential when men who do not
basically experience themselves as losers find themselves
caught up in a losing relation in the course of living in
the organisation. In a less extreme form, informal relations within an organisation can function to give certain
members an experience of winning when their official
status in the organisation may not allow for this. However, we should expect that informal 'winners' will be
acknowledged by the formal organisation only to the extent
that they do not interfere with the formal patterns of
winning and losing.
   Winning in the central areas of daily life is always
from a position of strength. The underground winner
operates from a base which cannot be controlled by the
formally designated winners. The informal winner is
often a winner in appearance only; his experience of
winning is 'allowed him' by the formally designated winners. However, the informal winner can increase the
strength of his position. To do this he must gain control over the access which others have to his experiences
and actions. If the others have need of his experience
and actions he can then require that they take account of
what he notices and the sense he makes of that he notices
in the course of relating to them.
   If the clients of social workers are to experience
authentic winning in a society based on unilateral affir-
mation/sacrifice they may find that the only options open
to them are underground winning, and winning by conflict.
The client who cheats the gas board, who obtains social

security beyond his entitlement, who steals from chain
stores, who lives by his wits, who terrorises the neighbourhood (or the residential establishment) falls into the
first group.   The client who uses a manifest failure by
an official or department to belabour them, or who com-
bines with other clients to demand what is rightfully, or
perhaps not rightfully theirs, falls into the second.

A third way by which a social work client can experience and express himself as a 'winner' in relation to
others is when he can find others who will relate to him
as losers.   Included may be virtually anyone who either
cannot affirm themselves in relation to him, or who decide that they should give up their self-affirmation 'for
his sake' - his family, his employer, government officials, neighbours.   The social worker who is troubled by
his client's susceptibility to being treated as a loser
may exercise substantial pressure on such people to persuade them to relate to his client as losers, so that his
client can experience himself as a winner and hopefully
begin to modify his self-image and his conduct in other
areas of daily life.   Amongst those whom he expects to
make such a sacrifice, the social worker may place himself.   He gives up a part of himself by allowing his
client to say and do things which run counter to what the
worker would prefer to live with.

Making oneself a loser in relation to a client may,
however, create resentment in either the worker or the
client.   The worker's resentment at what he is experiencing 'for the sake of the client' may be associated with
guilt (for after all, 'the client deserves some experience
of winning').   When he gives an account of himself in relation to the client he is aware of not being true to himself and so cannot present a strong case.   He affirms the
stance of his client (needs, stresses, lack of rights,
etc.), rather than the nature of his own activity.   He
speaks of himself as not being able to do things, needing
more skills, more knowledge, more training.   He may begin
to move into blaming other people for not supplying the
necessary backing and resources (colleagues, officials,
society in general), or into blaming the client for not
using the opportunities which are provided.   In his turn
the client may resent being made the object of another
person's guilt.   He finds himself under pressure to
assuage the worker's guilt by pretending that his experiences and actions are less sacrificial than they are.
He is, in fact, being asked to sacrifice a true expression
of his condition 'for the worker's sake'.   If he refuses
he may still find himself forced to experience his sacrificial status, this time perhaps by being defined as

'beyond help', or 'in need of further training'.   His
resentment expresses his awareness that he is being held
responsible for aspects of his condition which in substantial part are the work of the people who are holding him
responsible.

Under such conditions it is tempting for the social
worker to seek out ways of relating to his client which
allow both his client and himself to experience themselves
as winners.   However, unless he has moved beyond the unilateral approach to winning and losing, he is in fact
attempting the impossible.   The more he wins in respect
of a given area of concern, the more the client must lose,
and vice versa.   The appearance of joint winning can be
arrived at, however, in three ways.   First, worker and
client may agree to distribute their experiences of winning and losing in relation to one another - you win this
time, I win next.   Second, they may ally themselves
against a third party so that they win as a team.   (Hence
the often remarked tendency for 'people who help' to be
attracted to clients whose styles of life are informed by
principles similar to their own.)

Third, as has been noted in the last paragraph but one,
they may collude in understating the difference between
what they admit to each other about the clients experiences and actions, and the actual nature of those experiences and actions.

These approaches can only work for as long as worker
and client avoid facing the limits set by society as to
'who each can be'.   Hence the attraction of focusing
social work on the 'office interview' or on 'residential
living'.

LIMITS TO THE EXPERIENCE AND EXPRESSION OF THE SOCIAL WORK
CLIENT AS A WINNER

The social work client may experience himself as a winner
in domains of living which do not directly contribute to
his status as client.   He may be held in high regard in
his employment whilst experiencing failure as a husband or
a father.   Other people may treat him as successful in
respect of important matters which he experiences as being
beyond him (his marriage, his job, his friendships).
Finally, he may experience and express himself as a winner
in domains of living which are essentially marginal to his
major concerns.

The contrast between experiences of winning and experiences of failing can persuade the social work client to
redoubled efforts to win where hitherto he has failed.

Yet these efforts may themselves be doomed to failure because of his sacrificial position.   The man who is a
success at work may be the shared object of hostility at
home: his wife and children may need the shared experience of a 'failed father' in order to be able to relate
satisfyingly to one another.   The erratic employee may
be unable to live with the constraints which a work situation imposes on his self-expression: though he may have
control of his debts and have the backing of his wife, the
effects may be chiefly to make him aware how badly he
fills the roles of husband and breadwinner.   The impoverished single mother may give love to her child and receive it in return yet find that the world of social
agencies and businessmen have no regard for her private
riches.

The stresses of life which brings together experiences
of winning and losing may persuade the client to focus on
one or other definitions of who he is.   The question for
him will be 'Can he break away from the experiences he
wishes to escape?'   He may find that to experience success he must publicly and privately deny those parts of
his life which point up his failure.   He may find it
easier to give up his experiences of success, and commit
himself to the private and public image of being a
failure.

Some people find it more tolerable to be a 'whole
failure' rather than part failure, part success.   Alternatively, a style of being which society treats as failing may offer the client the opportunity to experience
success provided he gives up society's standards.   A
life of crime may be the only way an individual can experience and express himself successfully if society in
all other respects allocates to him a sacrificial status.

The social worker who seeks to do his job on the basis
of unilateral win/lose relationships of everyday life
faces dilemmas of his own.   If he builds for himself a
strong style of 'being a social worker' then in relation
to his clients he must reinforce their experience of being
losers.   He sets the direction, he ensures that the direction is sustained, he maintains and controls changes in
direction.   Alternatively, if he affirms his client's
right to be a winner then either he must do so in respect
of socially marginal issues, or if he focuses on socially
central issues then one of two consequences, both unfortunate for his client, tend to occur.   Either, his client
may be faced with the need to act as if he was experiencing winning when in fact he is not doing so.   Or, social
processes may operate against the endeavours of the social
worker, so that instead of resulting in the client exper-

iencing himself as a winner (in relation to education,
housing and so forth), he suffers yet one more defeat, his
self-image as a loser is subject to yet one more reinforc-
ement.   Social workers must then deal with the effects
on them of society's tendency to ensure that their endeavours fail if they attempt seriously to change the sacrificial status of their clients.   Many must feel an an-
tagonism towards society and its representatives which
they cannot easily express, but which appears in the
accounts they give of their work in the form of defensive-
ness or lack of clarity and specificity.

Overall, we see that commitment to unilateral affirma-
tion/sacrifice at the level of competitive relationships
is incompatible with the majority of social work clients
experiencing themselves as winners in certain central
areas of daily living.   When this dimension of their condition is not given due regard then they, and the social
worker, may enter into a state of false consciousness and
lack of personal authenticity.   They interpret experiences and actions according to principles which do not inform them, and they give correspondingly false accounts of
these experiences and actions.   At the same time the policies and models by which the social worker operates display internal contradictions.   He promises outcomes which
he cannot deliver, and he claims for his programmes a
relevance to his client's condition which they do not
have.   Eventually he must live with the fact that his
endeavours only make marginal differences to the central
areas of his client's life-style.   What is true for the
social worker in these respects is, of course, equally
true for other representatives of society who seek to modify the condition of the socially sacrificed - as it is
also true for the sacrificed themselves.

RECIPROCAL RELATIONS

The argument would therefore seem inescapable that if
social workers are genuinely to work towards informing
their client's experiences and actions with initiative,
success and winning, they must reach beyond unilateral
relationships of affirmation/sacrifice.   The question
that must be answered by any social work that seeks to
develop the life-styles of its clients beyond socially
marginal achievements is: 'Are reciprocal relations of
affirmation/sacrifice possible for social work?'

As our earlier reflections indicated, reciprocal relations of affirmation/sacrifice entail that all who take
part affirm 'who I am' in as full a recognition as pos-

sible of 'who you are'.   The content of such affirmation
cannot be discussed here, and indeed cannot be adequately
discussed except in the context of ongoing reciprocal relations.   What can be said, however, is that whoever in
the relationship is at any given time 'giving up' aspects
of his experience and action so that others can affirm
theirs is doing so of his own intended accord, and is
doing so within a relationship which will allow him to
enter the state of affirming himself in those same areas
whilst others will, in relation to him, freely give up
appropriate areas of their experience and action.

Thus we can see that reciprocal relationships of affir-
mation/sacrifice presuppose at least three ground conditions.   In the first place those who take part in them
must be aware of the nature of unilateral relationships
and how these define the experience and action of all who
live by them.   In the second place, they must be able to
apply this awareness to their current, and to past and
prospective, situations.   They must be able to direct
their perspective on to the way each individual is committed to 'being in relation to others', in the modes of unilateral affirmation or sacrifice, and also on to the presence in identified social roles and positions of 'rights
to affirm' or 'obligations to sacrifice'.   In the third
place, having identified the sources of unilateral affirmation and sacrifice they must be able to free themselves
from their influence.   This is more than simply a matter
of not observing the principles which inform unilateral
relations.   Simply to do this would be to leave experience and action directionless.   Instead, what is called
for is a positive commitment to others in terms of the
principles of reciprocal relations.

Living in terms of reciprocal relations is essentially
living in the light of change.   The 'openness' to others
which such relations entail requires of us that we change
our ways of 'being who we are' in relation to them as they
express aspects of being which challenge our established
ways in a manner we can acknowledge.   As we relate to
others we experience the effect we have on them: this
experience may be another stimulus to change.   Other
people change in time and in so doing make demands for us
to change correspondingly.   Relationships as such can
change as traditions become established or satisfactions
alter, and these again demand change of those of us who
take part in them.   Finally, outside influences can be
sources of demand on us for us to change what we notice
and what we do about what we notice.

To live reciprocally is to live in a condition of continuing change.   We must change in respect of given other

individuals.   We must live with other people who we require to change in relation to us, and we must enable
them to live with the effects of the change we require of
them.   We must change our demands of other people when
experience shows them to be more than they can meet, yet
we must continue to seek change in ourselves and others
in terms of the sense we have of the possibilities for
'being who I am' which each of us has in the presence of
the other.   The other person in his turn must be able to
change what he expects of us without being met by a failure to change on our part.

In unilateral relationships the occasion of change
necessarily means that stress is generated for one or
other of the participants, or both.   This is because
change is focused essentially on only one of the participants.   Typically either I work for my personal change
and leave you to deal with any effects my changing ways
may have on you;   or alternatively I try to bring about
your personal change without expecting to have to make any
changes on my part, and often without expecting your
changes to have any effect on me except that you become
more acceptable to me as I already am.

In reciprocal relationships change is essentially con-
joint.   The openness of each participant to the experience and action of each other participant means that
change in one participant must in some way lead to change
in others.   These changes are essentially rhythmic, with
each participant taking his turn whilst the other provides a reference point in respect of which the change is
taking place.

All relations need a base line of stability against
which participants can identify change.   There is need
for an unchanging element in a relationship which can set
limits to the changing element.   Unilateral relationships
display stability around the ongoing experience and action
of one of the participants.   'I change whilst you remain
as you are, or vice versa.'   In reciprocal relations
stability is expressed through the balance of concern
which the participants display for one another: 'I change
whilst you remain as you are, but I do so in ways which
then allow you to change whilst I remain as I am.'   Overall, our respective changes facilitate one another.

In a society basically committed to unilateral relationships of affirmation/sacrifice, such a commitment
should be expected to be of a developing nature rather
than of a completed one.   People so committed should expect to be seeking out opportunities to experience and
express the reciprocal life-style wherever they can find
or produce the 'social space' to do so in everyday life.

Two qualifications have to be made to this description
of the way reciprocal relations might be observed in
everyday life today.   First, we must acknowledge that
certain individuals and certain roles and social positions
are more favourably placed than are others to find or produce appropriate 'social space'.   Usually these people
will live more towards the margins than the centre of
society.   Second, we must recognise that the more an individual is subject to the influences of society the more
he needs support from his more marginally placed fellows
if he is to hold on to any effective commitment to reciprocal relationships.

RECIPROCAL RELATIONS IN SOCIAL WORK

What do these reflections on the nature of reciprocal relations of affirmation/sacrifice mean for social work?
In seeking a preliminary answer to this question we should
perhaps begin by acknowledging the extent to which social
work is committed to society's everyday expectations about
the experiences and actions of its members.   Certainly
some forms and agencies of social work, as well as some
individual social workers, are more committed to socially
established relationships than are others.   None the
less, all must work to some extent within the context of
existing society, if only because their clients are constantly engaging in relationships with members of that
society.
It is perhaps appropriate at this point to reflect on
what social workers are doing when they attempt to engage
in reciprocal relationships within the context of social
work today.   Clearly if we are right to argue that the
everyday practice of social work is grounded on society's
commitment to unilateral affirmation/sacrifice such
attempts can at best only give the appearance of reBecipro-
cal relationships.   If a social worker is able freely to
give to his client the opportunity to 'be who he is in
relation to the worker', is the client able to take up
that opportunity?   How far is he constrained by what the
role of 'social worker' means to him, how far by a self-
image which prevents him from being fully committed to
self-affirmation, how far by fears of what may happen to
him in other areas of his life if he begins to be a person
who can affirm himself in relation to social workers and
other authority figures?   If then, he is not able to take
up the worker's gift of 'an opportunity to be himself' how
can he begin to offer in return a similar gift to the
worker?   Instead, what may happen, and what may pass for

a reciprocal relationship between worker and client is
that both combine to plan, and perhaps implement, a course
of action which is variously geared to the affirmation
(and therefore the alternate sacrifice) of one or other
of the parties.   Thus they may work together on a budgeting scheme, a way of getting to school or work, an
approach to understanding the behaviour of another family
member, and what they are doing in no way raises fundamental questions about 'who each is' in relation to the
other or in relation to society.

However, care must be taken not to lose sight of occasions when the worker and client, or the client and others
do relate to one another with genuine reciprocity.   This
is perhaps most likely to happen in a family where the
members have sufficiently profound a concern for one another that they step outside the bounds of society's commitment to unilateral affirmation/sacrifice.   It can also
be seen to occur in the case of certain social workers who
are relatively marginal in their commitment to social
values, nor should we be surprised to find that at times
of crisis, or strong involvement, social workers from all
areas of practice may reach across to their clients and
their clients may reach back, if only briefly (and thereby provide an occasion for nostalgia).

Reciprocal relationships of affirmation/sacrifice offer
the prospects of a richer life for client and worker
alike.   However, their practicality is constantly at risk
in contemporary British society.   Social workers, having
once recognised the necessity of moving beyond unilateral
relationships if certain goals for clients themselves, and
society at large are to be achieved, must learn to identify where and when they can reasonably expect to live
according to reciprocal principles.   They must learn to
identify areas of living for their clients and others
where reciprocity is possible, if only briefly.   Certain
areas may prove to be amenable to the development of reciprocal relations.

In terms of a more personal commitment, social workers
must encourage reciprocity in relation to themselves.
They must learn to experience and express themselves auth-
entically in relation to others, not pretending to be who
they are not, and not using their position to force from
others defended or distorted experiences and expressions
of 'who they are'.   In this way they give to others an
opportunity to reveal and discover 'who they are' in the
company of a social worker who is trying to live according
to similar principles.   For this to happen the worker
must be able to 'take up' the experience and actions of
the other in ways which enable the other to feel confirmed

in 'who he is', and in a position to 'take up' in his turn
the experiences and actions of the social worker.
   The worker's concern to bring reciprocal relations into
the life of others must also take the form of supporting
and reinforcing all attempts by others to live according
to reciprocal principles, in whatever social context they
may occur.   In order to do so he may establish 'learning
environments' or 'supportive environments' geared to reciprocal principles, or he may move into the lives of his
clients and work directly with their everyday experiences
and expressions of reciprocal relationships.   Such approaches will involve him in enabling his clients and
others to stand back from situations, to identify and give
due weight to the perspectives and needs of other people,
to experience a rewarding expression of self through the
activities of planning, organising and implementing programmes of daily living, and to use other people's perspectives on situations and expressions of self in the
processes of building up their programme.
   Relationships are concerned not only with 'who the
individual is' but also with 'who he is able to become'.
The unfolding of his power to be requires that those who
relate to him give him the opportunity to become.   The
individual undergoing personal development challenges
those in contact with him to rise to his changing style of
being.   He seeks in their behaviour a matching capacity
to be.   All involved can experience a striving to match
their respective experiences and actions.   Personal development can come to resonate throughout the relationship.
A widespread example of this happening is the effects
which a growing child has on other members of his family.
   Reciprocal relationships offer the prospect of greatly
enriched development.   The openness of the participants
to one another in a reciprocal relationship means first,
that the potential of each is fully acknowledged by each,
and second that every movement of that potential is in-
corporated into the way each is 'who he is' in relation to
the other.   To the extent that each participant is open
to the challenges of the other, each offers to the other
possibilities for development.
   However, the world of affirmation/sacrifice is always
present to influence the path which personal development
takes.   When an individual seeks to realise his potential
in the world of affirmation/sacrifice, the opportunity to
be which he experiences is in part given by the affirmation of others, in part by the sacrifice of others.   He
may be confronted by people who affirm themselves by seeking to get him to affirm himself.   What they are seeking
is not to know him as he is, but to get him to be a person

in whose company they would feel comfortable.   Alternatively he may be expected to sacrifice his potential for
development so that others can exercise theirs.   Yet
again, he may meet people who have no sense of potential
for development in themselves.   They are available for
him to use to 'develop himself'.   In all instances the
resources available for personal development are substan-
tially less than those provided through reciprocal relationships.   Indeed personal development in relationships
of affirmation/sacrifice would seem to be restricted to
the 'potential' residing in the individual as such, whereas in the case of reciprocal relationships it resides in
the relationship between all who take part.

The processes of development offer to the social worker
a focus for working reciprocally.   Examples of how he
might work according to this focus are: (i) by seeking
out and encouraging instances of reciprocal development
(in the lives of families for example); (ii) by being
ready to relate, reciprocally, to any signs of development
which a client may show in relation to him; and (iii) by
seeking to involve other people (including colleagues) in
reciprocal relations focusing on their mutual development.

In the final analysis, social workers cannot expect to
move far beyond the norms of society.   Society's commitment to unilateral relationships of affirmation/sacrifice
permeate the lives of social work clients and all those
with whom they share their everyday life - including the
social worker himself.   If social workers are to engage
in realistic programmes of service, and in the process
become able to give a clear account of what they are
doing, they must recognise their commitment to unilateral
relationships of affirmation/sacrifice, and what this
means for their work in terms of both the possibilities
and limits which such principles set for the lives of the
members of society.   They must also identify the necessity of reciprocal relationships if certain opportunities
for 'being who I am' are ever to be realistically made
available to their clients, and learn to use and develop
these relationships whenever they can.

The practice of social work requires in effect, a con-
stant awareness of the limits of what can be achieved,
and a continuing search for ways by which what is beyond
their endeavours today comes within their reach tomorrow.

Bibliography

ABBATE, FRED J. (1974), The Conspiracy Doctrine: A Critique, 'Philosophy and Public Affairs', vol. 3, pp. 295-311.
ACTON, H.B. (1971), 'The Morals of Markets', London, Longman in conjunction with The Institute of Economic Affairs.
ARROW, K.J. (1972), Gifts and Exchanges, 'Philosophy and Public Affairs', vol. 1, no. 4.
BAKER, R. (1973), The Challenge for British Casework, 'Social Work Today', vol. 4, no. 10, pp. 290-3.
BASW (1973a), A Code of Ethics for Social Work, 'Discussion Paper No. 2', British Association of Social Workers.
BASW (1973b), The Inalienable Element in Social Work', 'Discussion Paper No. 3', British Association of Social Workers.
BENN, S.I. and PETERS, R.S. (1959), 'Social Principles and the Democratic State', London, George Allen & Unwin.
BEVERIDGE, Sir WILLIAM (1942), 'Social Insurance and Allied Services', London, HMSO, Cmd 6404.
BIESTEK, F.P. (1957), 'The Casework Relationship', Loyola University Press; London, George Allen & Unwin, 1961.
BUTLER, Bishop J. (1726), 'Fifteen Sermons', with Introduction, analyses and notes by W.R. Mathews, London, G. Bell & Sons, 1964.
CAMPBELL, T.D. (1974), Humanity before Justice, 'British Journal of Political Science', 4.
'Case Con' (April 1972).
COHEN, CARL (1971), 'Civil Disobedience - Conscience, Tactics and the Law', New York, Columbia University Press.
COOPER, M.H. and CULYER, A.J. (1968), 'The Price of Blood', London, The Institute of Economic Affairs.
CORNFORD, F.M. (1941), translation, with Introduction and notes, of Plato's 'Republic', Oxford, Clarendon Press.
CULYER, A.J. (1974), A Dialogue on Blood: I, 'New Society', 21 March.

DAVIS, KENNETH C. (1969), 'Discretionary Justice, a Preliminary Enquiry', Louisiana State University Press.
DOWNIE, R.S., LOUDFOOT, EILEEN M. and TELFER, ELIZABETH (1974), 'Education and Personal Relationships', London, Methuen.
DOWNIE, R.S. and TELFER, E. (1969), 'Respect for Persons', London, George Allen & Unwin.
ETZIONI, A. (ed.) (1969), 'The Semi-Professions and their Organisation', New York, Free Press; London, Macmillan.
FEINBERG, JOEL (1973), 'Social Philosophy', Englewood Cliffs, Prentice-Hall.
FOWLER, D.A. (1975), Ends and Means, in 'Towards a New Social Work', ed. Howard Jones, London, Routledge & Kegan Paul.
FRANKL, V. (1967), 'Psychotherapy and Existentialism', Harmondsworth, Penguin.
FRANKS (1957), Report of the Committee on Administrative Tribunals and Enquiries, Cmnd 218, London, HMSO.
GELLNER, E. (1959), 'Words and Things', London, Victor Gollancz, pp. 231-2.
GOLDBERG, E.M. (1972), 'The Use of Research in Social Work Education', paper presented at the International Congress Schools of Social Work.
GRAAFF, J. deV. (1957), 'Theoretical Welfare Economics', Cambridge University Press.
GROSSBARD, HYMAN (1967), Ego Deficiency in Delinquents, in ed. E. Younghusband, 'Social Work and Social Values', pp. 130-41.
HALMOS, PAUL (1965), 'The Faith of the Counsellors', London, Constable.
HALMOS, PAUL (1970), 'The Personal Service Society', London, Constable,
HARE, R.M. (1962), 'The Language of Morals', Oxford, Clarendon Press.
HARRIS, E.E. (1968), Respect for Persons, in 'Ethics and Society', ed. R.T. DeGeorge, London, Macmillan.
HOBBES, T. (1651), 'Leviathan', published with an introduction by John Plamenatz, Glasgow, Collins, 1962.
HOLLIS, FLORENCE (1949), 'Women in Marital Conflict', New York, Family Service Association of America.
HOLLIS, FLORENCE (1961), Principles and Assumptions Underlying Casework Practice, a lecture reprinted in 'An Introduction to Teaching Casework Skills', ed. Jean Heywood, London, Routledge & Kegan Paul.
HOLLIS, FLORENCE (1963), Contemporary Issues for Social Workers, in 'Ego-oriented Casework: problems and perspectives', ed. Howard J. Parad and Roger R. Miller, New York, Family Service Association of America.
HOLLIS, FLORENCE (1964), 'Casework: a Psychosocial Therapy', New York, Random House.

Home Office (1973), 'The Probation and After-Care Service
in England and Wales', London, HMSO, 5 edn.
HOROWITZ, I. (1961), 'Philosophy, Science and the Socio-
logy of Knowledge', Charles C. Thomas, Springfield, Ill-
inois.
JONES, HOWARD (1971), 'Crime in a Changing Society', Har-
mondsworth, Penguin.
JUSTICE (1961), 'Justice: The Citizen and the Administra-
tion', London, Stevens.
KEITH-LUCAS, ALAN (1953), The Political Theory Implicit in
Social Casework Theory, 'American Political Science Re-
view', 47.
KEITH-LUCAS, ALAN (1957), 'Decisions about People in
Need', University of North Carolina Press.
KILBRANDON (1964), 'Report on Children and Young Persons
(Scotland)', London, HMSO, Cmnd 2306.
LUCAS, J.R. (1966), 'The Principles of Politics', Oxford,
Clarendon Press.
MCDERMOTT, F.E. (ed.) (1975), 'Self-Determination in
Social Work', London, Routledge & Kegan Paul.
MACLAGAN, W.G. (1960), Respect for Persons as a Moral
Principle - I, 'Philosophy', vol. 35, no. 134.
MANNHEIM, K. (1936), 'Ideology and Utopia', New York, Har-
court Brace.
MARSHALL, A. (1966), 'Principles of Economics', London,
Macmillan, 8 edn.
MARSHALL, T.H. (1965), The Right to Welfare, 'Sociological
Review', NS 213.   Reprinted in 'Talking about Welfare',
ed. Noel Timms and David Watson, London, Routledge & Kegan
Paul, 1976.
MAYER, J.E. and TIMMS, N. (1970), 'The Client Speaks',
London, Routledge & Kegan Paul.
MILL, J.S. (1863), 'Utilitarianism', ed. Mary Warnock,
Glasgow, Collins, 1962.
MISHAN, E.J. (1969), '21 Popular Economic Fallacies', Har-
mondsworth, Penguin.
MOFFETT, J. (1968), 'Concepts in Casework Treatment',
London, Routledge & Kegan Paul.
MORISON (1962), Report of the Departmental Committee on
the Probation Service, Cmnd 1650, London, HMSO.
MURDOCH, I. (1962), Metaphysics and Ethics, in 'The Nature
of Metaphysics', ed. D.F. Pears, London, Macmillan.
MURDOCH, I. (1970), 'Sovereignty of Good', London, Rout-
ledge & Kegan Paul.
NIELSEN, KAI (1968), On Moral Truth, in 'Studies in Moral
Philosophy', ed. Nicholas Rescher, Oxford, Blackwell, pp.
9-25.
PARSLOE, PHYLLIDA (1967), 'The Work of the Probation and
After-Care Officer', London, Routledge & Kegan Paul.

PATON, H.J. (1948), 'The Moral Law', London, Hutchinson
University Library.   Translation of Kant's 'Groundwork of
the Metaphysic of Morals'.   References to the paperback
edn.
PEARSON, G. (1975), The Politics of Uncertainty, in 'To-
wards a New Social Work', ed. Howard Jones, London, Rout-
ledge & Kegan Paul.
PINKER, R. (1971), 'Social Theory and Social Policy',
London, Heinemann.
PINKER, R. (1974), Social Policy and Social Justice,
'Journal of Social Policy', vol. 3, no. 1.
PLANT, R. (1970), 'Social and Moral Theory in Casework',
London, Routledge & Kegan Paul.
PLANT, R. (1974), 'Community and Ideology', London, Rout-
ledge & Kegan Paul.
POLLAK, OTTO (1967), Treatment of Character Disorders: a
Dilemma in Casework Culture, in 'Social Work and Social
Values', ed. E. Younghusband, pp. 121-9.
POPPLESTONE, G. (1971), The Ideology of Professional Com-
munity Workers, 'British Journal of Social Work', vol. 1,
no. 1, April.
RICHMOND, MARY E. (1917), 'Social Diagnosis', New York,
Russell Sage Foundation.
The Right to Know - an Investigation into Secrecy, 'Lis-
tener', vol. 91, no. 2353 (2 May 1974), pp. 559-62.
ROBERTSON, GEOFF (1974), 'Whose Conspiracy?', London,
National Council for Civil Liberties.
ROBSON, WILLIAM A. (1928), 'Justice and Administrative
Law', London, Stevens.
ROBSON, WILLIAM A. and CRICK, BERNARD (1970), 'The Future
of the Social Services', Harmondsworth, Penguin.
RODGERS, BARBARA N. and DIXON, JULIA (1960), 'Portrait of
Social Work', Oxford University Press.
ROGERS, C. (1961), 'On Becoming a Person (A Therapist's
View of Psychotherapy)', Boston, Houghton & Mifflin.
ROWE, A. (1974), Some Implications of the Career Struc-
ture for Social Workers, in 'Management in the Social and
Safety Services', ed. W.D. Reekie and N. Hunt, London,
Tavistock Publications.
SEEBOHM (1968), Report of the Committee on Local Authority
and Allied Personal Services, Cmnd 3703, London, HMSO.
SINGER, PETER (1973a), 'Democracy and Disobedience',
Oxford, Clarendon Press.
SINGER, PETER (1973b), Altruism and Commerce: A defense
of Titmuss Against Arrow, 'Philosophy and Public Affairs',
vol. 2, no. 3.
SLACK, KATHLEEN (1966), 'Social Administration and the
Citizen', London, Michael Joseph.
SMITH, C. (1973), Consensus or Conflict?, 'Social Work
Today', vol. 4, no. 18.

STEVENSON, O. (1971), Knowledge for Social Work, 'British Journal of Social Work', vol. 1, no. 2.

Supplementary Benefits Handbook (1972), 3rd edn, London, HMSO.

TITMUSS, R.M. (1968), 'Commitment to Welfare', London, George Allen & Unwin.

TITMUSS, R.M. (1970), 'The Gift Relationship', London, George Allen & Unwin.

TITMUSS, R.M. (1971), Welfare 'Rights', Law and Discretion, 'Political Quarterly', vol. 42.

TOREN, N. (1969), Semi-Professionalism and Social Work: A Theoretical Perspective, in 'The Semi-Professions and their Organization', ed. A. Etzioni, New York, Free Press.

URMSON, J.O. (1968), 'The Emotive Theory of Ethics', London, Hutchinson.

WADE, H.W.R. (1963), 'Towards Administrative Justice', Ann Arbor, University of Michigan Press.

WARNOCK, G.J. (1971), 'The Object of Morality', London, Methuen.

WASSERSTROM, RICHARD A. (1963), The Obligation to Obey the Law, 'University of California Los Angeles Law Review', vol. 10, pp. 780-807.

WATSON, D. (1973), Paraffin and Matches, a discussion of BASW (1973b), 'Social Work Today', vol. 4, no. 7.

WATSON, D. (1975), Freedom from Welfare, 'Social Work Today', vol. 6, no. 8.

WILENSKY, H. and LEBEAUX, C. (1958), 'Industrial Society and Social Welfare', New York, Free Press.

WILKES, R. (1973), Divided and Distinguished Worlds, 'Social Work Today', vol. 3, no. 21.

WINCH, D.M. (1971), 'Analytical Welfare Economics', Harmondsworth, Penguin.

WOODROOFE, KATHLEEN (1962), 'From Charity to Social Work', London, Routledge & Kegan Paul.

WOOTTON, B. (1975), A Philosophy for the Social Services, Rita Hinden Memorial Lecture, 'Socialist Commentary', January.

YOUNGHUSBAND, E. (1964), 'Social Work and Social Change', London, George Allen & Unwin.

YOUNGHUSBAND, E. (ed.) (1967), 'Social Work and Social Values', London, George Allen & Unwin.

YOUNGHUSBAND, E. (1973), The Future of Social Work, 'Social Work Today', vol. 4, no. 2.

Routledge Social Science Series

Routledge & Kegan Paul   London, Henley and Boston

39 Store Street, London WC1E 7DD
Broadway House, Newtown Road, Henley-on-Thames,
Oxon RG9 1EN
9 Park Street, Boston, Mass. 02108

Contents

*Authors wishing to submit manuscripts for any series in
this catalogue should send them to the Social Science Editor,
Routledge & Kegan Paul Ltd, 39 Store Street,
London WC1E 7DD*

● *Books so marked are available in paperback
All books are in Metric Demy 8vo format (216 × 138mm approx.)*

International Library of Sociology

General Editor John Rex

GENERAL SOCIOLOGY

Barnsley, J. H. The Social Reality of Ethics. *464 pp.*
Belshaw, Cyril. The Conditions of Social Performance. *An Exploratory Theory. 144 pp.*
Brown, Robert. Explanation in Social Science. *208 pp.*
● Rules and Laws in Sociology. *192 pp.*
Bruford, W. H. Chekhov and His Russia. *A Sociological Study. 244 pp.*
Cain, Maureen E. Society and the Policeman's Role. *326 pp.*
●**Fletcher, Colin.** Beneath the Surface. *An Account of Three Styles of Sociological Research. 221 pp.*
Gibson, Quentin. The Logic of Social Enquiry. *240 pp.*
Glucksmann, M. Structuralist Analysis in Contemporary Social Thought. *212 pp.*
Gurvitch, Georges. Sociology of Law. *Preface by Roscoe Pound. 264 pp.*
Hodge, H. A. Wilhelm Dilthey. *An Introduction. 184 pp.*
Homans, George C. Sentiments and Activities. *336 pp.*
Johnson, Harry M. Sociology: *a Systematic Introduction. Foreword by ᐧ Robert K. Merton. 710 pp.*
●**Keat, Russell,** and **Urry, John.** Social Theory as Science. *278 pp.*
Mannheim, Karl. Essays on Sociology and Social Psychology. *Edited by Paul Kecskemeti. With Editorial Note by Adolph Lowe. 344 pp.*
Systematic Sociology: *An Introduction to the Study of Society. Edited by J. S. Erös and Professor W. A. C. Stewart. 220 pp.*
Martindale, Don. The Nature and Types of Sociological Theory. *292 pp.*
●**Maus, Heinz.** A Short History of Sociology. *234 pp.*
Mey, Harald. Field-Theory. *A Study of its Application in the Social Sciences. 352 pp.*
Myrdal, Gunnar. Value in Social Theory: *A Collection of Essays on Methodology. Edited by Paul Streeten. 332 pp.*
Ogburn, William F., and **Nimkoff, Meyer F.** A Handbook of Sociology. *Preface by Karl Mannheim. 656 pp. 46 figures. 35 tables.*
Parsons, Talcott, and **Smelser, Neil J.** Economy and Society: *A Study in the Integration of Economic and Social Theory. 362 pp.*
Podgórecki, Adam. Practical Social Sciences. *About 200 pp.*
●**Rex, John.** Key Problems of Sociological Theory. *220 pp.*
Sociology and the Demystification of the Modern World. *282 pp.*
●**Rex, John** (Ed.) Approaches to Sociology. *Contributions by Peter Abell, Frank Bechhofer, Basil Bernstein, Ronald Fletcher, David Frisby, Miriam Glucksmann, Peter Lassman, Herminio Martins, John Rex, Roland Robertson, John Westergaard and Jock Young. 302 pp.*
Rigby, A. Alternative Realities. *352 pp.*
Roche, M. Phenomenology, Language and the Social Sciences. *374 pp.*

3

Sahay, A. Sociological Analysis. *220 pp.*

Simirenko, Alex (Ed.) Soviet Sociology. *Historical Antecedents and Current Appraisals. Introduction by Alex Simirenko. 376 pp.*

Strasser, Hermann. The Normative Structure of Sociology. *Conservative and Emancipatory Themes in Social Thought. About 340 pp.*

Urry, John. Reference Groups and the Theory of Revolution. *244 pp.*

Weinberg, E. Development of Sociology in the Soviet Union. *173 pp.*

FOREIGN CLASSICS OF SOCIOLOGY

●**Durkheim, Emile.** Suicide. *A Study in Sociology. Edited and with an Introduction by George Simpson. 404 pp.*

●**Gerth, H. H., and Mills, C. Wright.** From Max Weber: *Essays in Sociology. 502 pp.*

●**Tönnies, Ferdinand.** Community and Association. (*Gemeinschaft und Gesellschaft.) Translated and Supplemented by Charles P. Loomis. Foreword by Pitirim A. Sorokin. 334 pp.*

SOCIAL STRUCTURE

Andreski, Stanislav. Military Organization and Society. *Foreword by Professor A. R. Radcliffe-Brown. 226 pp. 1 folder.*

Carlton, Eric. Ideology and Social Order. *Preface by Professor Philip Abrahams. About 320 pp.*

Coontz, Sydney H. Population Theories and the Economic Interpretation. *202 pp.*

Coser, Lewis. The Functions of Social Conflict. *204 pp.*

Dickie-Clark, H. F. Marginal Situation: *A Sociological Study of a Coloured Group. 240 pp. 11 tables.*

Glaser, Barney, and Strauss, Anselm L. Status Passage. *A Formal Theory. 208 pp.*

Glass, D. V. (Ed.) Social Mobility in Britain. *Contributions by J. Berent, T. Bottomore, R. C. Chambers, J. Floud, D. V. Glass, J. R. Hall, H. T. Himmelweit, R. K. Kelsall, F. M. Martin, C. A. Moser, R. Mukherjee, and W. Ziegel. 420 pp.*

Johnstone, Frederick A. Class, Race and Gold. *A Study of Class Relations and Racial Discrimination in South Africa. 312 pp.*

Jones, Garth N. Planned Organizational Change: *An Exploratory Study Using an Empirical Approach. 268 pp.*

Kelsall, R. K. Higher Civil Servants in Britain: *From 1870 to the Present Day. 268 pp. 31 tables.*

König, René. The Community. *232 pp. Illustrated.*

●**Lawton, Denis.** Social Class, Language and Education. *192 pp.*

McLeish, John. The Theory of Social Change: *Four Views Considered. 128 pp.*

Marsh, David C. The Changing Social Structure of England and Wales, 1871-1961. *288 pp.*

Menzies, Ken. Talcott Parsons and the Social Image of Man. *About 208 pp.*

●**Mouzelis, Nicos.** Organization and Bureaucracy. *An Analysis of Modern Theories. 240 pp.*

Mulkay, M. J. Functionalism, Exchange and Theoretical Strategy. *272 pp.*

Ossowski, Stanislaw. Class Structure in the Social Consciousness. *210 pp.*

●**Podgórecki, Adam.** Law and Society. *302 pp.*

Renner, Karl. Institutions of Private Law and Their Social Functions. *Edited, with an Introduction and Notes, by O. Kahn-Freud. Translated by Agnes Schwarzschild. 316 pp.*

SOCIOLOGY AND POLITICS

Acton, T. A. Gypsy Politics and Social Change. *316 pp.*

Clegg, Stuart. Power, Rule and Domination. *A Critical and Empirical Understanding of Power in Sociological Theory and Organisational Life. About 300 pp.*

Hechter, Michael. Internal Colonialism. *The Celtic Fringe in British National Development, 1536–1966. 361 pp.*

Hertz, Frederick. Nationality in History and Politics: *A Psychology and Sociology of National Sentiment and Nationalism. 432 pp.*

Kornhauser, William. The Politics of Mass Society. *272 pp. 20 tables.*

●**Kroes, R.** Soldiers and Students. *A Study of Right- and Left-wing Students. 174 pp.*

Laidler, Harry W. History of Socialism. *Social-Economic Movements: An Historical and Comparative Survey of Socialism, Communism, Co-operation, Utopianism; and other Systems of Reform and Reconstruction. 992 pp.*

Lasswell, H. D. Analysis of Political Behaviour. *324 pp.*

Martin, David A. Pacifism: *an Historical and Sociological Study. 262 pp.*

Martin, Roderick. Sociology of Power. *About 272 pp.*

Myrdal, Gunnar. The Political Element in the Development of Economic Theory. *Translated from the German by Paul Streeten. 282 pp.*

Wilson, H. T. The American Ideology. *Science, Technology and Organization of Modes of Rationality. About 280 pp.*

Wootton, Graham. Workers, Unions and the State. *188 pp.*

CRIMINOLOGY

Ancel, Marc. Social Defence: *A Modern Approach to Criminal Problems. Foreword by Leon Radzinowicz. 240 pp.*

Cain, Maureen E. Society and the Policeman's Role. *326 pp.*

Cloward, Richard A., and **Ohlin, Lloyd E.** Delinquency and Opportunity: *A Theory of Delinquent Gangs. 248 pp.*

Downes, David M. The Delinquent Solution. *A Study in Subcultural Theory. 296 pp.*

Dunlop, A. B., and **McCabe, S.** Young Men in Detention Centres. *192 pp.*

Friedlander, Kate. The Psycho-Analytical Approach to Juvenile Delinquency: *Theory, Case Studies, Treatment. 320 pp.*

Glueck, Sheldon, and **Eleanor.** Family Environment and Delinquency. *With the statistical assistance of Rose W. Kneznek. 340 pp.*

Lopez-Rey, Manuel. Crime. *An Analytical Appraisal. 288 pp.*

Mannheim, Hermann. Comparative Criminology: *a Text Book. Two volumes. 442 pp. and 380 pp.*

Morris, Terence. The Criminal Area: *A Study in Social Ecology. Foreword by Hermann Mannheim. 232 pp. 25 tables. 4 maps.*

Rock, Paul. Making People Pay. *338 pp.*

● **Taylor, Ian, Walton, Paul,** and **Young, Jock.** The New Criminology. *For a Social Theory of Deviance. 325 pp.*

● **Taylor, Ian, Walton, Paul,** and **Young, Jock** (Eds). Critical Criminology. *268 pp.*

SOCIAL PSYCHOLOGY

Bagley, Christopher. The Social Psychology of the Epileptic Child. *320 pp.*

Barbu, Zevedei. Problems of Historical Psychology. *248 pp.*

Blackburn, Julian. Psychology and the Social Pattern. *184 pp.*

● **Brittan, Arthur.** Meanings and Situations. *224 pp.*

Carroll, J. Break-Out from the Crystal Palace. *200 pp.*

● **Fleming, C. M.** Adolescence: Its Social Psychology. *With an Introduction to recent findings from the fields of Anthropology, Physiology, Medicine, Psychometrics and Sociometry. 288 pp.*

● The Social Psychology of Education: *An Introduction and Guide to Its Study. 136 pp.*

● **Homans, George C.** The Human Group. *Foreword by Bernard DeVoto. Introduction by Robert K. Merton. 526 pp.*

● Social Behaviour: *its Elementary Forms. 416 pp.*

● **Klein, Josephine.** The Study of Groups. *226 pp. 31 figures. 5 tables.*

Linton, Ralph. The Cultural Background of Personality. *132 pp.*

● **Mayo, Elton.** The Social Problems of an Industrial Civilization. *With an appendix on the Political Problem. 180 pp.*

Ottaway, A. K. C. Learning Through Group Experience. *176 pp.*

Plummer, Ken. Sexual Stigma. *An Interactionist Account. 254 pp.*

● **Rose, Arnold M.** (Ed.) Human Behaviour and Social Processes: *an Interactionist Approach. Contributions by Arnold M. Rose, Ralph H. Turner, Anselm Strauss, Everett C. Hughes, E. Franklin Frazier, Howard S. Becker, et al. 696 pp.*

Smelser, Neil J. Theory of Collective Behaviour. *448 pp.*

Stephenson, Geoffrey M. The Development of Conscience. *128 pp.*

Young, Kimball. Handbook of Social Psychology. *658 pp. 16 figures. 10 tables.*

SOCIOLOGY OF THE FAMILY

Banks, J. A. Prosperity and Parenthood: *A Study of Family Planning among The Victorian Middle Classes. 262 pp.*

Bell, Colin R. Middle Class Families: *Social and Geographical Mobility. 224 pp.*

Burton, Lindy. Vulnerable Children. *272 pp.*
Gavron, Hannah. The Captive Wife: *Conflicts of Household Mothers.* *190 pp.*
George, Victor, and **Wilding, Paul.** Motherless Families. *248 pp.*
Klein, Josephine. Samples from English Cultures.
  1. Three Preliminary Studies and Aspects of Adult Life in England. *447 pp.*
  2. Child-Rearing Practices and Index. *247 pp.*
Klein, Viola. The Feminine Character. *History of an Ideology. 244 pp.*
McWhinnie, Alexina M. Adopted Children. *How They Grow Up. 304 pp.*
● **Morgan, D. H. J.** Social Theory and the Family. *About 320 pp.*
● **Myrdal, Alva,** and **Klein, Viola.** Women's Two Roles: *Home and Work.* *238 pp. 27 tables.*
Parsons, Talcott, and **Bales, Robert F.** Family: Socialization and Interaction Process. *In collaboration with James Olds, Morris Zelditch and Philip E. Slater. 456 pp. 50 figures and tables.*

SOCIAL SERVICES

Bastide, Roger. The Sociology of Mental Disorder. *Translated from the French by Jean McNeil. 260 pp.*
Carlebach, Julius. Caring For Children in Trouble. *266 pp.*
George, Victor. Foster Care. *Theory and Practice. 234 pp.*
  Social Security: *Beveridge and After. 258 pp.*
George, V., and **Wilding, P.** Motherless Families. *248 pp.*
● **Goetschius, George W.** Working with Community Groups. *256 pp.*
Goetschius, George W., and **Tash, Joan.** Working with Unattached Youth. *416 pp.*
Hall, M. P., and **Howes, I. V.** The Church in Social Work. *A Study of Moral Welfare Work undertaken by the Church of England. 320 pp.*
Heywood, Jean S. Children in Care: *the Development of the Service for the Deprived Child. 264 pp.*
Hoenig, J., and **Hamilton, Marian W.** The De-Segregation of the Mentally Ill. *284 pp.*
Jones, Kathleen. Mental Health and Social Policy, 1845-1959. *264 pp.*
King, Roy D., Raynes, Norma V., and **Tizard, Jack.** Patterns of Residential Care. *356 pp.*
Leigh, John. Young People and Leisure. *256 pp.*
● **Mays, John.** (Ed.) Penelope Hall's Social Services of England and Wales. *About 324 pp.*
Morris, Mary. Voluntary Work and the Welfare State. *300 pp.*
Nokes, P. L. The Professional Task in Welfare Practice. *152 pp.*
Timms, Noel. Psychiatric Social Work in Great Britain (1939-1962). *280 pp.*
● Social Casework: *Principles and Practice. 256 pp.*
Young, A. F. Social Services in British Industry. *272 pp.*

SOCIOLOGY OF EDUCATION

Banks, Olive. Parity and Prestige in English Secondary Education: a Study in Educational Sociology. *272 pp.*

Bentwich, Joseph. Education in Israel. *224 pp. 8 pp. plates.*

●**Blyth, W. A. L.** English Primary Education. *A Sociological Description.*
1. Schools. *232 pp.*
2. Background. *168 pp.*

Collier, K. G. The Social Purposes of Education: *Personal and Social Values in Education. 268 pp.*

Dale, R. R., and **Griffith, S.** Down Stream: *Failure in the Grammar School. 108 pp.*

Evans, K. M. Sociometry and Education. *158 pp.*

●**Ford, Julienne.** Social Class and the Comprehensive School. *192 pp.*

Foster, P. J. Education and Social Change in Ghana. *336 pp. 3 maps.*

Fraser, W. R. Education and Society in Modern France. *150 pp.*

Grace, Gerald R. Role Conflict and the Teacher. *150 pp.*

Hans, Nicholas. New Trends in Education in the Eighteenth Century. *278 pp. 19 tables.*

● Comparative Education: *A Study of Educational Factors and Traditions. 360 pp.*

●**Hargreaves, David.** Interpersonal Relations and Education. *432 pp.*

● Social Relations in a Secondary School. *240 pp.*

Holmes, Brian. Problems in Education. *A Comparative Approach. 336 pp.*

King, Ronald. Values and Involvement in a Grammar School. *164 pp.*

School Organization and Pupil Involvement. *A Study of Secondary Schools.*

●**Mannheim, Karl,** and **Stewart, W. A. C.** An Introduction to the Sociology of Education. *206 pp.*

Morris, Raymond N. The Sixth Form and College Entrance. *231 pp.*

●**Musgrove, F.** Youth and the Social Order. *176 pp.*

●**Ottaway, A. K. C.** Education and Society: An Introduction to the Sociology of Education. *With an Introduction by W. O. Lester Smith. 212 pp.*

Peers, Robert. Adult Education: *A Comparative Study. 398 pp.*

Pritchard, D. G. Education and the Handicapped: *1760 to 1960. 258 pp.*

Stratta, Erica. The Education of Borstal Boys. *A Study of their Educational Experiences prior to, and during, Borstal Training. 256 pp.*

Taylor, P. H., Reid, W. A., and **Holley, B. J.** The English Sixth Form. *A Case Study in Curriculum Research. 200 pp.*

SOCIOLOGY OF CULTURE

Eppel, E. M., and **M.** Adolescents and Morality: *A Study of some Moral Values and Dilemmas of Working Adolescents in the Context of a changing Climate of Opinion. Foreword by W. J. H. Sprott. 268 pp. 39 tables.*

●**Fromm, Erich.** The Fear of Freedom. *286 pp.*

● The Sane Society. *400 pp.*

Mannheim, Karl. Essays on the Sociology of Culture. *Edited by Ernst Mannheim in co-operation with Paul Kecskemeti. Editorial Note by Adolph Lowe. 280 pp.*
Weber, Alfred. Farewell to European History: *or The Conquest of Nihilism. Translated from the German by R. F. C. Hull. 224 pp.*

SOCIOLOGY OF RELIGION

Argyle, Michael and **Beit-Hallahmi, Benjamin.** The Social Psychology of Religion. *About 256 pp.*
Glasner, Peter E. The Sociology of Secularisation. *A Critique of a Concept. About 180 pp.*
Nelson, G. K. Spiritualism and Society. *313 pp.*
Stark, Werner. The Sociology of Religion. *A Study of Christendom.*
Volume I. *Established Religion. 248 pp.*
Volume II. *Sectarian Religion. 368 pp.*
Volume III. *The Universal Church. 464 pp.*
Volume IV. *Types of Religious Man. 352 pp.*
Volume V. *Types of Religious Culture. 464 pp.*
Turner, B. S. Weber and Islam. *216 pp.*
Watt, W. Montgomery. Islam and the Integration of Society. *320 pp.*

SOCIOLOGY OF ART AND LITERATURE

Jarvie, Ian C. Towards a Sociology of the Cinema. *A Comparative Essay on the Structure and Functioning of a Major Entertainment Industry. 405 pp.*
Rust, Frances S. Dance in Society. *An Analysis of the Relationships between the Social Dance and Society in England from the Middle Ages to the Present Day. 256 pp. 8 pp. of plates.*
Schücking, L. L. The Sociology of Literary Taste. *112 pp.*
Wolff, Janet. Hermeneutic Philosophy and the Sociology of Art. *150 pp.*

SOCIOLOGY OF KNOWLEDGE

Diesing, P. Patterns of Discovery in the Social Sciences. *262 pp.*
Douglas, J. D. (Ed.) Understanding Everyday Life. *370 pp.*
Hamilton, P. Knowledge and Social Structure. *174 pp.*
Jarvie, I. C. Concepts and Society. *232 pp.*
Mannheim, Karl. Essays on the Sociology of Knowledge. *Edited by Paul Kecskemeti. Editorial Note by Adolph Lowe. 353 pp.*
Remmling, Gunter W. The Sociology cf Karl Mannheim. *With a Bibliographical Guide to the Sociology of Knowledge, Ideological Analysis, and Social Planning. 255 pp.*

Remmling, Gunter W. (Ed.) Towards the Sociology of Knowledge. *Origin and Development of a Sociological Thought Style. 463 pp.*
Stark, Werner. The Sociology of Knowledge: *An Essay in Aid of a Deeper Understanding of the History of Ideas. 384 pp.*

URBAN SOCIOLOGY

Ashworth, William. The Genesis of Modern British Town Planning: *A Study in Economic and Social History of the Nineteenth and Twentieth Centuries. 288 pp.*
Cullingworth, J. B. Housing Needs and Planning Policy: *A Restatement of the Problems of Housing Need and 'Overspill' in England and Wales. 232 pp. 44 tables. 8 maps.*
Dickinson, Robert E. City and Region: *A Geographical Interpretation 608 pp. 125 figures.*
The West European City: *A Geographical Interpretation. 600 pp. 129 maps. 29 plates.*
● The City Region in Western Europe. *320 pp. Maps.*
Humphreys, Alexander J. New Dubliners: *Urbanization and the Irish Family. Foreword by George C. Homans. 304 pp.*
Jackson, Brian. Working Class Community: *Some General Notions raised by a Series of Studies in Northern England. 192 pp.*
Jennings, Hilda. Societies in the Making: *a Study of Development and Re-development within a County Borough. Foreword by D. A. Clark. 286 pp.*
●**Mann, P. H.** An Approach to Urban Sociology. *240 pp.*
Morris, R. N., and **Mogey, J.** The Sociology of Housing. *Studies at Berinsfield. 232 pp. 4 pp. plates.*
Rosser, C., and **Harris, C.** The Family and Social Change. *A Study of Family and Kinship in a South Wales Town. 352 pp. 8 maps.*
●**Stacey, Margaret, Batsone, Eric, Bell, Colin,** and **Thurcott, Anne.** Power, Persistence and Change. *A Second Study of Banbury. 196 pp.*

RURAL SOCIOLOGY

Haswell, M. R. The Economics of Development in Village India. *120 pp.*
Littlejohn, James. Westrigg: *the Sociology of a Cheviot Parish. 172 pp. 5 figures.*
Mayer, Adrian C. Peasants in the Pacific. *A Study of Fiji Indian Rural Society. 248 pp. 20 plates.*
Williams, W. M. The Sociology of an English Village: *Gosforth. 272 pp. 12 figures. 13 tables.*

SOCIOLOGY OF INDUSTRY AND DISTRIBUTION

Anderson, Nels. Work and Leisure. *280 pp.*

●**Blau, Peter M.**, and **Scott, W. Richard.** Formal Organizations: *a Comparative approach. Introduction and Additional Bibliography by J. H. Smith. 326 pp.*

Dunkerley, David. The Foreman. *Aspects of Task and Structure. 192 pp.*

Eldridge, J. E. T. Industrial Disputes. *Essays in the Sociology of Industrial Relations. 288 pp.*

Hetzler, Stanley. Applied Measures for Promoting Technological Growth. *352 pp.*
Technological Growth and Social Change. *Achieving Modernization. 269 pp.*

Hollowell, Peter G. The Lorry Driver. *272 pp.*

●**Oxaal, I., Barnett, T.,** and **Booth, D.** (Eds). Beyond the Sociology of Development. *Economy and Society in Latin America and Africa. 295 pp.*

Smelser, Neil J. Social Change in the Industrial Revolution: *An Application of Theory to the Lancashire Cotton Industry, 1770–1840. 468 pp. 12 figures. 14 tables.*

ANTHROPOLOGY

Ammar, Hamed. Growing up in an Egyptian Village: *Silwa, Province of Aswan. 336 pp.*

Brandel-Syrier, Mia. Reeftown Elite. *A Study of Social Mobility in a Modern African Community on the Reef. 376 pp.*

Dickie-Clark, H. F. The Marginal Situation. *A Sociological Study of a Coloured Group. 236 pp.*

Dube, S. C. Indian Village. *Foreword by Morris Edward Opler. 276 pp. 4 plates.*
India's Changing Villages: *Human Factors in Community Development. 260 pp. 8 plates. 1 map.*

Firth, Raymond. Malay Fishermen. *Their Peasant Economy. 420 pp. 17 pp. plates.*

Gulliver, P. H. Social Control in an African Society: a Study of the Arusha, Agricultural Masai of Northern Tanganyika. *320 pp. 8 plates. 10 figures.*
Family Herds. *288 pp.*

Ishwaran, K. Tradition and Economy in Village India: *An Interactionist Approach.*
Foreword by Conrad Arensburg. 176 pp.

Jarvie, Ian C. The Revolution in Anthropology. *268 pp.*

Little, Kenneth L. Mende of Sierra Leone. *308 pp. and folder.*
Negroes in Britain. *With a New Introduction and Contemporary Study by Leonard Bloom. 320 pp.*

Lowie, Robert H. Social Organization. *494 pp.*

Mayer, A. C. Peasants in the Pacific. *A Study of Fiji Indian Rural Society. 248 pp.*

Meer, Fatima. Race and Suicide in South Africa. *325 pp.*

Smith, Raymond T. The Negro Family in British Guiana: *Family Structure and Social Status in the Villages. With a Foreword by Meyer Fortes. 314 pp. 8 plates. 1 figure. 4 maps.*

Smooha, Sammy. Israel: Pluralism and Conflict. *About 320 pp.*

SOCIOLOGY AND PHILOSOPHY

Barnsley, John H. The Social Reality of Ethics. *A Comparative Analysis of Moral Codes. 448 pp.*

Diesing, Paul. Patterns of Discovery in the Social Sciences. *362 pp.*

● **Douglas, Jack D.** (Ed.) Understanding Everyday Life. *Toward the Reconstruction of Sociological Knowledge. Contributions by Alan F. Blum. Aaron W. Cicourel, Norman K. Denzin, Jack D. Douglas, John Heeren, Peter McHugh, Peter K. Manning, Melvin Power, Matthew Speier, Roy Turner, D. Lawrence Wieder, Thomas P. Wilson and Don H. Zimmerman. 370 pp.*

Gorman, Robert A. The Dual Vision. *Alfred Schutz and the Myth of Phenomenological Social Science. About 300 pp.*

Jarvie, Ian C. Concepts and Society. *216 pp.*

● **Pelz, Werner.** The Scope of Understanding in Sociology. *Towards a more radical reorientation in the social humanistic sciences. 283 pp.*

Roche, Maurice. Phenomenology, Language and the Social Sciences. *371 pp.*

Sahay, Arun. Sociological Analysis. *212 pp.*

Sklair, Leslie. The Sociology of Progress. *320 pp.*

Slater, P. Origin and Significance of the Frankfurt School. *A Marxist Perspective. About 192 pp.*

Smart, Barry. Sociology, Phenomenology and Marxian Analysis. *A Critical Discussion of the Theory and Practice of a Science of Society. 220 pp.*

International Library of Anthropology

General Editor Adam Kuper

Ahmed, A. S. Millenium and Charisma Among Pathans. *A Critical Essay in Social Anthropology. 192 pp.*

Brown, Paula. The Chimbu. *A Study of Change in the New Guinea Highlands. 151 pp.*

Gudeman, Stephen. Relationships, Residence and the Individual. *A Rural Panamanian Community. 288 pp. 11 Plates, 5 Figures, 2 Maps, 10 Tables.*

Hamnett, Ian. Chieftainship and Legitimacy. *An Anthropological Study of Executive Law in Lesotho. 163 pp.*

Hanson, F. Allan. Meaning in Culture. *127 pp.*

Lloyd, P. C. Power and Independence. *Urban Africans' Perception of Social Inequality. 264 pp.*

Pettigrew, Joyce. Robber Noblemen. *A Study of the Political System of the Sikh Jats. 284 pp.*

Street, Brian V. The Savage in Literature. *Representations of 'Primitive' Society in English Fiction, 1858–1920. 207 pp.*

Van Den Berghe, Pierre L. Power and Privilege at an African University. *278 pp.*

International Library of Social Policy

General Editor Kathleen Jones

Bayley, M. Mental Handicap and Community Care. *426 pp.*

Bottoms, A. E., and **McClean, J. D.** Defendants in the Criminal Process. *284 pp.*

Butler, J. R. Family Doctors and Public Policy. *208 pp.*

Davies, Martin. Prisoners of Society. *Attitudes and Aftercare. 204 pp.*

Gittus, Elizabeth. Flats, Families and the Under-Fives. *285 pp.*

Holman, Robert. Trading in Children. *A Study of Private Fostering. 355 pp.*

Jones, Howard, and **Cornes, Paul.** Open Prisons. *About 248 pp.*

Jones, Kathleen. History of the Mental Health Service. *428 pp.*

Jones, Kathleen, with **Brown, John, Cunningham, W. J., Roberts, Julian,** and **Williams, Peter.** Opening the Door. *A Study of New Policies for the Mentally Handicapped. 278 pp.*

Karn, Valerie. Retiring to the Seaside. *About 280 pp. 2 maps. Numerous tables.*

Thomas, J. E. The English Prison Officer since 1850: *A Study in Conflict. 258 pp.*

Walton, R. G. Women in Social Work. *303 pp.*

Woodward, J. To Do the Sick No Harm. *A Study of the British Voluntary Hospital System to 1875. 221 pp.*

International Library of Welfare and Philosophy

General Editors Noel Timms and David Watson

● **Plant, Raymond.** Community and Ideology. *104 pp.*

● **McDermott, F. E.** (Ed.) Self-Determination in Social Work. *A Collection of Essays on Self-determination and Related Concepts by Philosophers and Social Work Theorists. Contributors: F. P. Biestek, S. Bernstein, A. Keith-Lucas, D. Sayer, H. H. Perelman, C. Whittington, R. F. Stalley, F. E. McDermott, I. Berlin, H. J. McCloskey, H. L. A. Hart, J. Wilson, A. I. Melden, S. I. Benn. 254 pp.*

Ragg, Nicholas M. People Not Cases. *A Philosophical Approach to Social Work. About 250 pp.*

● **Timms, Noel,** and **Watson, David** (Eds). Talking About Welfare. *Readings in Philosophy and Social Policy. Contributors: T. H. Marshall, R. B. Brandt, G. H. von Wright, K. Nielsen, M. Cranston, R. M. Titmuss, R. S. Downie, E. Telfer, D. Donnison, J. Benson, P. Leonard, A. Keith-Lucas, D. Walsh, I. T. Ramsey. 320 pp.*

Primary Socialization, Language and Education

General Editor Basil Bernstein

Adlam, Diana S., *with the assistance of Geoffrey Turner and Lesley Lineker.* Code in Context. *About 272 pp.*

Bernstein, Basil. Class, Codes and Control. *3 volumes.*
   1. *Theoretical Studies Towards a Sociology of Language. 254 pp.*
   2. *Applied Studies Towards a Sociology of Language. 377 pp.*
●   3. *Towards a Theory of Educatiomal Transmission. 167 pp.*

Brandis, W., and **Bernstein, B.** Selection and Control. *176 pp.*

Brandis, Walter, and **Henderson, Dorothy.** Social Class, Language and Communication. *288 pp.*

Cook-Gumperz, Jenny. Social Control and Socialization. *A Study of Class Differences in the Language of Maternal Control. 290 pp.*

● **Gahagan, D. M.,** and **G. A.** Talk Reform. *Exploration in Language for Infant School Children. 160 pp.*

Hawkins, P. R. Social Class, the Nominal Group and Verbal Strategies. *About 220 pp.*

Robinson, W. P., and **Rackstraw, Susan D. A.** A Question of Answers. *2 volumes. 192 pp. and 180 pp.*

Turner, Geoffrey J., and **Mohan, Bernard A.** A Linguistic Description and Computer Programme for Children's Speech. *208 pp.*

Reports of the Institute of Community Studies

● **Cartwright, Ann.** Parents and Family Planning Services. *306 pp.*
   Patients and their Doctors. *A Study of General Practice. 304 pp.*

Dench, Geoff. Maltese in London. *A Case-study in the Erosion of Ethnic Consciousness. 302 pp.*

● **Jackson, Brian.** Streaming: *an Education System in Miniature. 168 pp.*

Jackson, Brian, and **Marsden, Dennis.** Education and the Working Class: *Some General Themes raised by a Study of 88 Working-class Children in a Northern Industrial City. 268 pp. 2 folders.*

Marris, Peter. The Experience of Higher Education. *232 pp. 27 tables.*
   Loss and Change. *192 pp.*

Marris, Peter, and **Rein, Martin.** Dilemmas of Social Reform. *Poverty and Community Action in the United States. 256 pp.*

Marris, Peter, and Somerset, Anthony. African Businessmen. *A Study of Entrepreneurship and Development in Kenya. 256 pp.*

Mills, Richard. Young Outsiders: *a Study in Alternative Communities. 216 pp.*

Runciman, W. G. Relative Deprivation and Social Justice. *A Study of Attitudes to Social Inequality in Twentieth-Century England. 352 pp.*

Willmott, Peter. Adolescent Boys in East London. *230 pp.*

Willmott, Peter, and Young, Michael. Family and Class in a London Suburb. *202 pp. 47 tables.*

Young, Michael. Innovation and Research in Education. *192 pp.*

●Young, Michael, and McGeeney, Patrick. Learning Begins at Home. *A Study of a Junior School and its Parents. 128 pp.*

Young, Michael, and Willmott, Peter. Family and Kinship in East London. *Foreword by Richard M. Titmuss. 252 pp. 39 tables.*

The Symmetrical Family. *410 pp.*

Reports of the Institute for Social Studies in Medical Care

Cartwright, Ann, Hockey, Lisbeth, and Anderson, John L. Life Before Death. *310 pp.*

Dunnell, Karen, and Cartwright, Ann. Medicine Takers, Prescribers and Hoarders. *190 pp.*

Medicine, Illness and Society

General Editor W. M. Williams

Robinson, David. The Process of Becoming Ill. *142 pp.*

Stacey, Margaret, *et al.* Hospitals, Children and Their Families. *The Report of a Pilot Study. 202 pp.*

Stimson, G. V., and Webb, B. Going to See the Doctor. *The Consultation Process in General Practice. 155 pp.*

Monographs in Social Theory

General Editor Arthur Brittan

●Barnes, B. Scientific Knowledge and Sociological Theory. *192 pp.*

Bauman, Zygmunt. Culture as Praxis. *204 pp.*

●Dixon, Keith. Sociological Theory. *Pretence and Possibility. 142 pp.*

Meltzer, B. N., Petras, J. W., and Reynolds, L. T. Symbolic Interactionism. *Genesis, Varieties and Criticisms. 144 pp.*

●Smith, Anthony D. The Concept of Social Change. *A Critique of the Functionalist Theory of Social Change. 208 pp.*

Routledge Social Science Journals

The British Journal of Sociology. *Editor – Angus Stewart; Associate Editor – Leslie Sklair. Vol. 1, No. 1 – March 1950 and Quarterly. Roy. 8vo. All back issues available. An international journal publishing original papers in the field of sociology and related areas.*
Community Work. *Edited by David Jones and Marjorie Mayo. 1973. Published annually.*
Economy and Society. *Vol. 1, No. 1. February 1972 and Quarterly. Metric Roy. 8vo. A journal for all social scientists covering sociology, philosophy, anthropology, economics and history. All back numbers available.*
Religion. Journal of Religion and Religions. *Chairman of Editorial Board, Ninian Smart. Vol. 1, No. 1, Spring 1971. A journal with an interdisciplinary approach to the study of the phenomena of religion. All back numbers available.*
Year Book of Social Policy in Britain, The. *Edited by Kathleen Jones. 1971. Published annually.*

Social and Psychological Aspects of Medical Practice

Editor Trevor Silverstone

Lader, Malcolm. Psychophysiology of Mental Illness. *280 pp.*
● **Silverstone, Trevor,** and **Turner, Paul.** Drug Treatment in Psychiatry. *232 pp.*

Printed in Great Britain by
Lowe & Brydone Printers Limited, Thetford, Norfolk